This beautiful book is a mindful investigation into the relationship between time, place and textile art. Explored through the lens of the author's textile art practice, this book outlines how cultural and personal context at different stages of your life can influence and shape the work you produce. Building on themes discussed in the author's previous books, *Slow Stitch* and *Resilient Stitch*, renowned textile artist Claire Wellesley-Smith takes us through local, seasonal and sustainable ways of taking on and interpreting the nebulous themes of time and place.

Here you will find a collection of rich photography illustrating the author's processes and finalised works as well as photos from artists from all over the world, alongside practical pointers and examples ready to be taken into your own work. Delve into the relationship between time and place through the mediums of daily embroidery journals, stitching with intention, making twine and the power of patterns. Learn about the symbiosis between different materials and how they act as markers in your work, and how they hold fast or deteriorate over time.

Along the inspiring and creative arc of this book, you'll learn the difference between creating as an individual and creating as a community, and how that affects each practice along the way.

Reflective Stitch

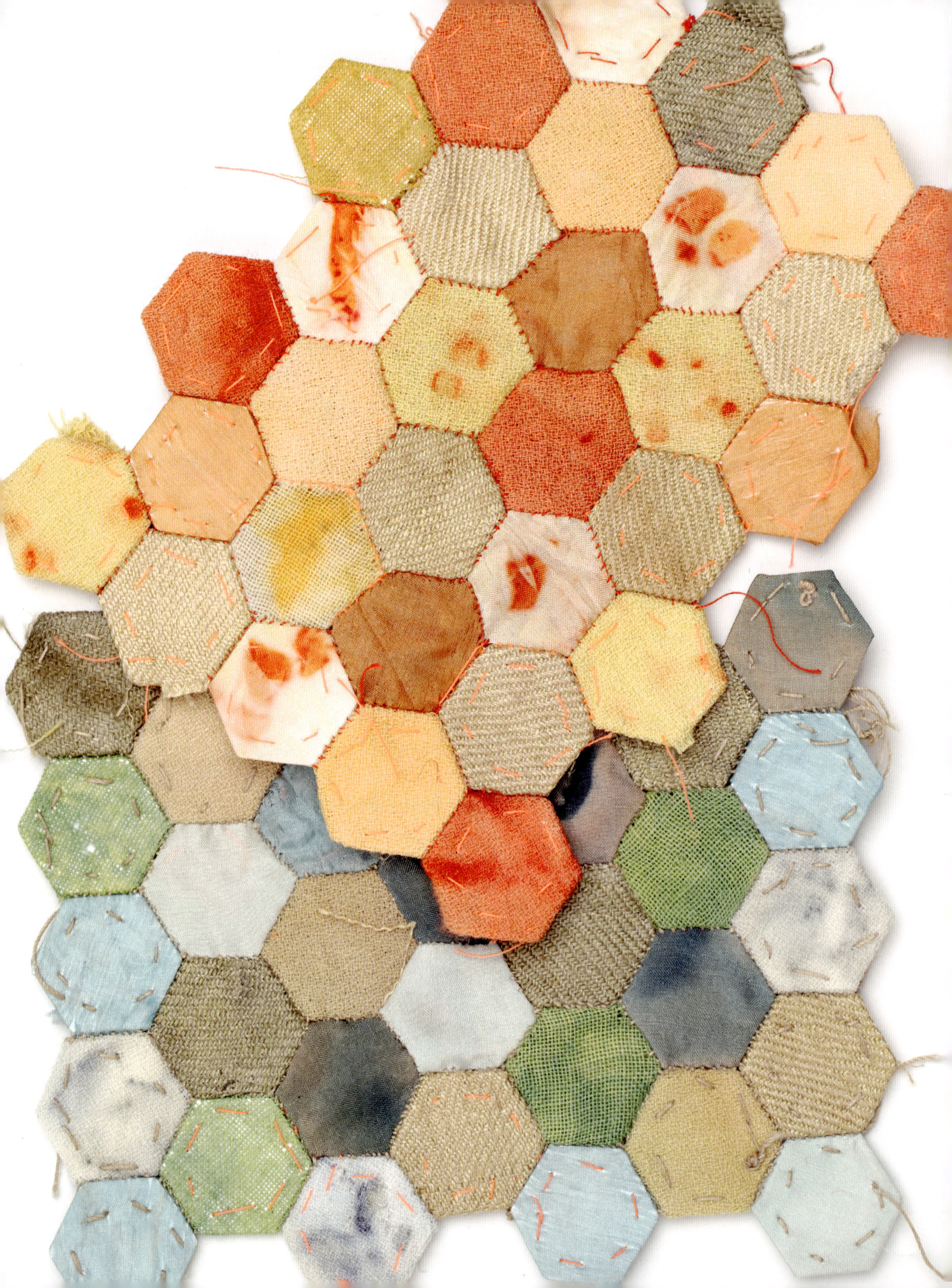

Reflective Stitch

Time and Place in Textile Art

Claire Wellesley-Smith

BATSFORD

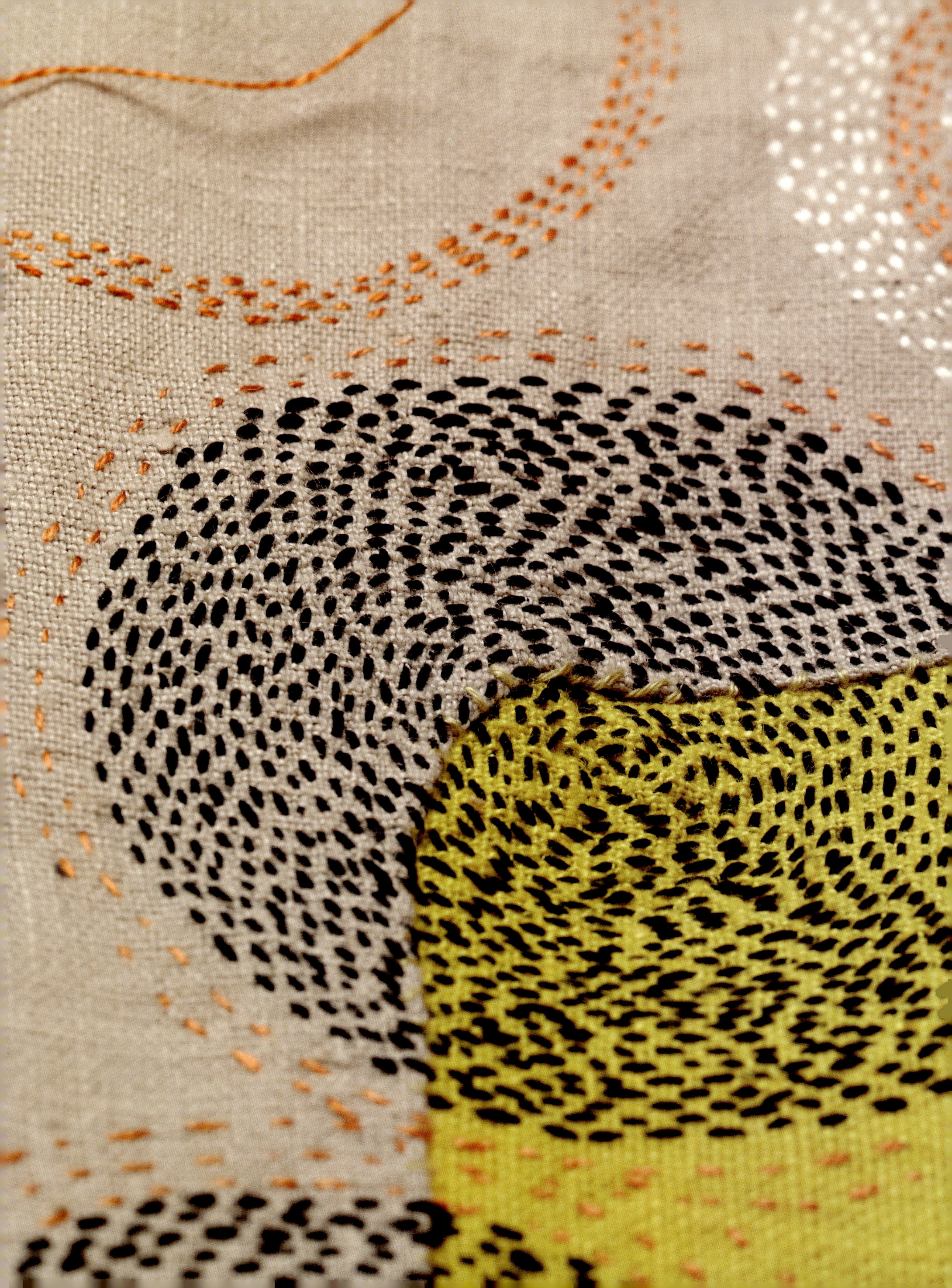

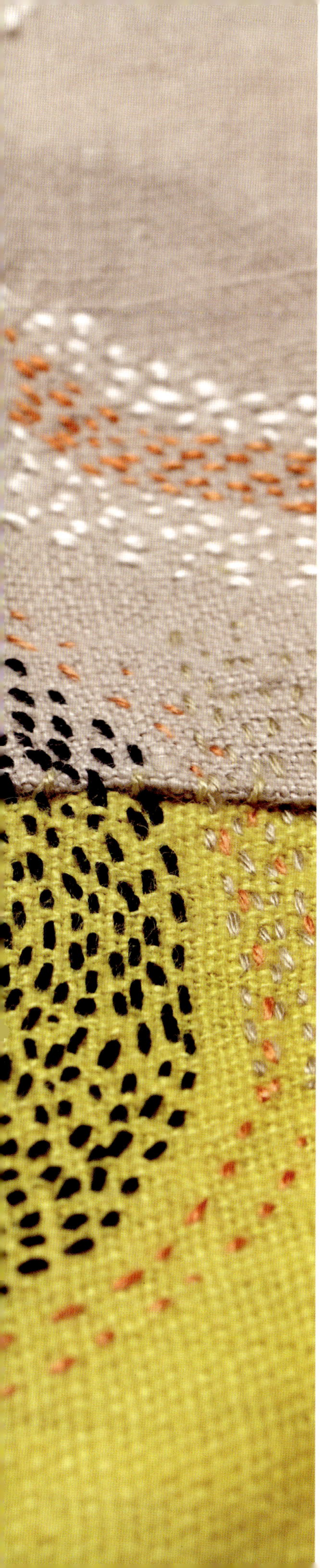

Contents

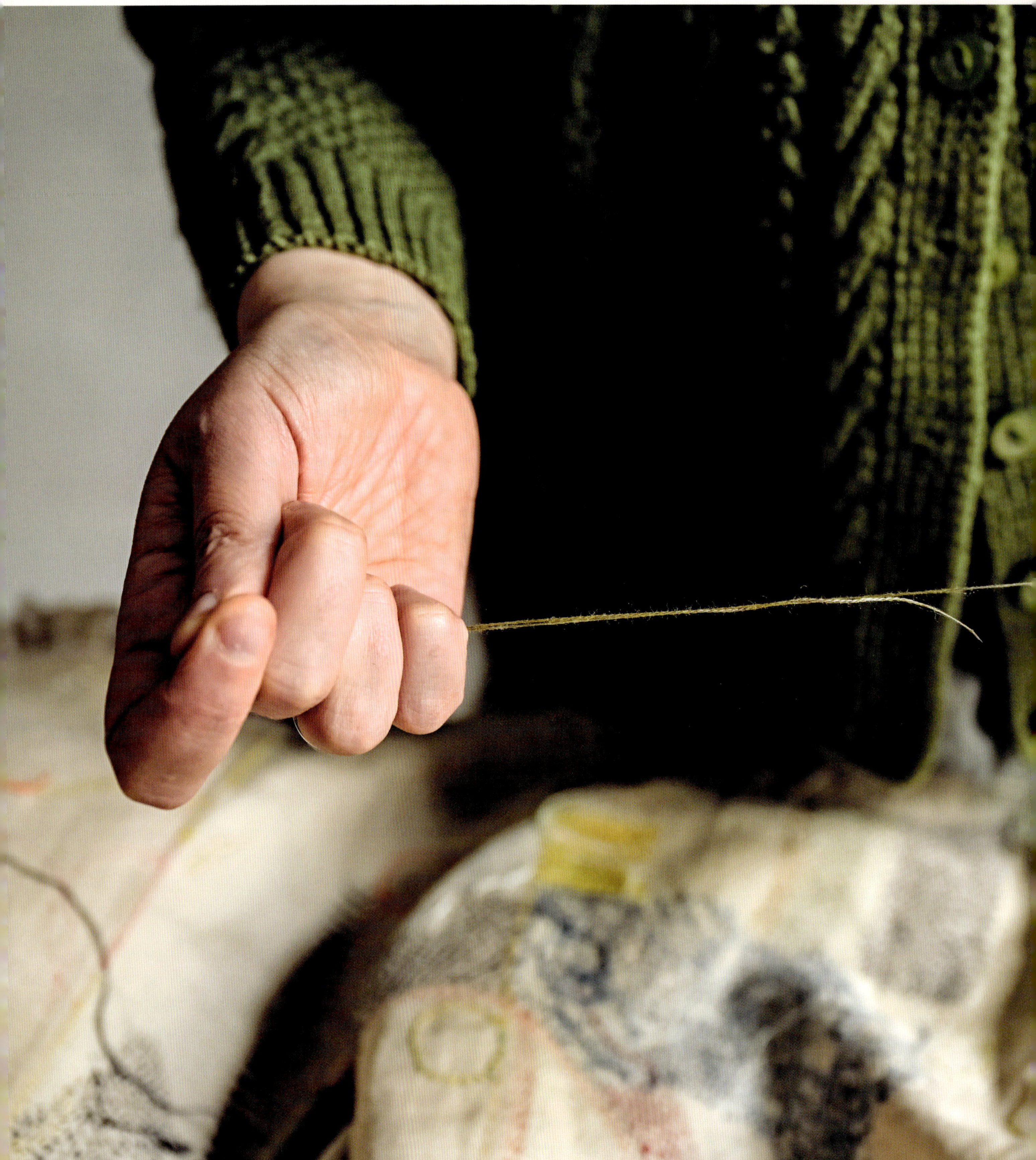

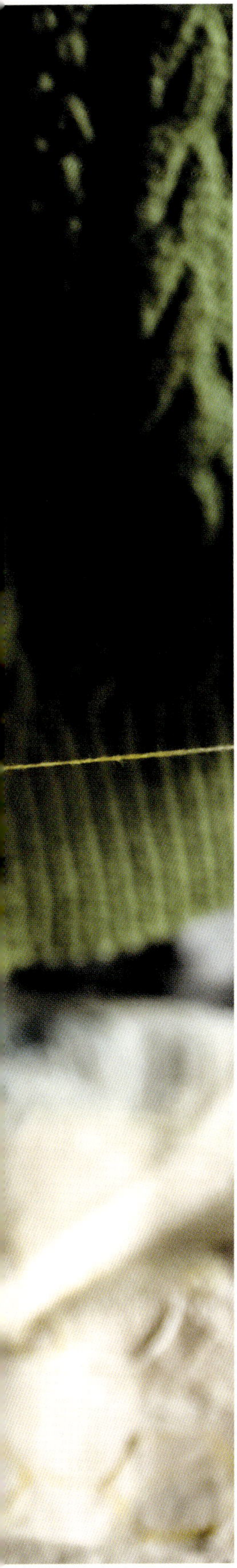

Introduction

This book explores reflective textile practices tied to time and place. The two are connected: we experience time through place and vice versa. Over the last decade, since my first two books, *Slow Stitch: Mindful and Contemplative Textile Art* (Batsford, 2015) and *Resilient Stitch: Wellbeing and Connection in Textile Art* (Batsford, 2021), were published I have continued to work with communities on site-specific textile work alongside a long period of academic research.

I find myself with the privilege of being able to reflect on years of practice, drawing on experience gained through studio practice, research, curatorial projects and working with and alongside multiple communities. I have continued to work with themes of time and place, but with a longitudinal approach. In this book I will offer thoughts about finding a place and working with it over time.

Is there somewhere that inspires you to learn or to observe more? What about interrupted places – those that have experienced huge change in their environment or structure? Does the time spent with a textile process connected to a place offer new ways of working with it?

The themes of both making and marking time and place are offered here, and the thread that runs through my first two books, connecting wellbeing to textile activity, will continue to emerge through a range of new projects, collaborations, ideas and the work of other artists.

Hand stitching continues to be my main technique; in my personal practice it offers me focus and a way of thinking through other projects. In community-based work it operates as a great connector in groups of people – sharing threads and threading needles for one another, learning stitches together, the easy conversation and silence that happens around the table.

For me, textile is the great connector. It joins and communicates in so many ways. It's the ordinary thing that we are surrounded by every day; it's the extraordinary thing that remembers and offers us ways of being storytellers of our own experience of our life in communities and in the geographies of the places where we live.

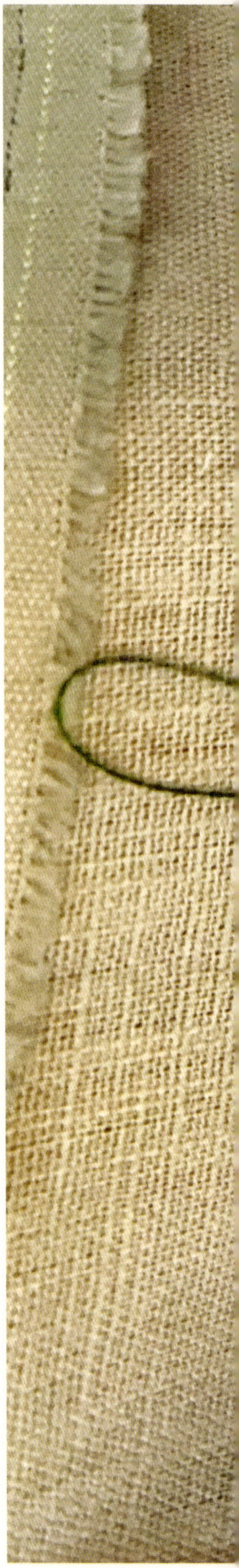

PREVIOUS PAGE
The author stitching at her kitchen table, 2021.
OPPOSITE
Community stitching session, Brontë Parsonage Museum, 2025.

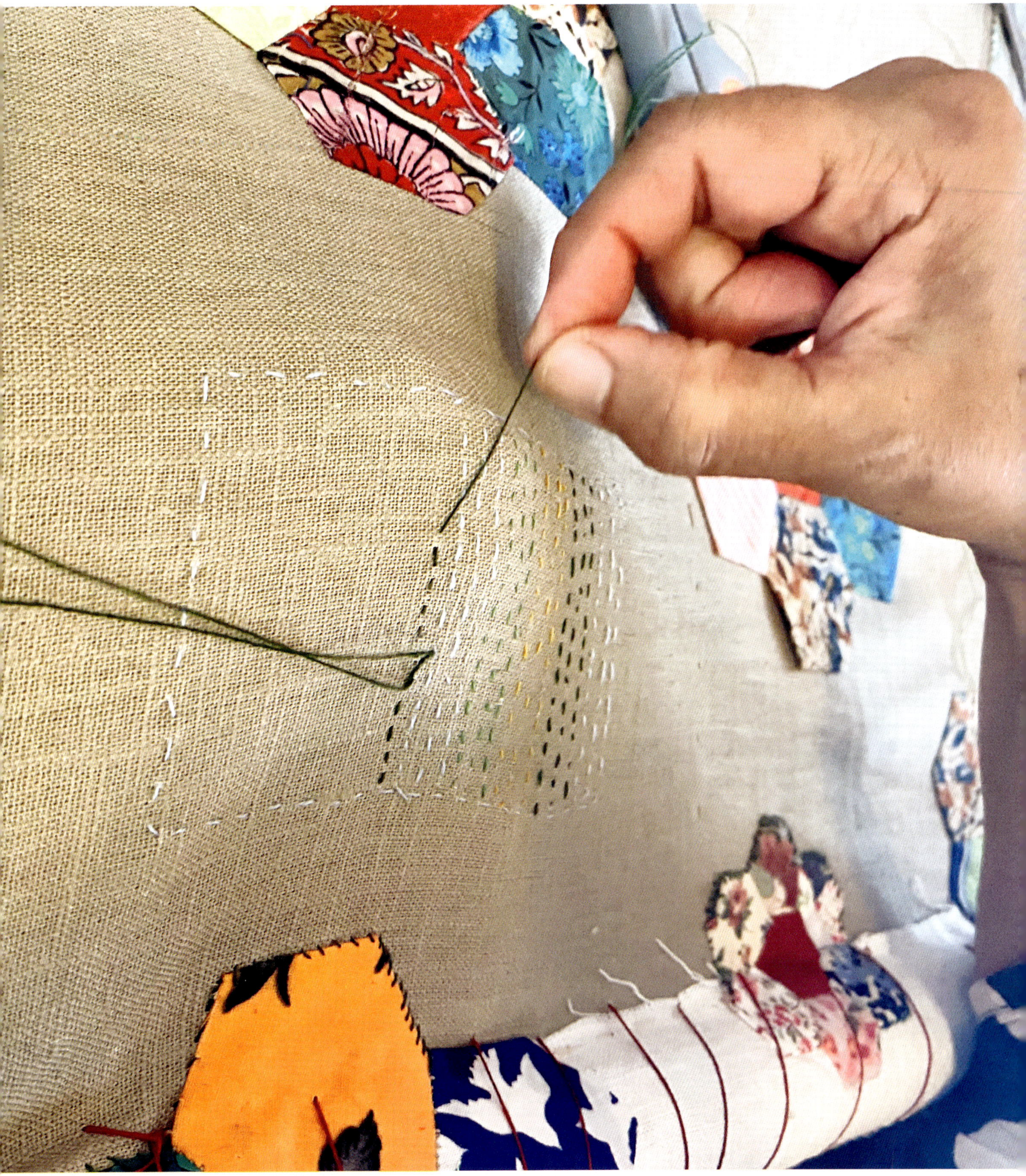

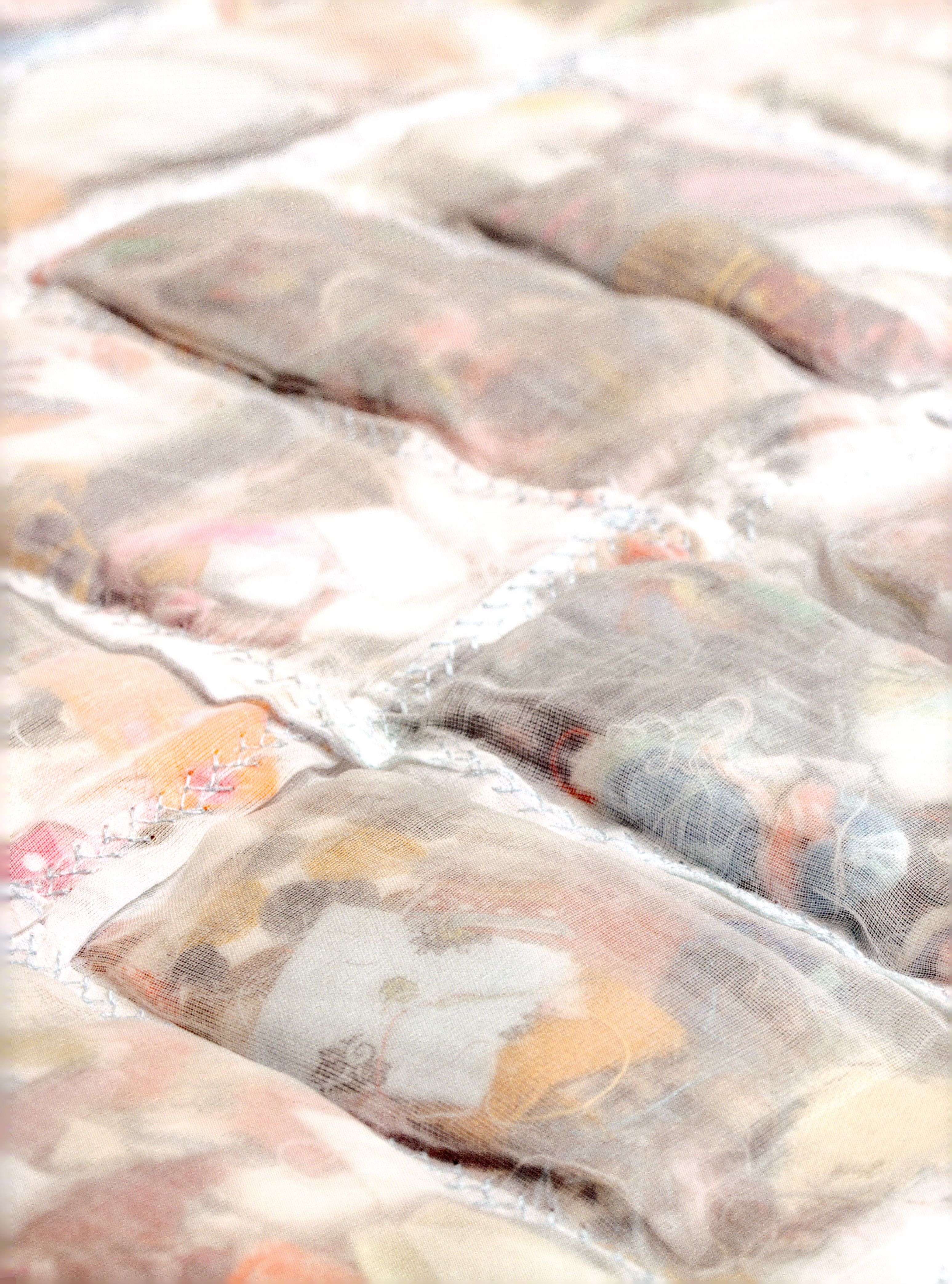

Gathering

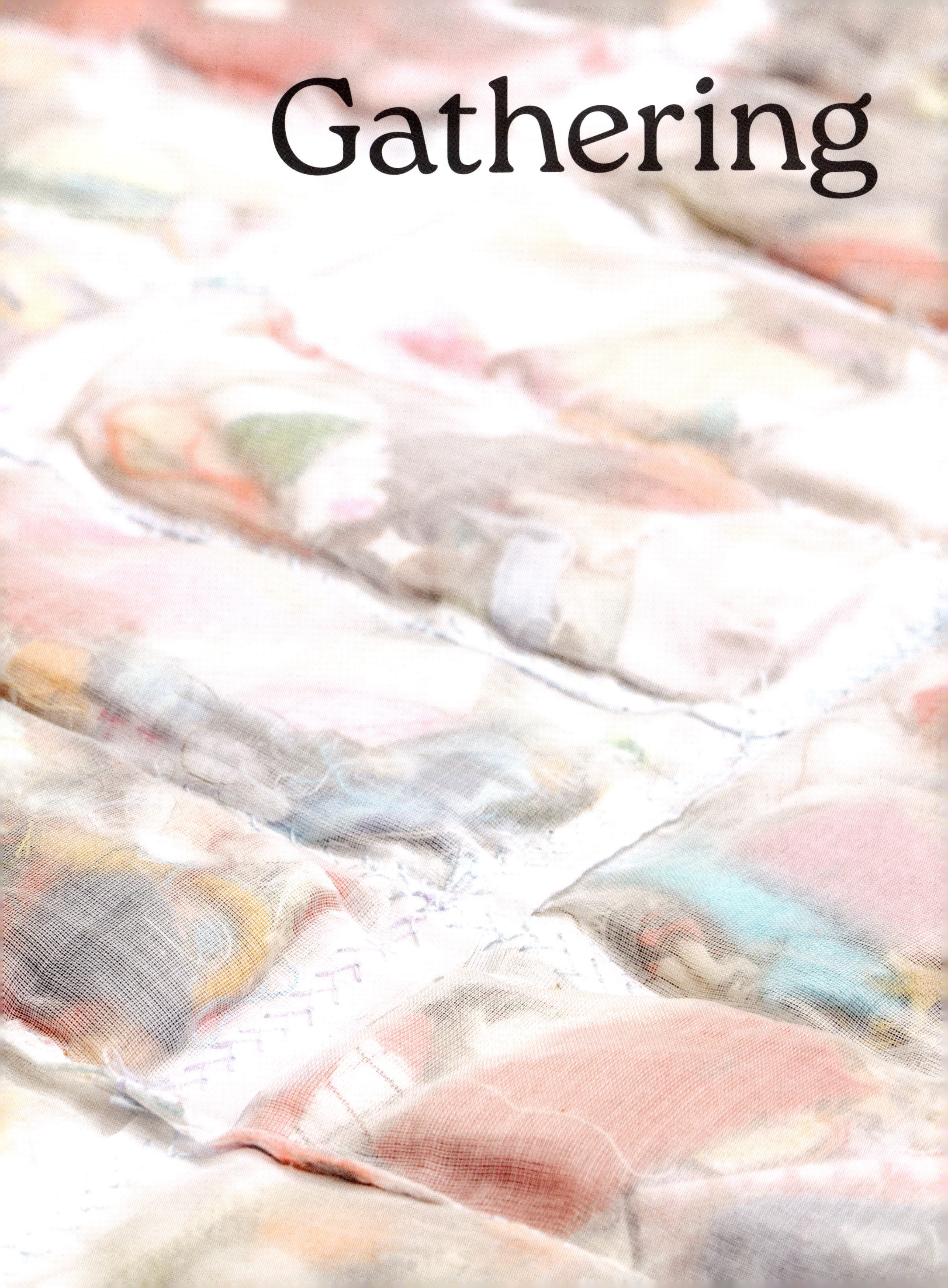

Twenty years ago I started work on a King's Fund project, *A Healing Environment*, for a mental-health NHS Trust in northern England. The first work I'd done in an in-patient hospital setting, the project explored the connections between green spaces, in this case a hospital garden, creativity and health.

A few things emerged from that project and the work with the patients, their families and the clinical staff. Of them, one relates to textile processes, from quiet making around a table to busy, faster paced dye workshops, or growing projects and all the precarities involved in gardening and growing dyes and fibres. Textiles offer all these different paces and ways of engaging for a short time – or over a long time. In all my projects since then I've thought hard about how impact is often informed by time spent, and how time offers different ways to engage.

My creative health-based practice has continued since then and the particular geographies and heritage of the now post-industrial textile areas of northern England have naturally been folded into this work.

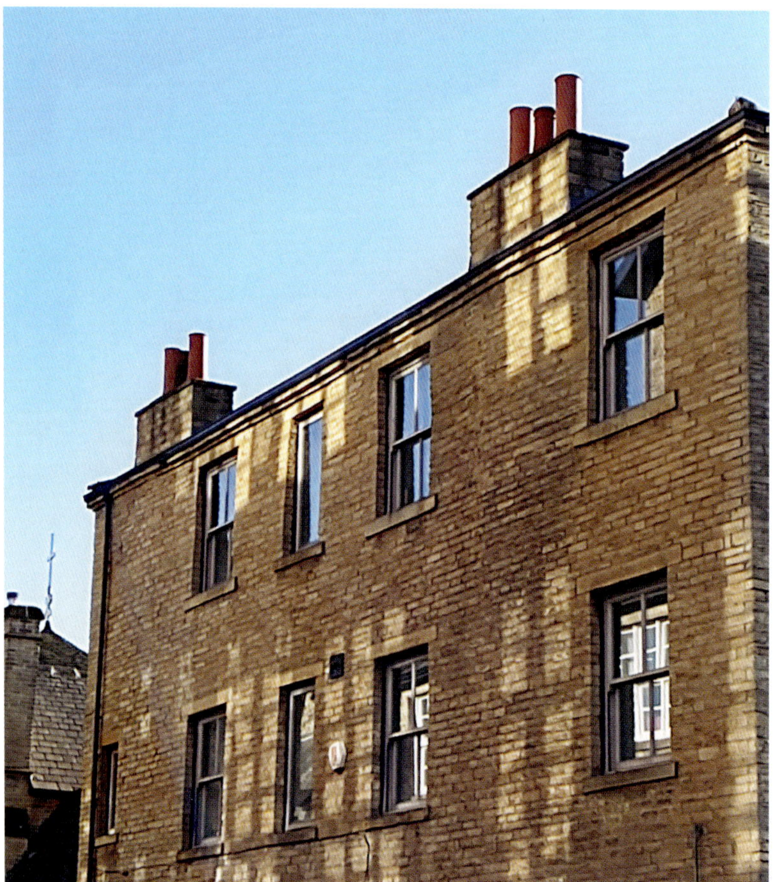

LEFT
Golden hour, Stott Hill, Bradford, 2025.

OPPOSITE
The author at her *Stitching Connections* exhibition, South Square Centre, Bradford, 2024.

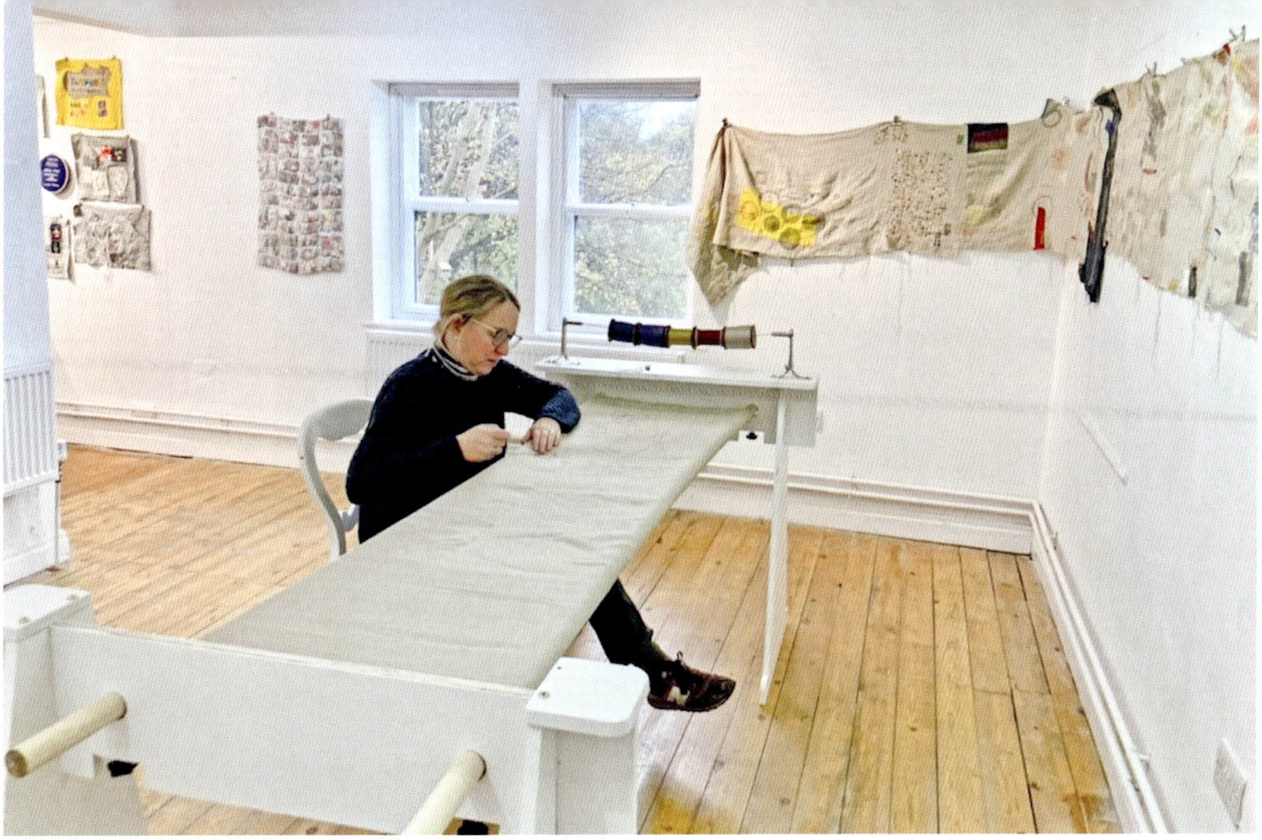

The sweep of mainly urban areas between Leeds and Liverpool and the textile specialities of the towns and cities in the region offer rich stories of production, the architecture of industry and the communities that live there – many of whom came to work in textile manufacture over a period of two centuries. Now, mainly post-industrial, these places also offer challenges, the spaces left and gradually filled, piecemeal, as a once-dominant industry declined.

Gathering work together for a retrospective exhibition in 2024 I thought about the afterlife of community textile projects. I retrieved things from storage and borrowed them back from organisations. Some of the pieces I would have liked to exhibit were lost, organisations now closed or priorities changed. And it is hard to convey in a finished textile on a wall the processes involved in getting to the point where something is made and can be shown as a thing.

The truth is, the process *is* the work. The sessions where hardly anyone comes, the sessions where you all sat in a shed with a cup of tea because it was too rainy to garden, the sessions when you were expecting eight people and 25 turned up and all the different ways that community spaces adapt to projects and people and how we gather together.

Documentary photography as projects progress shows groups making together. My photo library evidences this in the

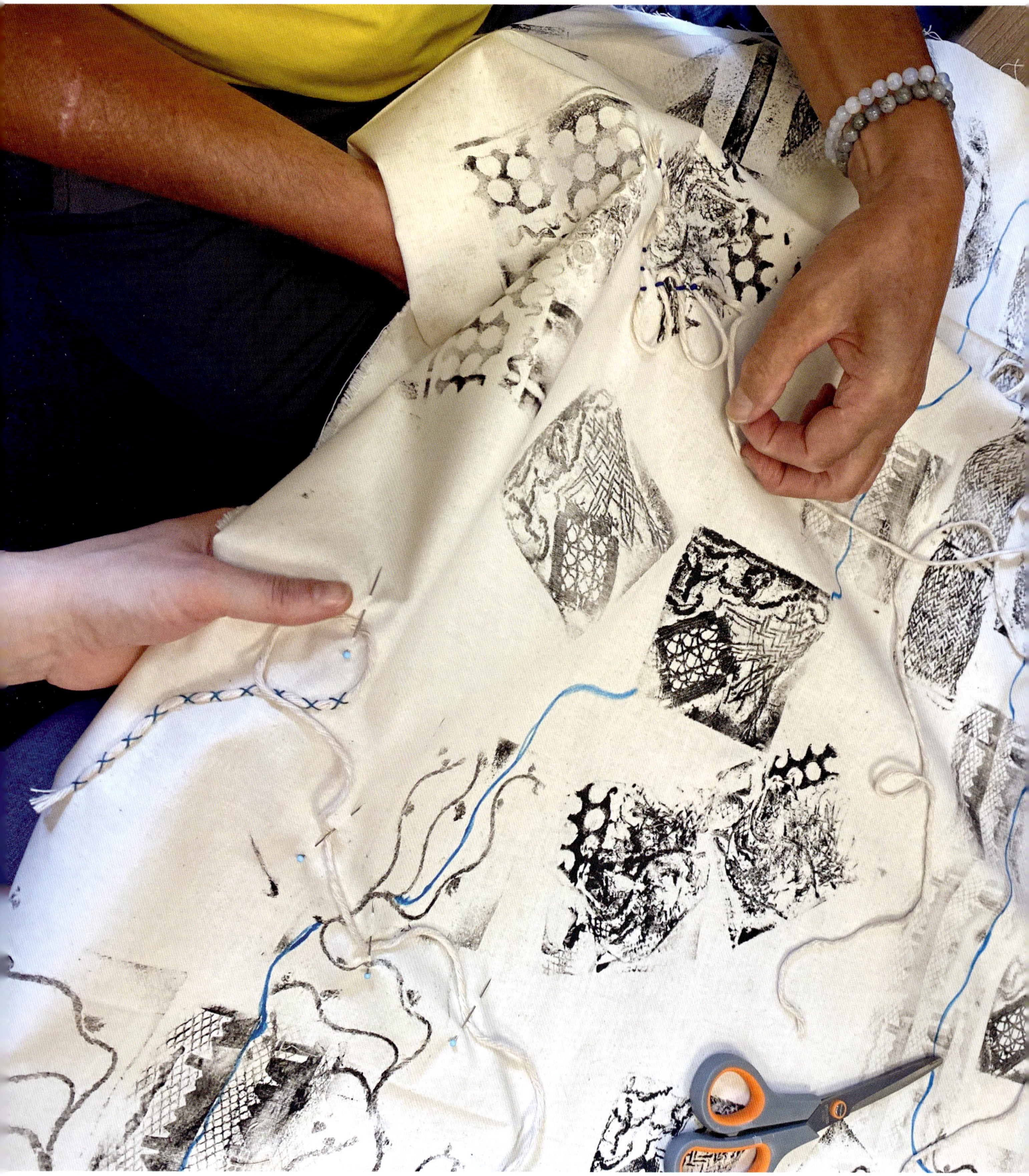

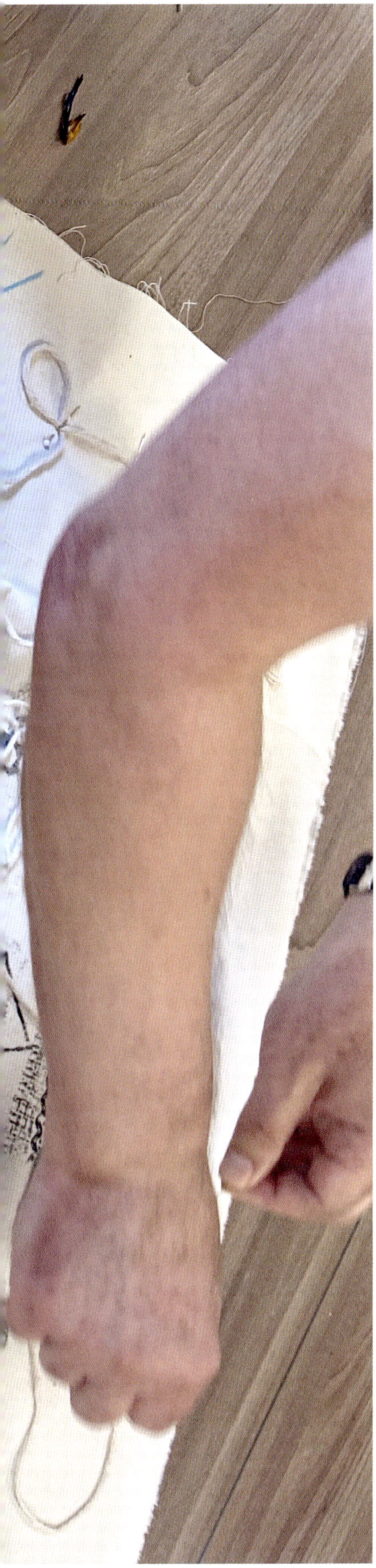

thousands of photographs of hands that I've taken over more than 20 years of practice. These are snapshots in time; they give the viewer visual clues to how the work came together but can never really illuminate the whole process. For that, one must be embedded, in the place and at the time, and for the duration of the work.

Gathering is a textile-adjacent word. Scattered sources come together, or fabric is gathered with stitches around tables in community centres. From church crypts and scout huts to portable classrooms and polytunnels, I've learned how best to set up space for the conversations that happen when people gather alongside textile-making activities. By the age of the tables I can divine when the most recent chunk of funding for the community organisation came – heavy melamine tops, lighter plastic, a wallpaper-pasting table brought in from my car in extremis.

The tabletop is a gathering space, 'a story so far'. It can just as easily be a quiet making space as it can host intense conversations about community renewal and repair. These are places of multiple languages and stories and advice sessions for new arrivals to the country.

Before the session starts, I wipe off the vestiges of the previous session – it could be carrot peelings from a grow, cook and eat project, or felt-tip pen marks from a crèche session with young children. The contents of my community scrap bag (written about in *Resilient Stitch*, 2021) are tipped out for participants to rummage through. The leftover threads and scraps are swept into another bag at the end of the session and kept. Eventually, they will serve as stuffing for an 'economy quilt' made by groups all over the city following instructions from a 1919 book, *Needlework Economies* by Flora Klickmann. Tapestry wool ends, a collection of printed cotton selvedges from a local sewing business and synthetics from a South Asian tailor all come together.

OPPOSITE
Pathways to Wellbeing project HALE Bradford, as part of Bradford 2025 City of Culture Creative Health delivery.

Out in the world the news headlines are populated by big stories about urban change; headline figures detail the 'most deprived' areas and a proliferation of data tells the story of unequal healthy life expectancies across communities living cheek by jowl. These harsh realities can be countered by small stories heard while passing the biscuit tin or sharing a pair of scissors. The table in the community space offers room for loose ends and missing links: where many kinds of dialogue emerge, where precarities are part of the story, where we can materialise big cities and identify unique characteristics of very local places.

Start where you are

Projects that explore place and time can be tempting – in the sense that these big themes offer you a space to explore anywhere you want. But, in this book I want to encourage a local approach. This involves thinking about the things around you now – the place you live, the green spaces adjacent to it, the materials you already have. This approach embraces local place and seasonal change, the potentialities of the area around you. The short walk to a local park or the dog-walking route you take every day can offer differences and unique perspectives on place every time you tread that path.

I encourage spending some time looking at the collection of materials and equipment you already have. Identify simple materials and tools: plain neutral-coloured fabric, fine black thread and a good needle – these can be used much as you would use a sketchbook page and a black fine-liner pen. They offer simple ways to make a mark, a place-based stitch drawing or a line that captures the story and route of a journey. Other scraps of thread and fabric in a collection can offer you ways of recollecting or reminiscing: materials used in other projects or threads used for making clothes, quilts or embellishments.

OPPOSITE
Community Economy Quilt, 2018, scrap fabrics with cotton organdie cover, part of the Worn Stories project at Hive, Bradford. 50×73cm (19.6×28.7in).

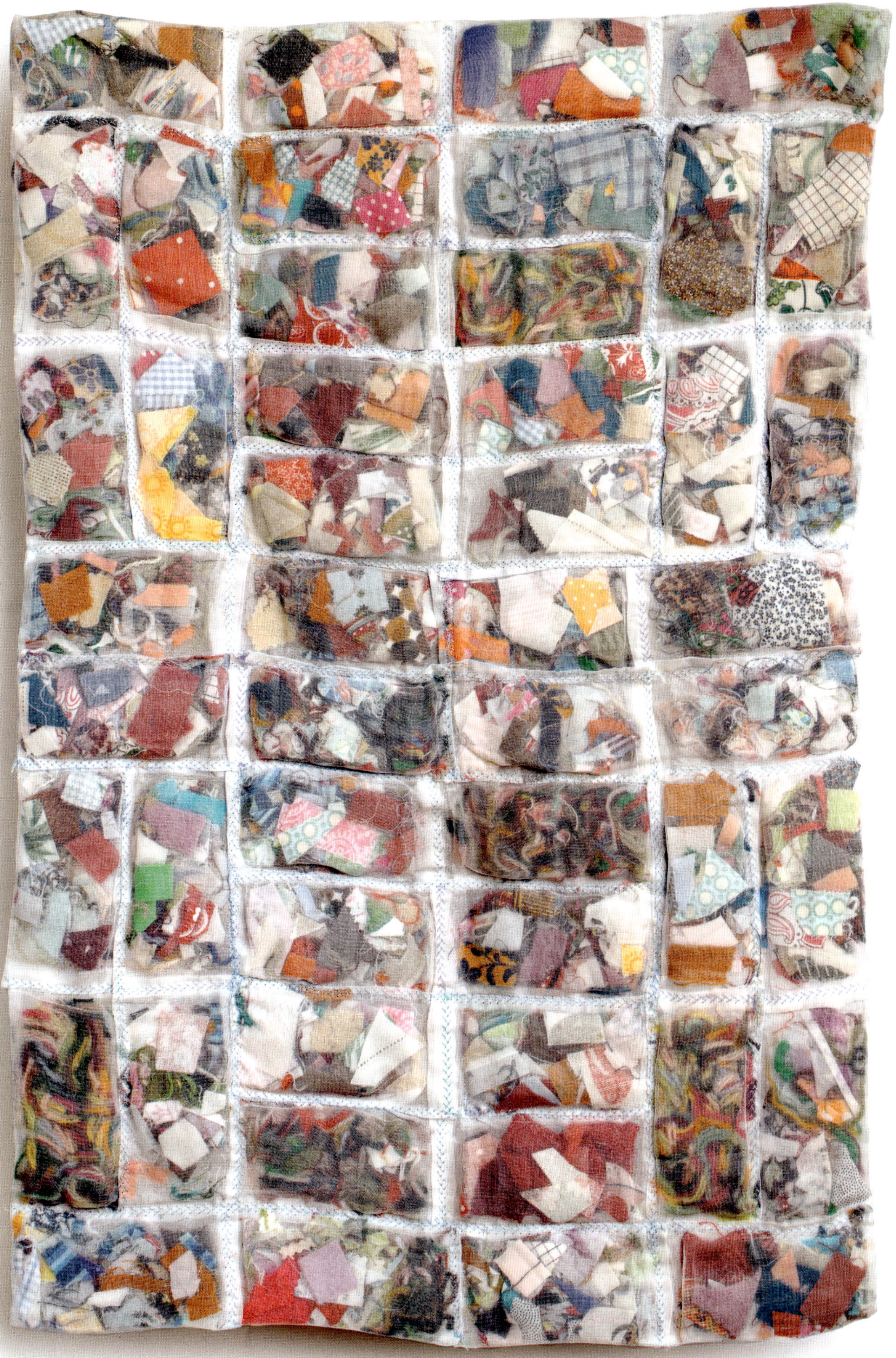

Conversations through Making

Conversations through Making is a piece of work begun during the COVID-19 lockdowns of 2020 when my working life changed abruptly. Used to the work of the community space, stitching alongside others, sharing tools, resources and conversations, I had to take my practice online, like so many.

The opening section of all my online workshops involved a simple prompt, to stitch a circle using basic running stitches and a single type of thread. My preference was to complete this activity alongside the online participants and, as we stitched, a growing pile of my semi-completed circles grew on the studio table. As the practitioner during these sessions, I was holding space for the participants so rarely had time to complete my own circles during the workshops.

Afterwards, I returned to my stitched circles and reflected on the conversations shared during these multiple sessions: observations about the pace of stitching, the quiet breathing space it offered, reminiscences about other projects worked on, the strange dislocation of lockdowns. To make a record of these shared stories I eventually appliquéd the circles together, framing them in a large quilt hoop. The connecting of them together is haphazard, the backing pieces uneven in size and sometimes colour. This is messy, often incomplete work but the circularity of the stories and the different kinds of stitching circle we created online are evidenced and gathered together as one.

OPPOSITE
Conversations through making (2020–22), recycled linen and thread, 48cm diameter (18.8in).

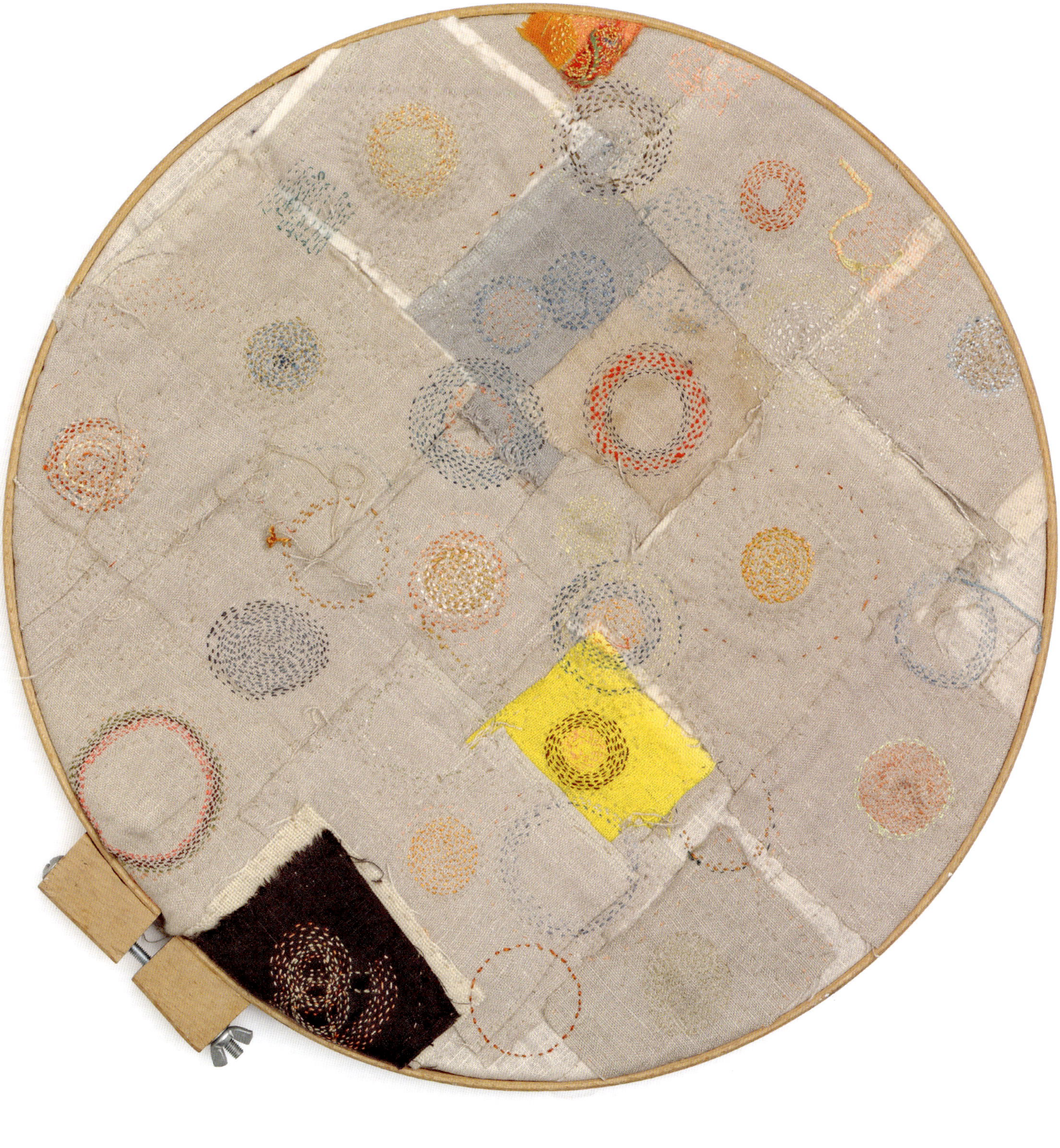

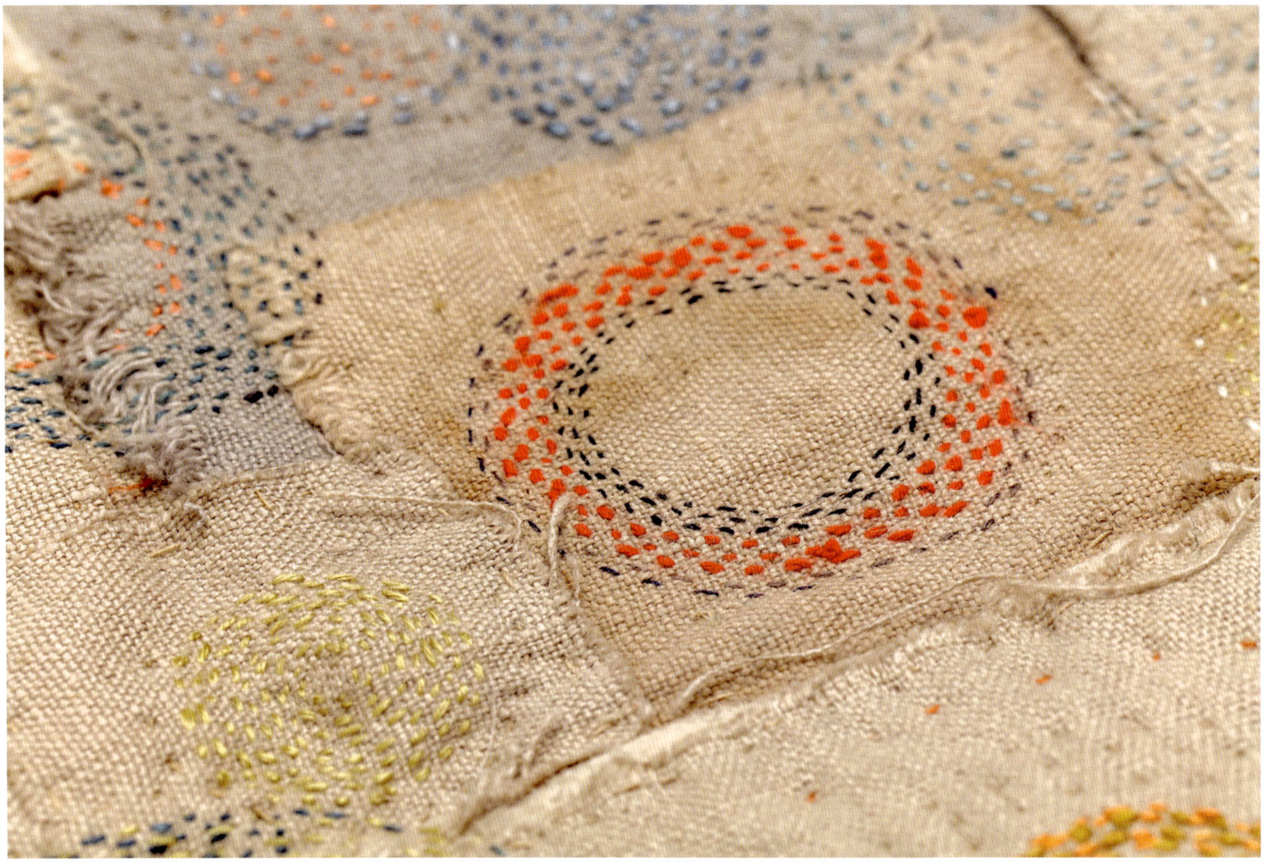

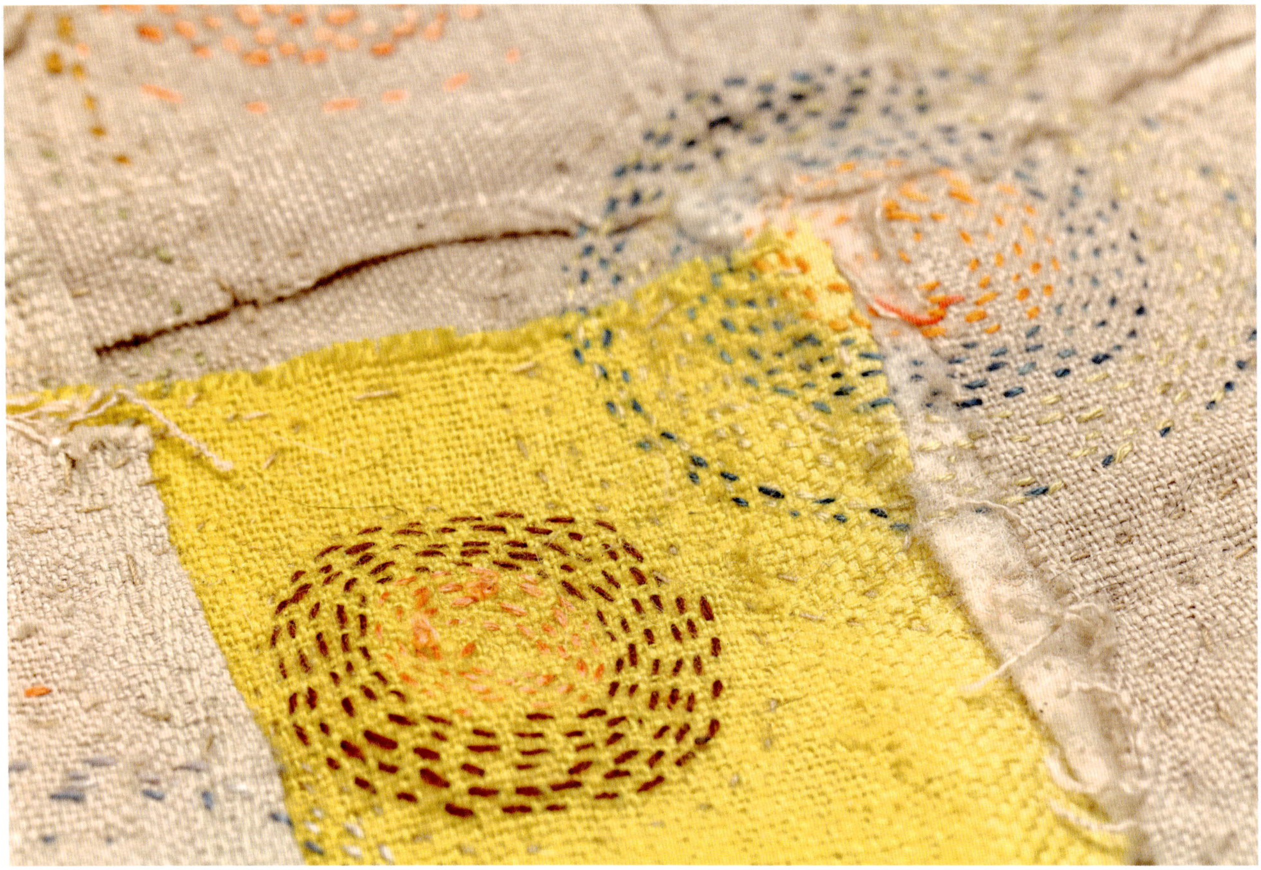

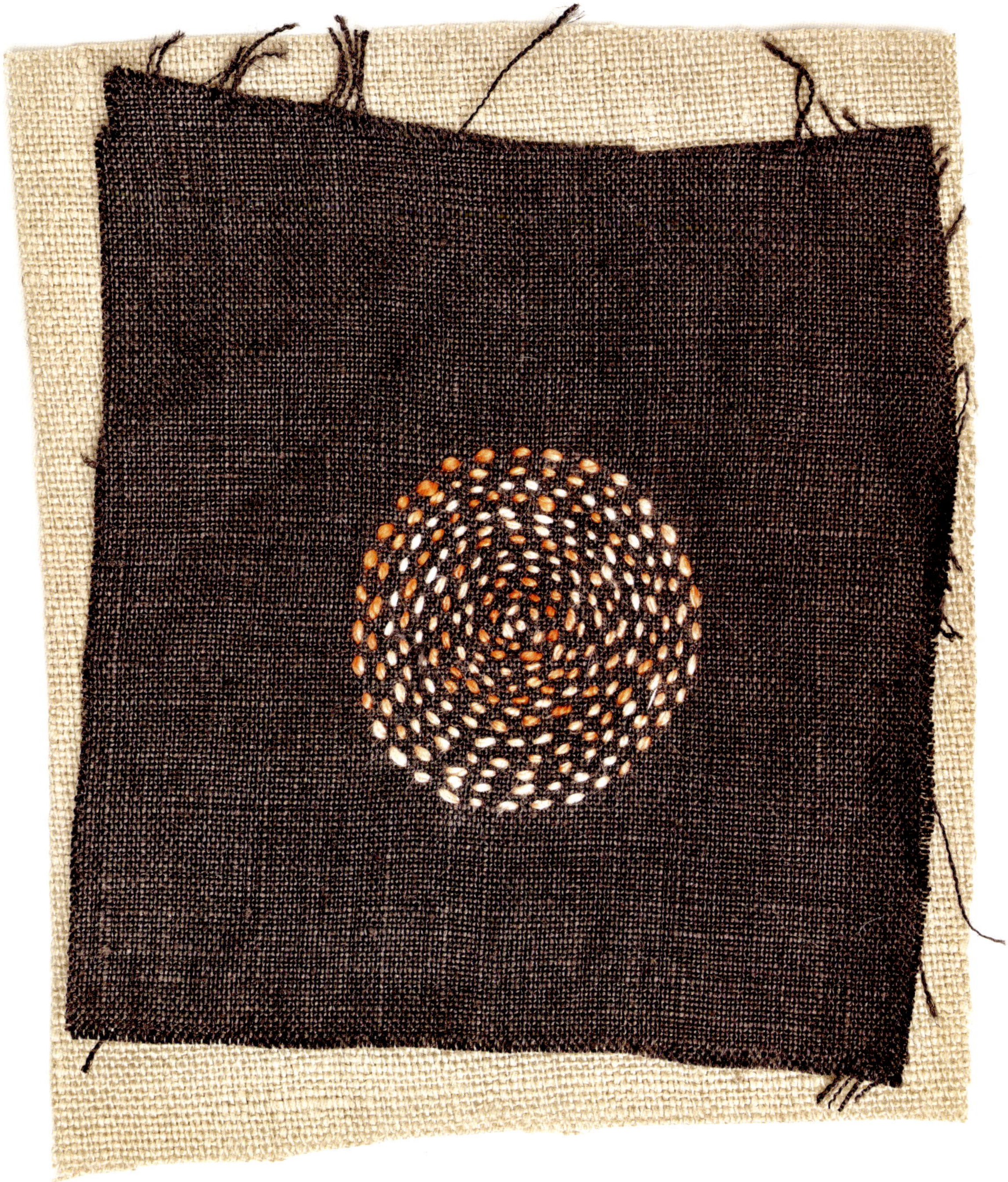

As described in *Conversations through making*, you could begin a practice that involves starting a period of reflection by stitching a circle yourself. Try to limit yourself to one colour of thread that easily stitches through your choice of fabric. A simple running stitch will offer you an opportunity to establish a stitching rhythm and an appreciation of the marks you make. This process can be grounding and can also open your mind to new ideas and directions.

OPPOSITE AND ABOVE
Conversations through making (details).

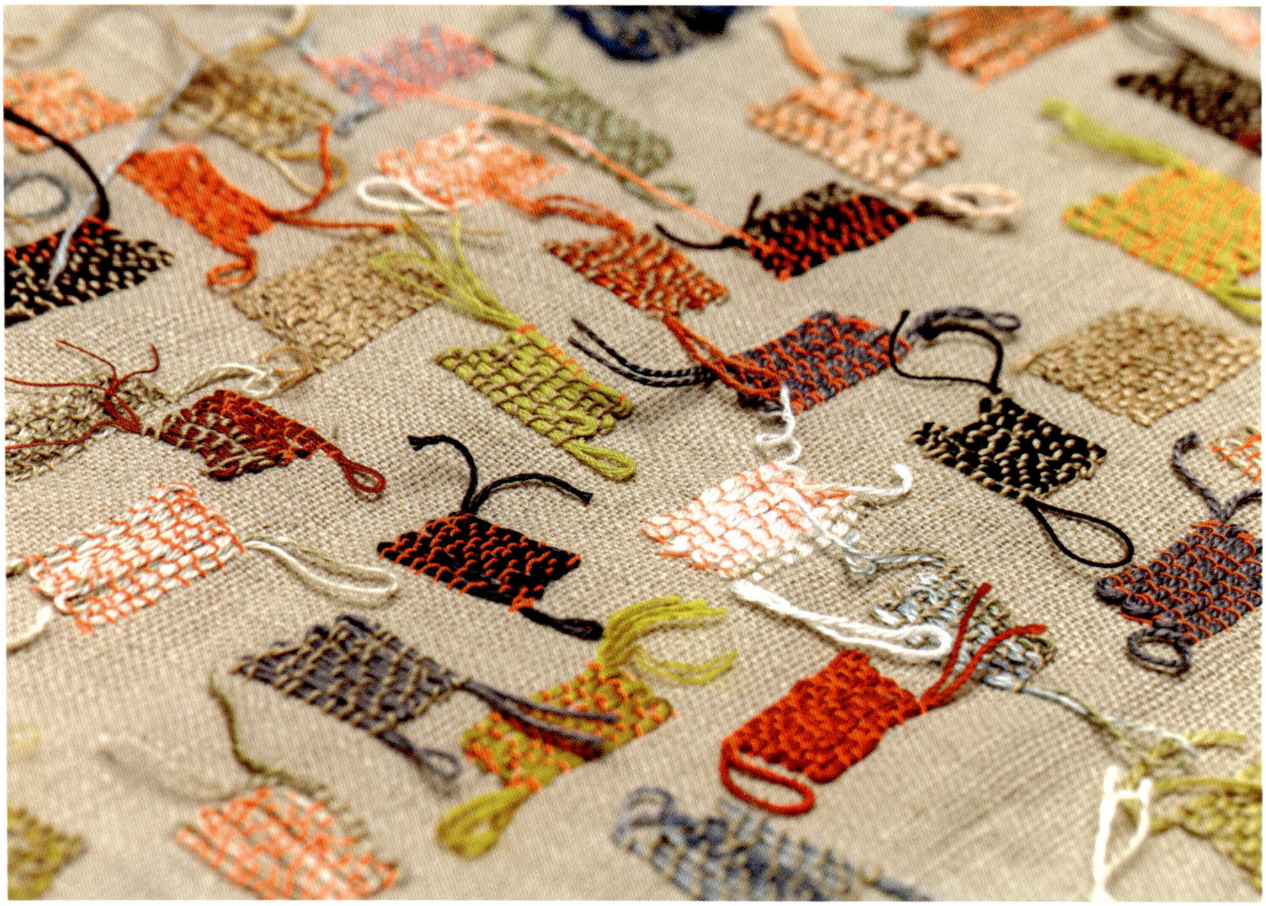

Praxis

This series of work emerged from a period of university-based research about extraction and its many meanings. I began to research extractive practices in textiles and started with my own studio practice – looking at the stripped-back and simplified processes of growing, dyeing, making and unmaking, and how I use the plants I grow at my allotment.

The extraction of beeswax and its use also became part of this story. The allotments where I garden are bounded by a railway line, nineteenth century and 1930s housing and major roads. Around the corner a large dyeworks was still working until the late 1960s, built on the remains of the first worsted mill in Bradford, which had started production in 1815.

Stories of textile industries and the post-industrial aftermath have informed my working life for 20 years. This constantly prompts me to try to make sense of a personal practice that is far removed from the industrial textile processes that happened

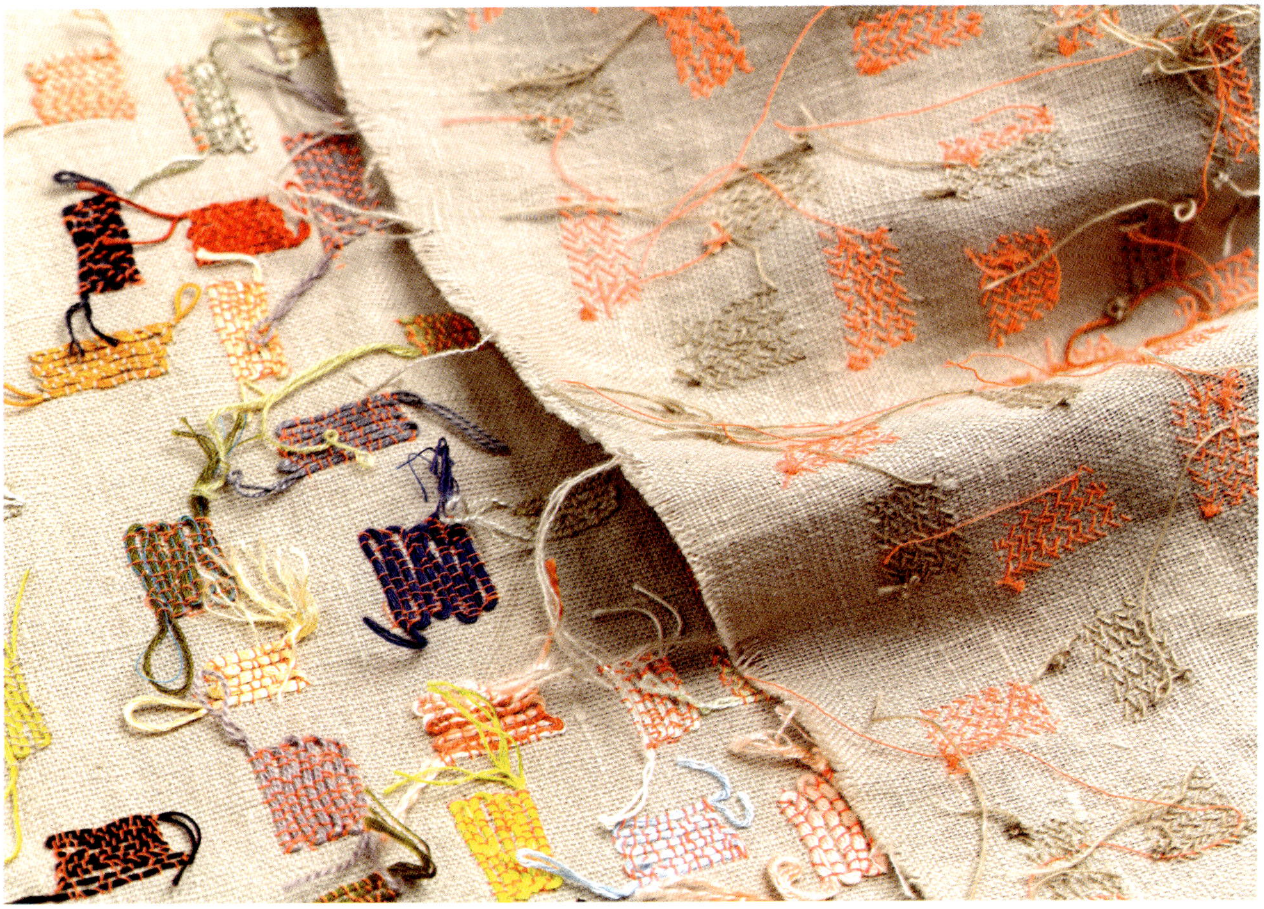

ABOVE
Praxis (details) (2024), recycled silk thread, cotton thread, on recycled linen.
OVERLEAF
Praxis (2024), recycled silk thread, beeswax, cotton thread, on recycled linen 78×43cm (30.7×16.9in).

around my allotment site. When I first rented the plot, the soil was full of glass and rubble, and after rainfall, fragments of broken clay smokers' pipes still rise to the surface of the beds, which I retrieve and save – another kind of extraction.

The shapes in this piece offer me a space for reflection. The beeswax I condition my threads with was extracted with small amounts of honey from the hives kept at my allotment. The beehives, hidden behind a shed in a tangle of bindweed and comfrey, house bee colonies that thrive on my planting and that of other gardeners and on the ample forage in the wild patches around the site. The process of refining dirty wax is quite immersive: melting it in water, letting it set, removing impurities, melting it again, letting it set – and on it goes. This, for me, was almost more enjoyable than the small number of jars of honey taken from the hives. The wax remains honey scented and I like that too.

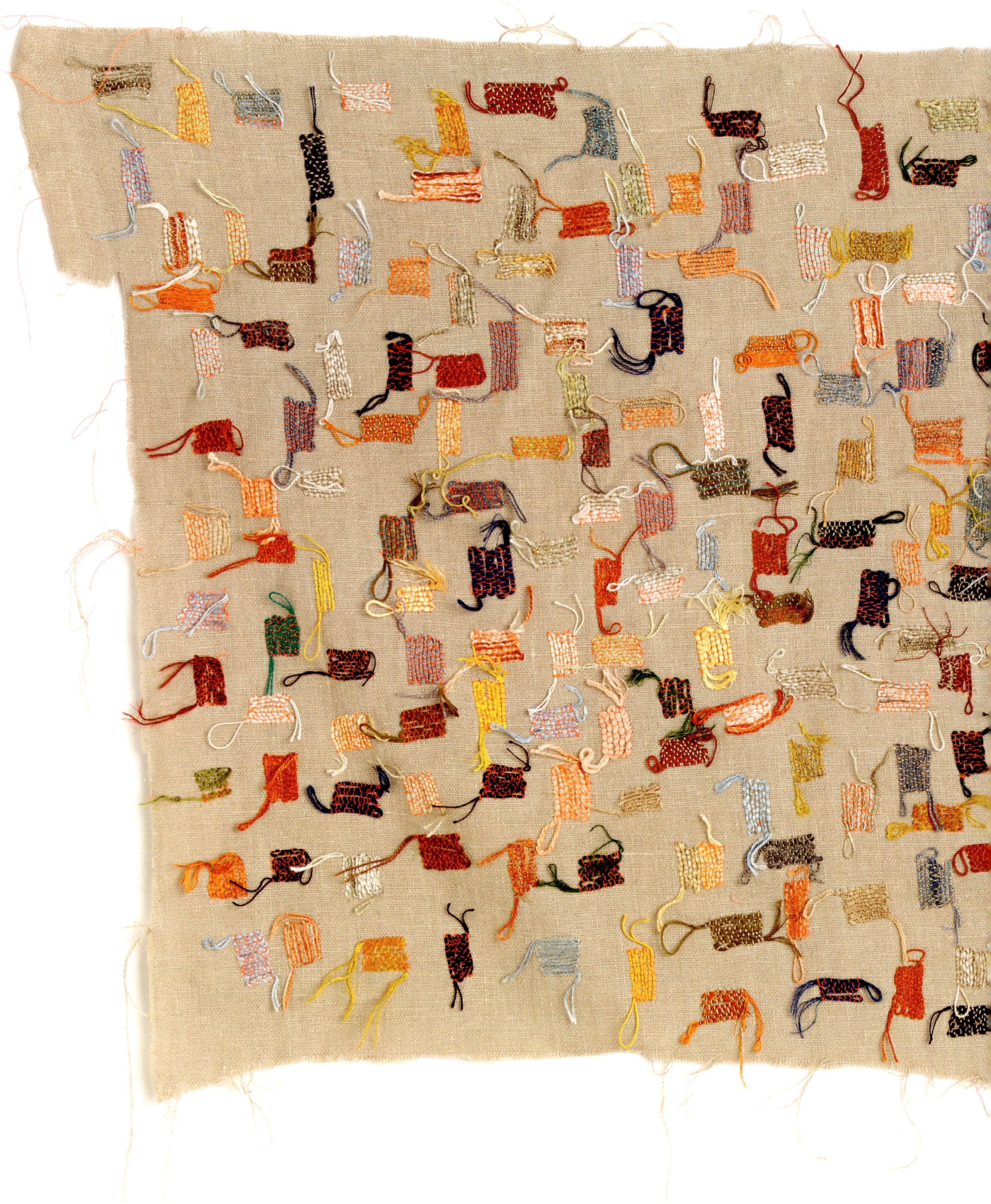

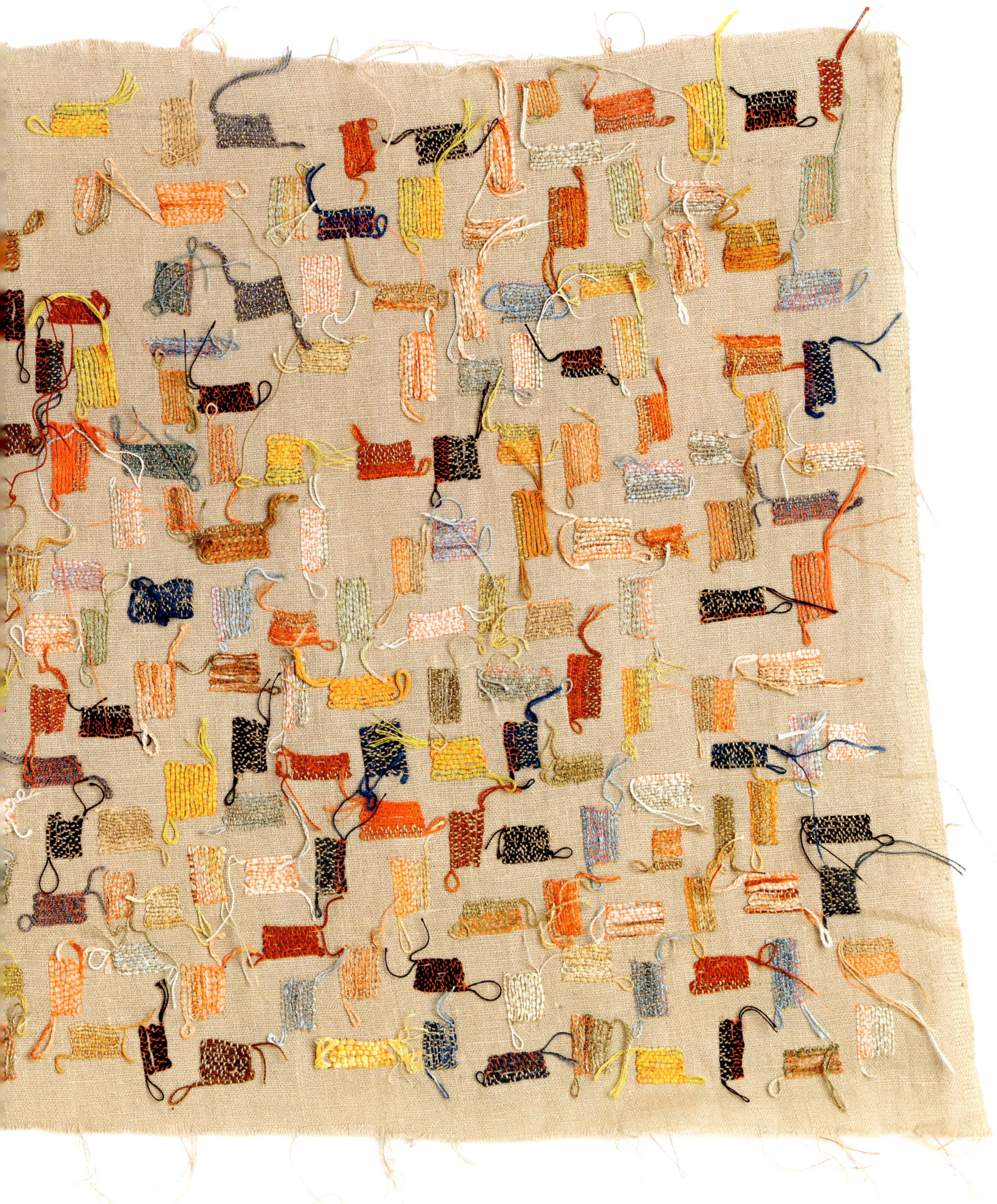

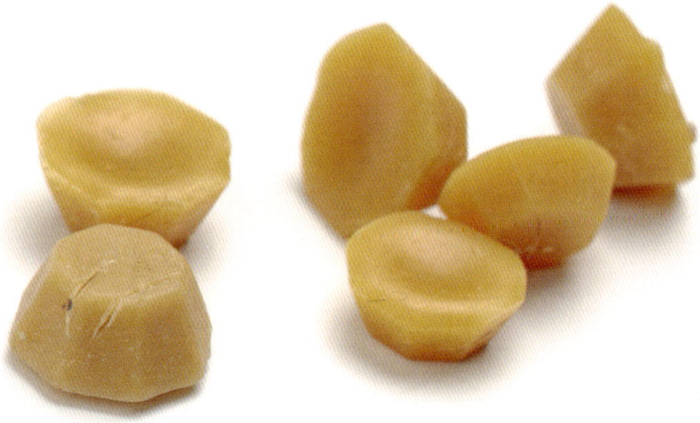

ABOVE
Beeswax pucks from the authors allotment hives.
BELOW
Praxis ii (2024) detail.
OPPOSITE
Praxis ii (2024), recycled silk thread, beeswax, cotton thread, on recycled linen 39×39cm (15.3×15.3in).

In *Praxis* all my stitching was accompanied by a block of this wax; on colder days I held it in my hand until it became slightly softened. The work includes couched and needle-woven silk threads which I dyed with plants from the same urban space where the bees live.

I pull a single thread, cutting through the wax, double the thread and run my finger and thumb along the thicker piece. The waxed thread pulls itself together and holds its shape although I sometimes pin it in place. I use a finer sewing cotton to couch it to my linen background. Working in blocks of stitches, laying the threads together, the wax holds the surface. It feels both malleable and robust.

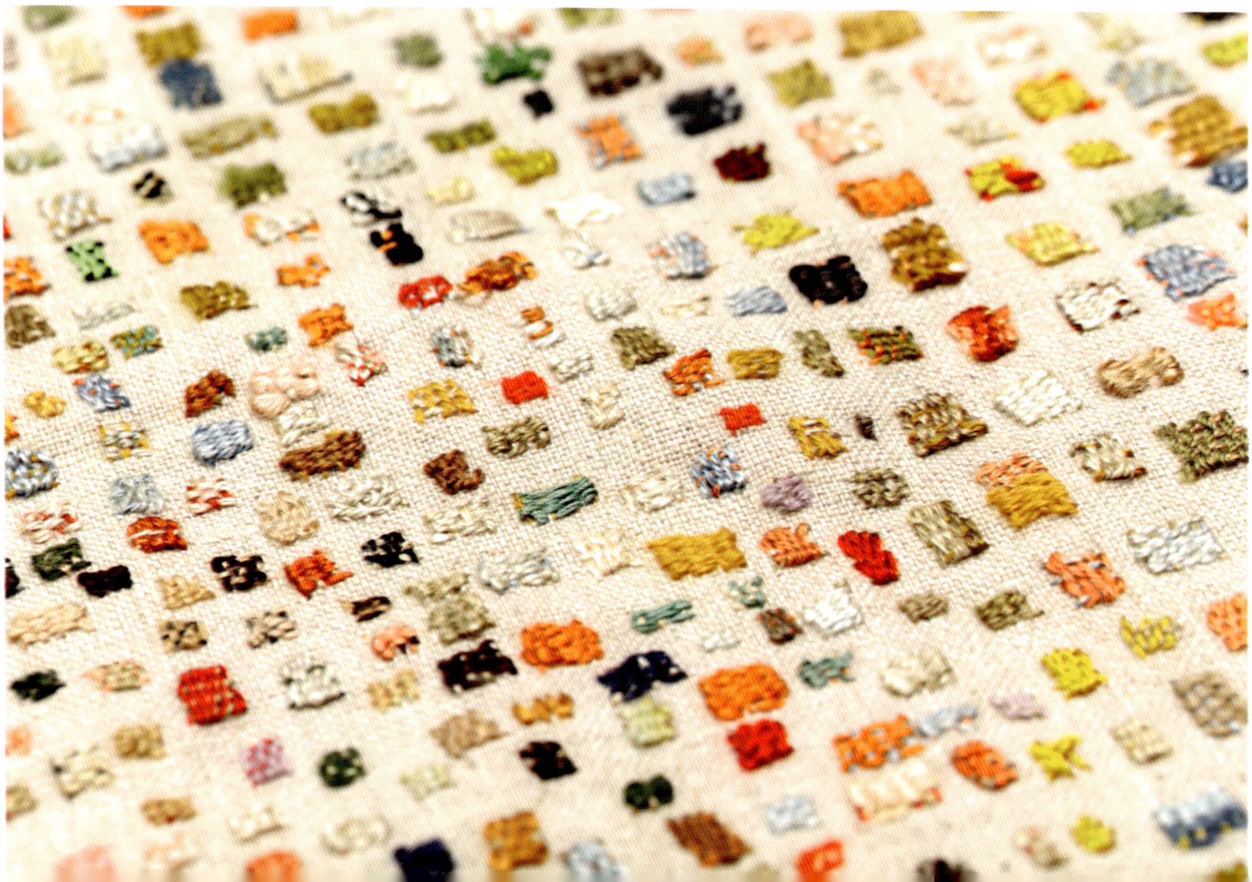

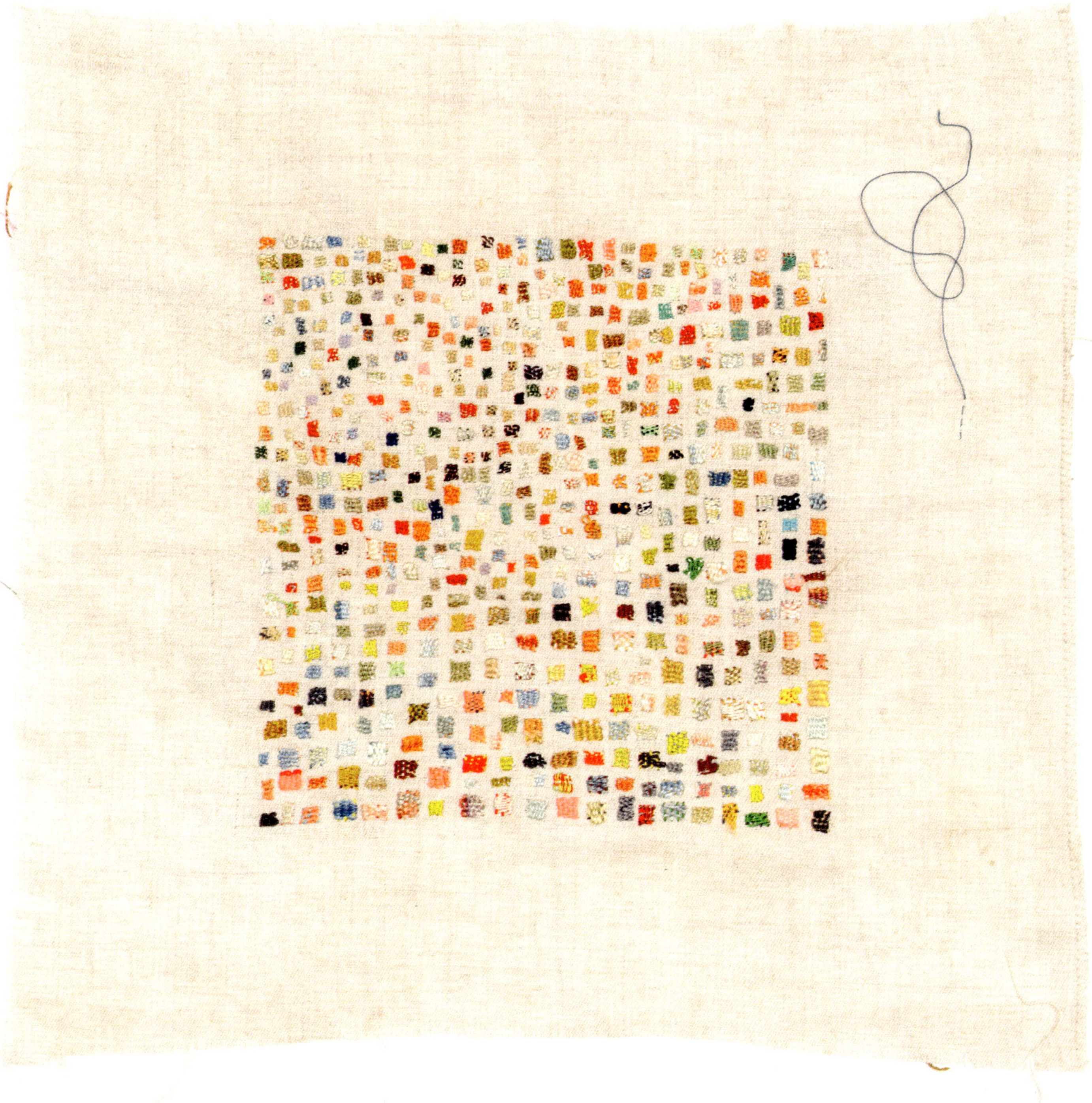

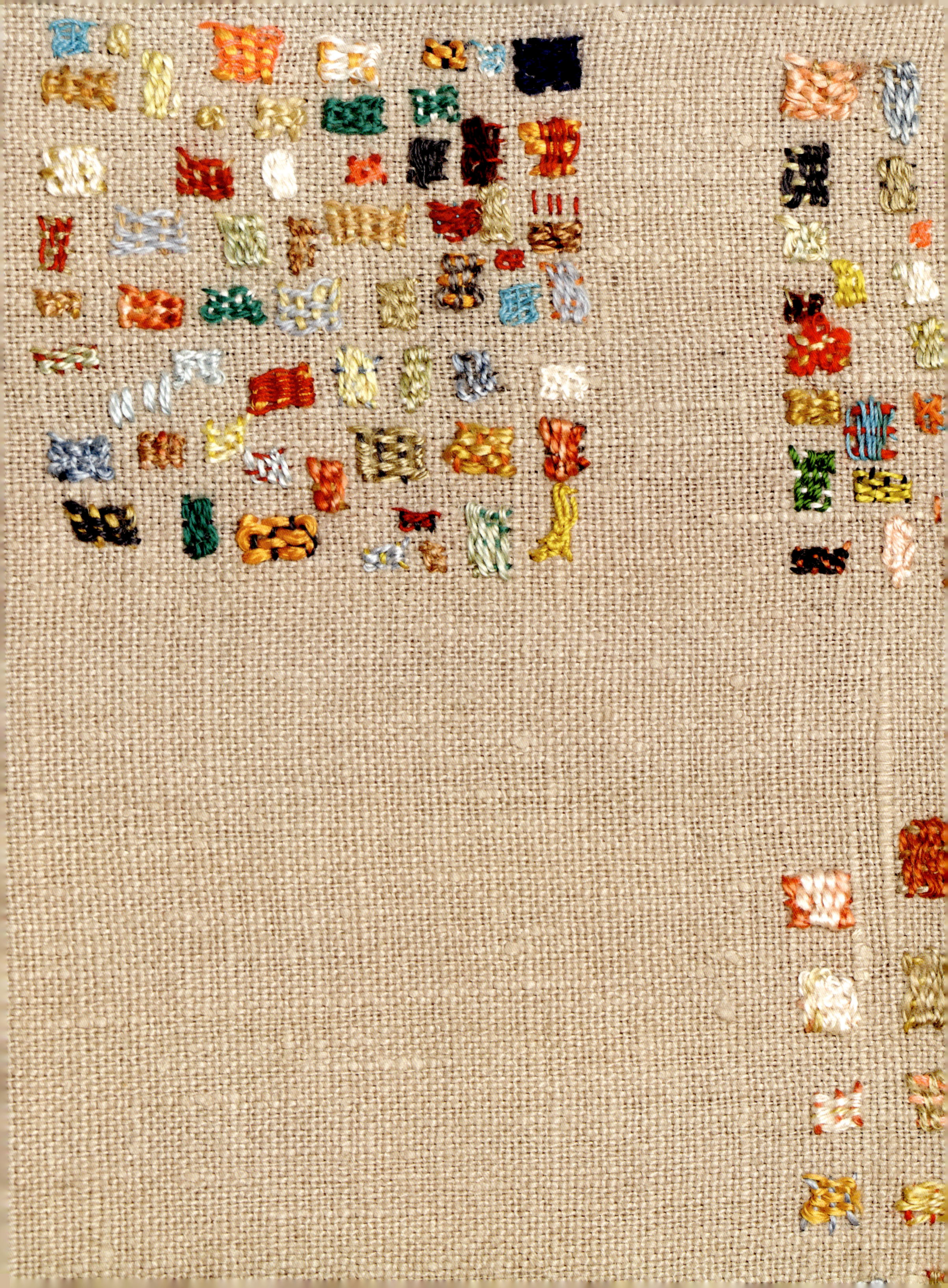

Time

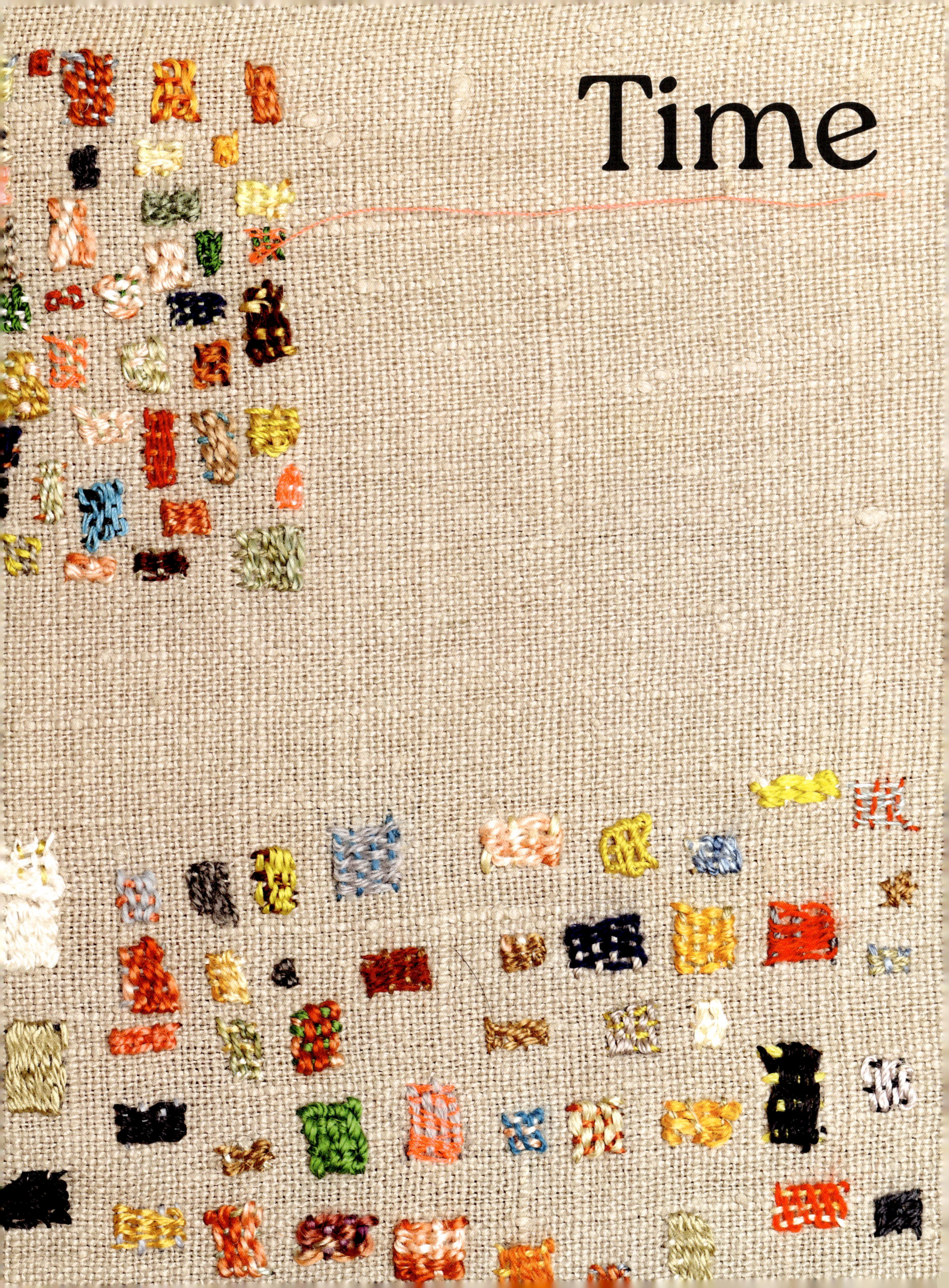

My preference is for projects where the appropriate amount of time is given to uncover a story, to complete a textile process, to grow something from seed and work with the harvest, so the project can come to full fruition. Alongside these pieces of work, often with communities, my personal practices have been durational. I have taken a period of time and worked within it, sometimes a fixed timeframe, sometimes ongoing. Everything from a decade to a single weekly stitched reflection over the course of a year has been part of my work.

The practices working with time that I have explored include the process of reworking projects, adding to them and bringing their stories up to date.

In this teaching sample I worked over existing stitches with thread dyed with allotment plants with some old gold-coloured silk thread dyed with the last of the *Tagetes* 'Burning Embers' grown at my allotment. The flower heads were still full of colour and scent when I dyed a little batch in early December, the growing season worryingly lengthening each year. The needle-weaving technique is one I use a lot when stitching while editing my writing.

Revisiting textile work and words over the decades offers me routes into remaking and reflecting, reinventing and redesigning. This reflective process often provides an entry point for new projects, and ways to reconsider themes. The colours processed with plants shift every season due to variations in colour and temperature. Over time, I appreciate colour as it fades, the impermanence of these often-improvised colour-collecting experiments. The working of needle and thread change too, as my hands become, at once, more experienced and less flexible with age.

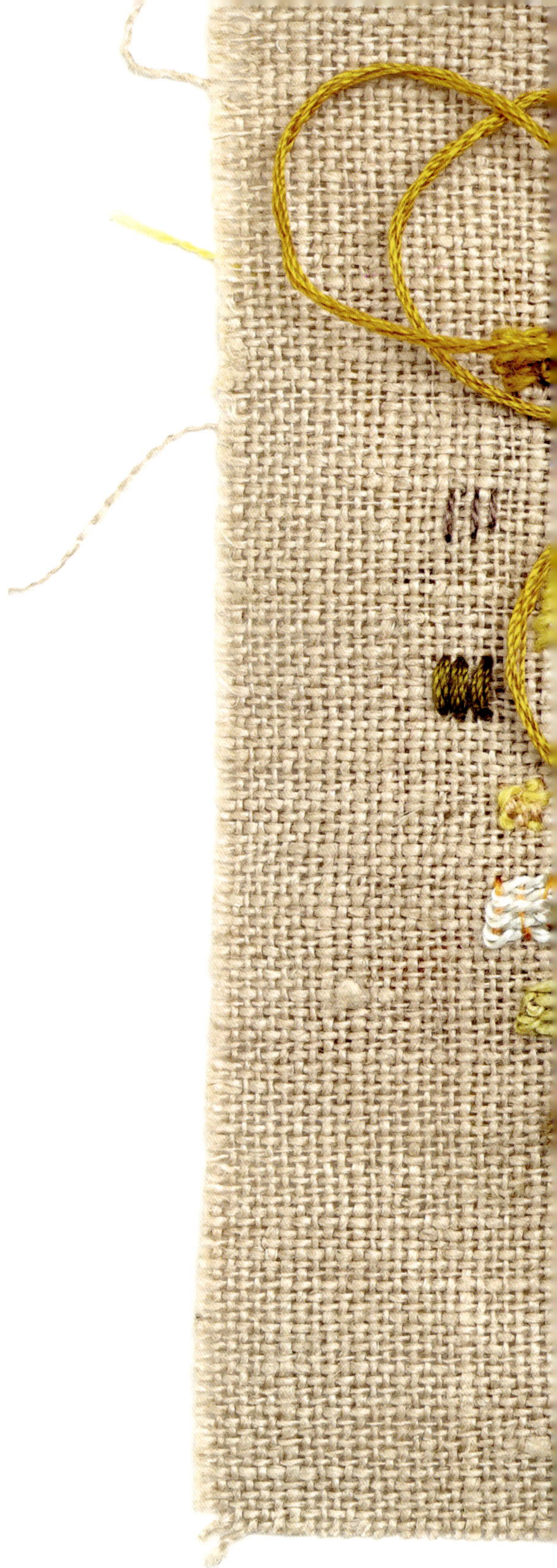

OPPOSITE
Sample with needle weaving, recycled silk and hand dyed silk threads (see p.38 for instructions).

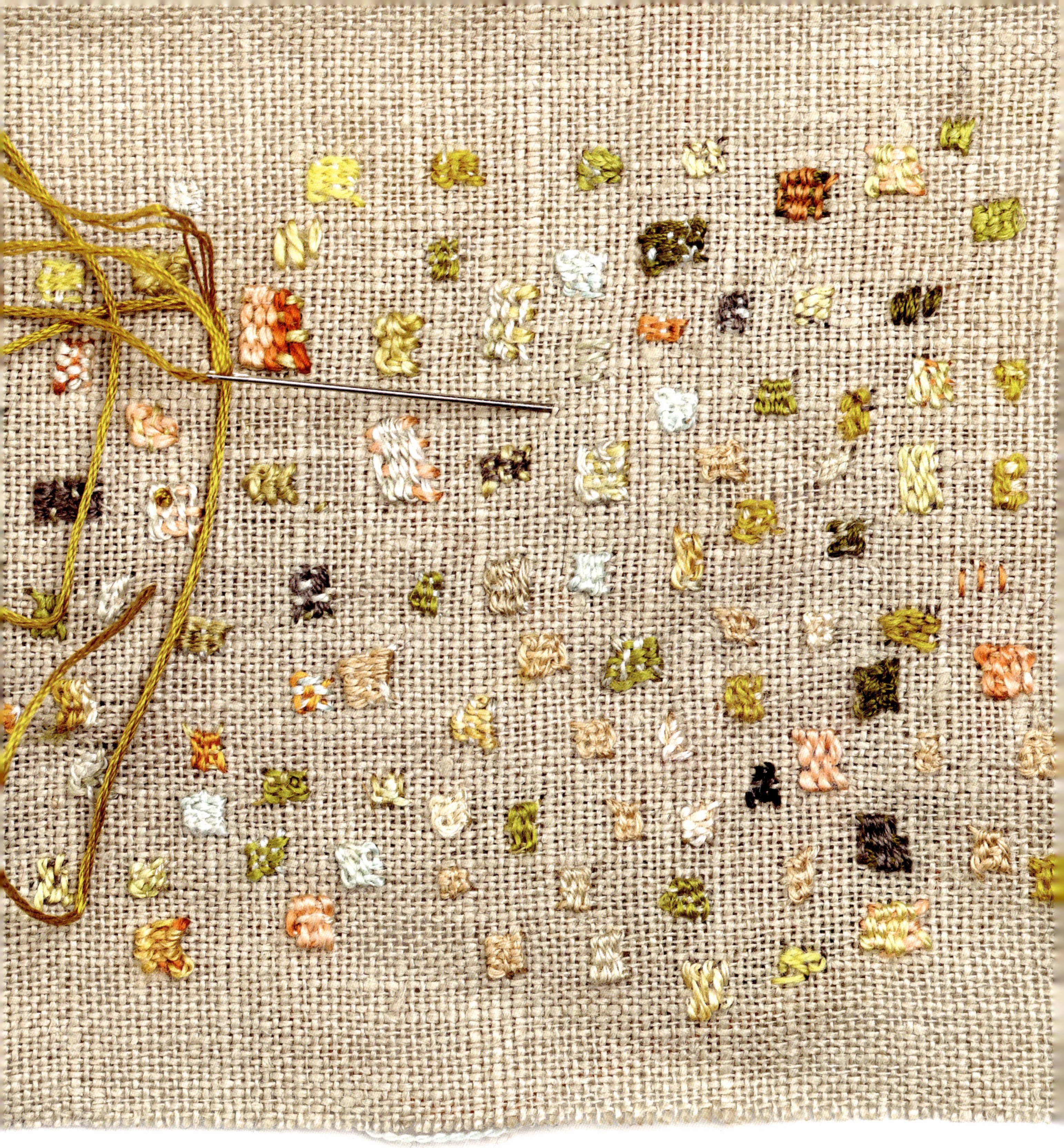

Durational pieces

Daily practices – Stitch Journal: A decade of daily stitching

Stitch Journal is a long length of linen cloth, pieces added in sections (I also wrote about it in *Slow Stitch*, 2015 and *Resilient Stitch*, 2021). It is covered in rhythmic, improvised, hand stitches. The use of textile as a creative recording method continued alongside my PhD and extended a practice I began in 2013.

This solitary activity in a working life based in socially engaged arts projects was a material-based method that carved out a different sort of thinking space. It acted as a counter to the busyness of community spaces, the constant reflexivity required as practitioner-researcher, offering stillness and quiet contemplation. During my research, I used it as another way of managing often messy real-world multi-site research and also as a mirror of it.

BELOW AND OPPOSITE
Stitch Journal (2013-2023) (details), hand stitch on recycled linen.
OVERLEAF
Stitch Journal (2013-2023), hand stitch on recycled linen 836×700cm (329×275.5 in) at widest point.

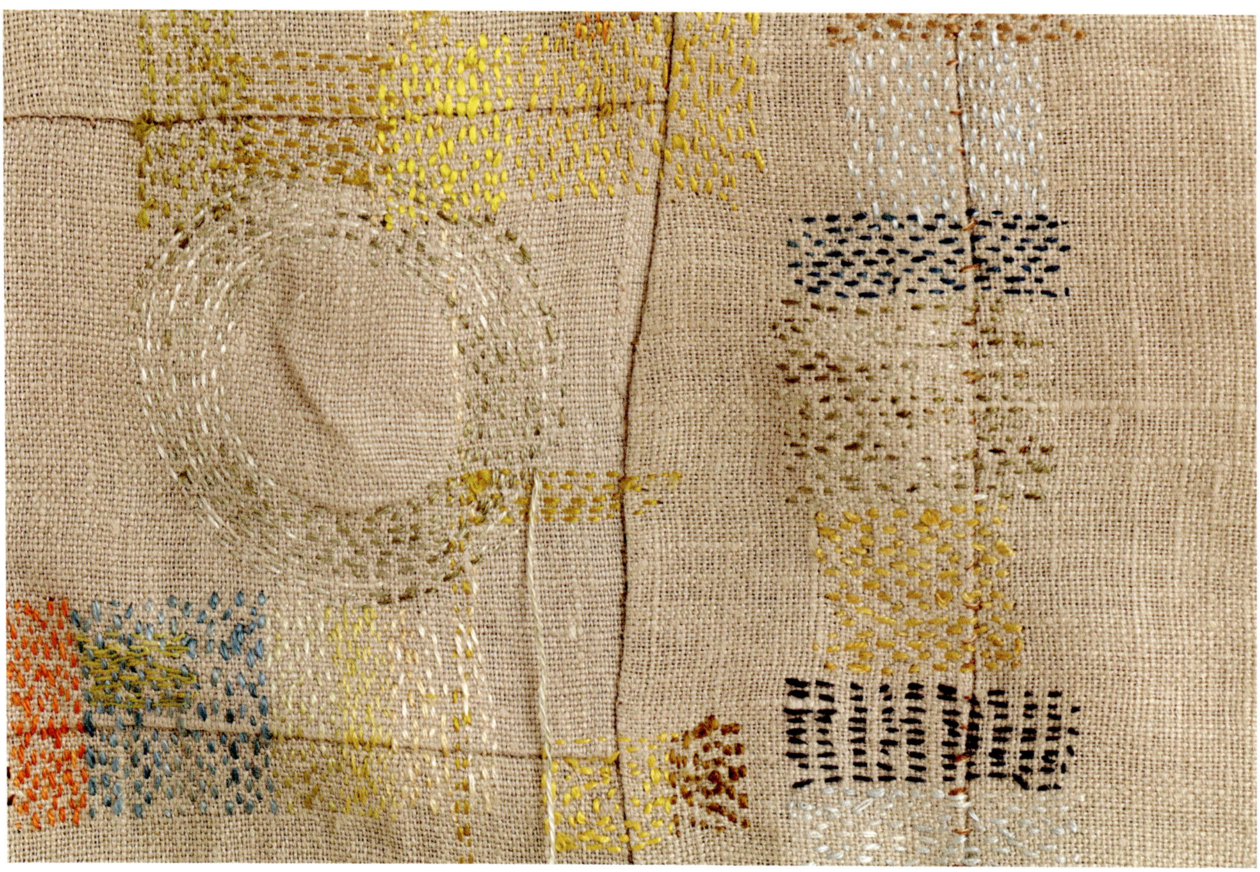

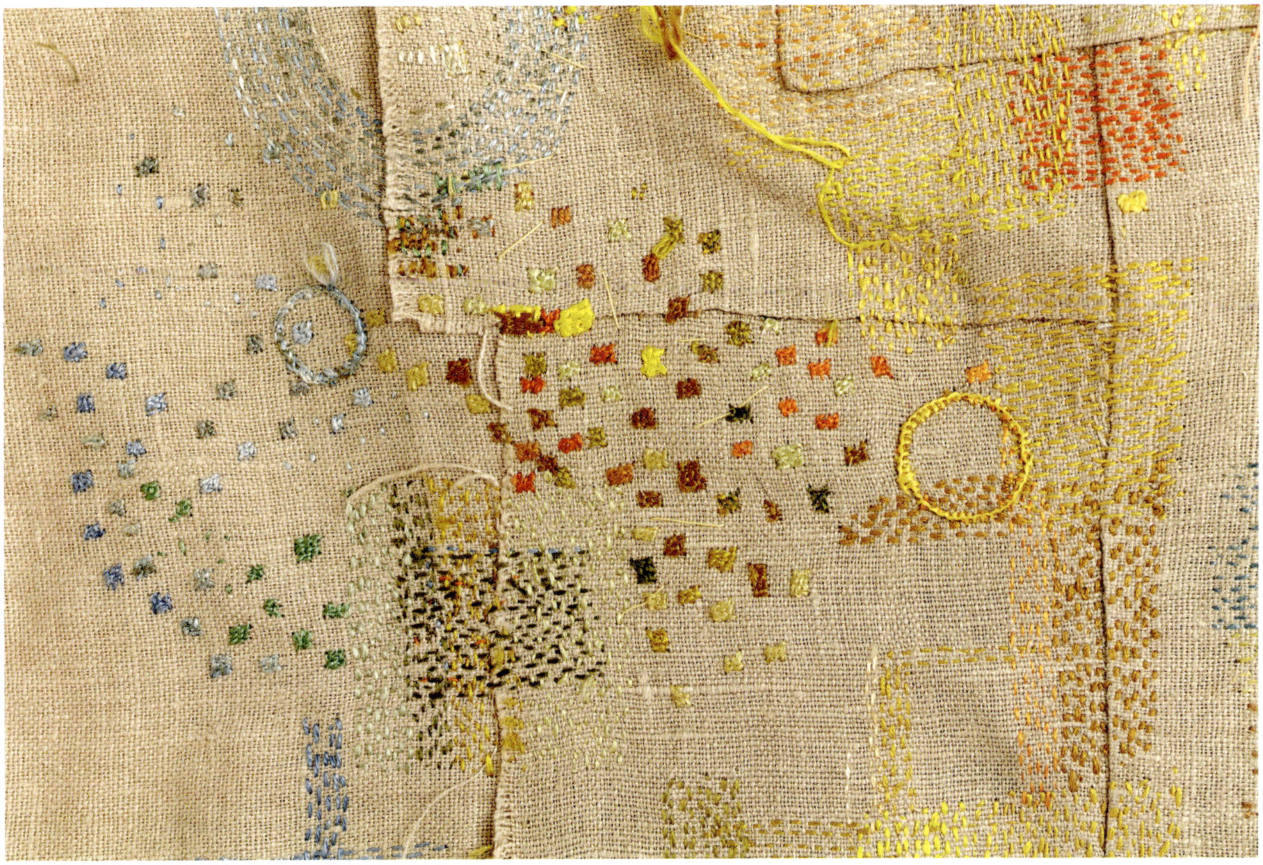

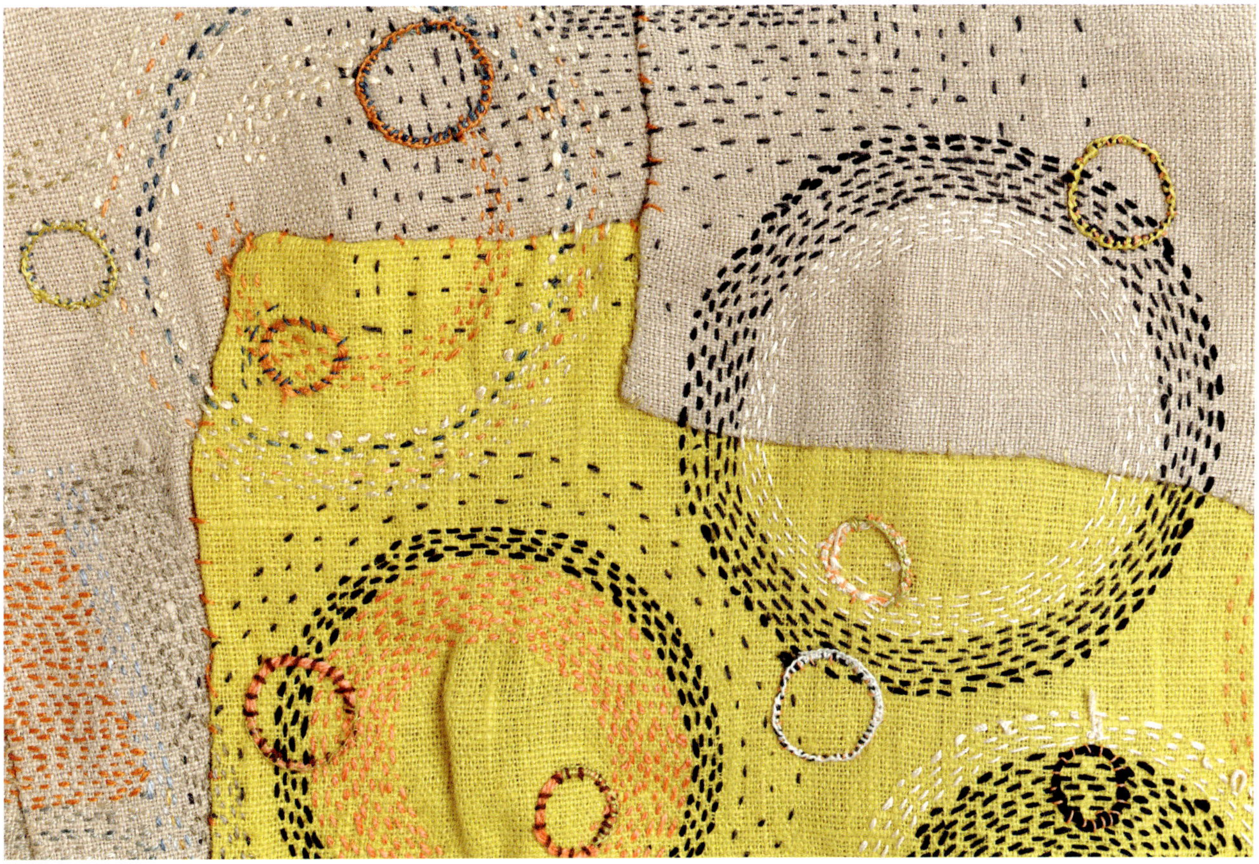

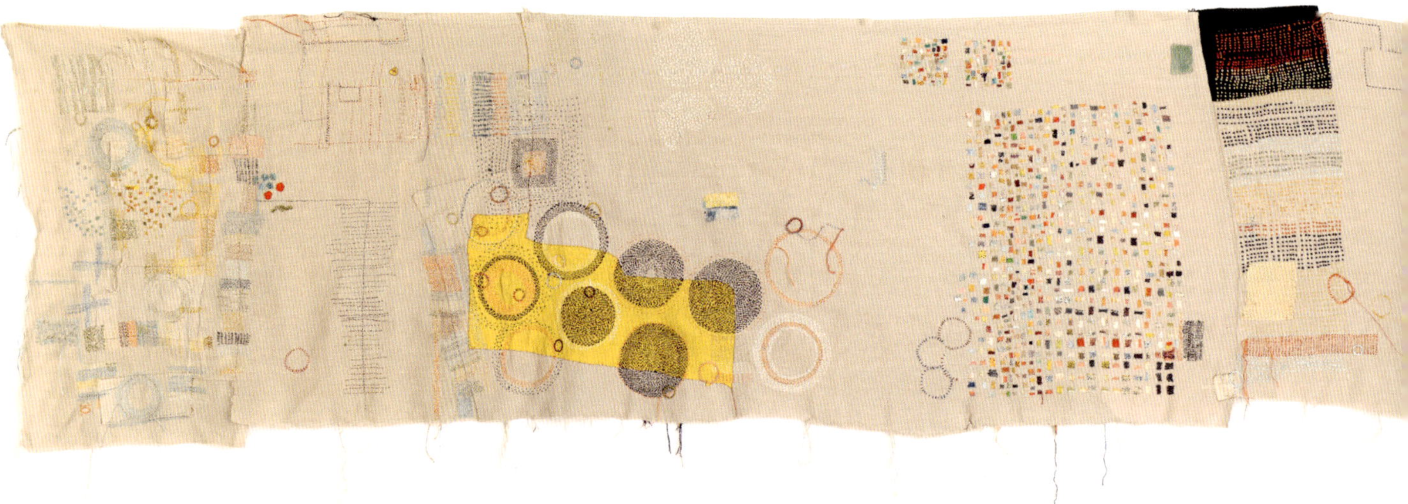

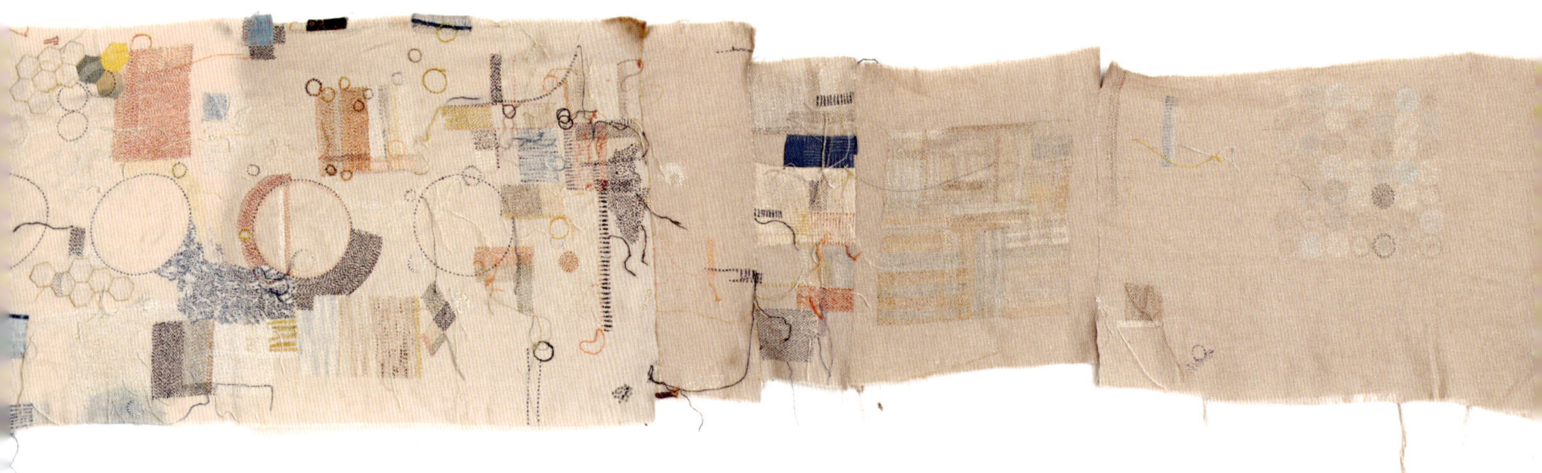

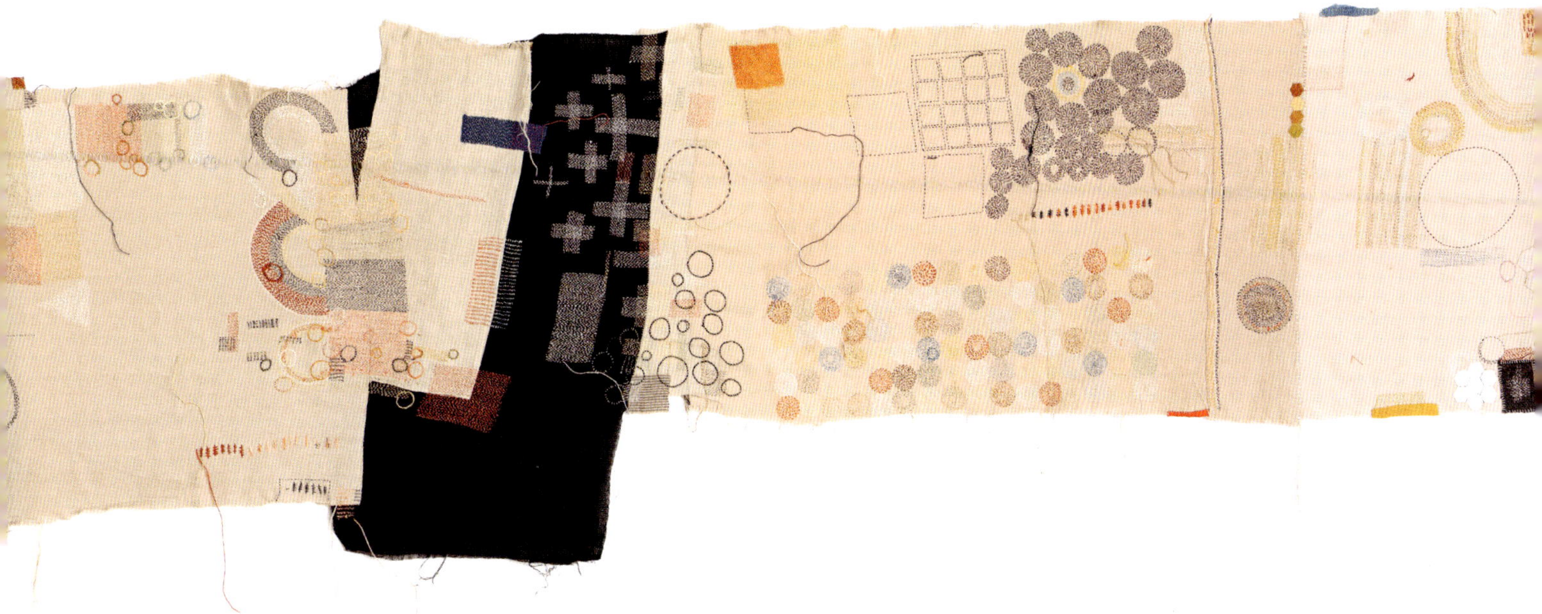

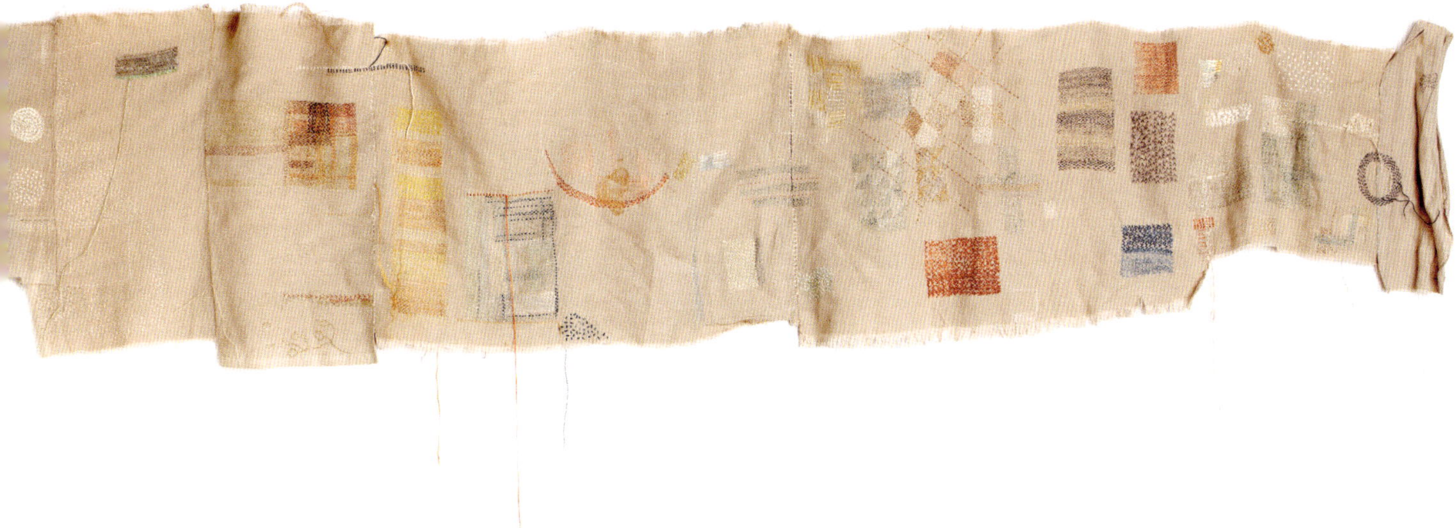

The threads I used were often dyed at community growing projects and at my allotment. I included the odd snippet of naturally dyed wools, silks and cottons, old Viyella shirting, prints and patterns from other projects, those fabrics related to conversations with people. Ironing these tiny scraps of cloth made them useable; they became precious reminders of engagement work. Some of this collection was gathered over many years of practice, with some ordinary and some more storied pieces of cloth. During teaching and community projects I liked seeing them reinvented by others. The idea of them being reconfigured and reimagined into new work out in the world is both comforting and exciting in its ongoing-ness.

As I approached a decade of daily stitching, the background fabrics that were my preference, originally a damaged linen curtain, other recycled linen offcuts and repurposed clothing, were running out. The final sections of the journal were small scraps of fabric stitched together, my daily stitching added to the pieced work. The process of piecing my stories and thinking through a decade felt like it was coming to a natural end.

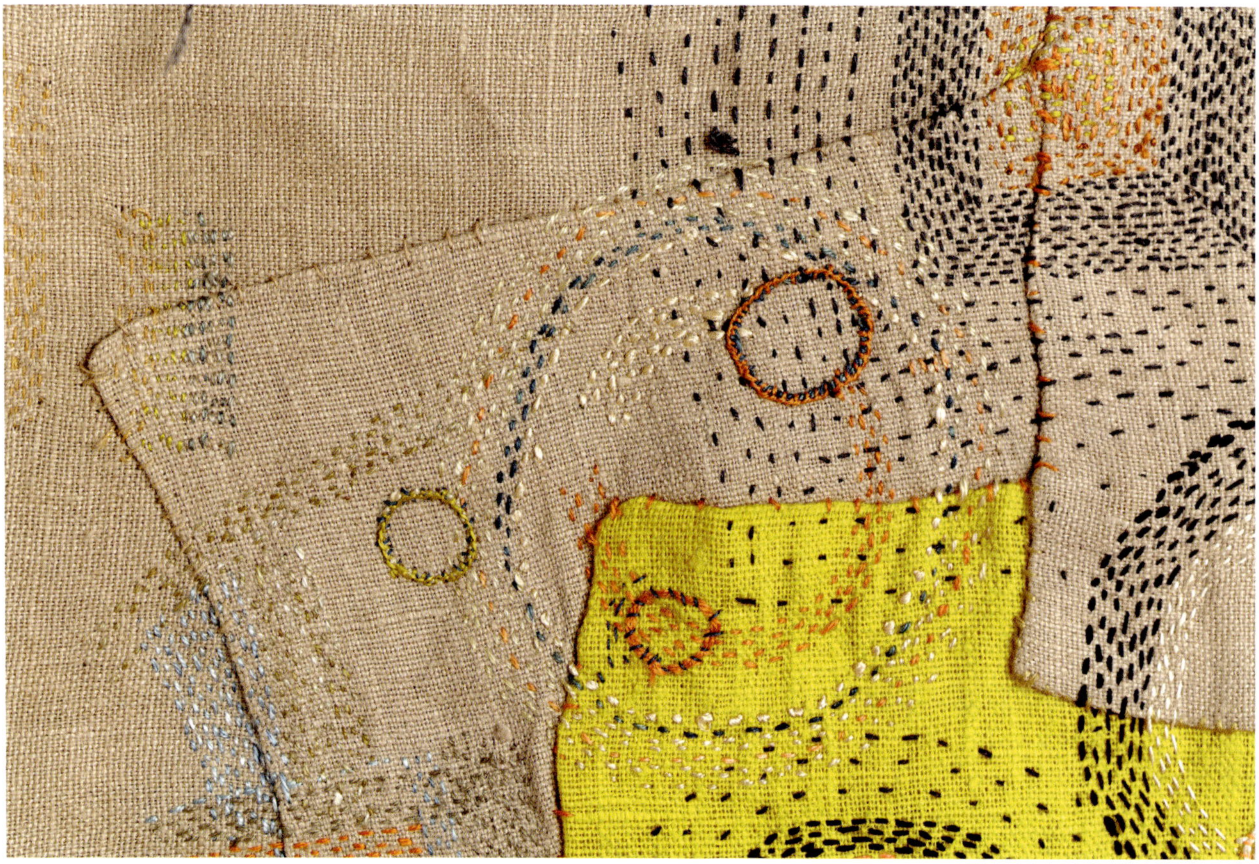

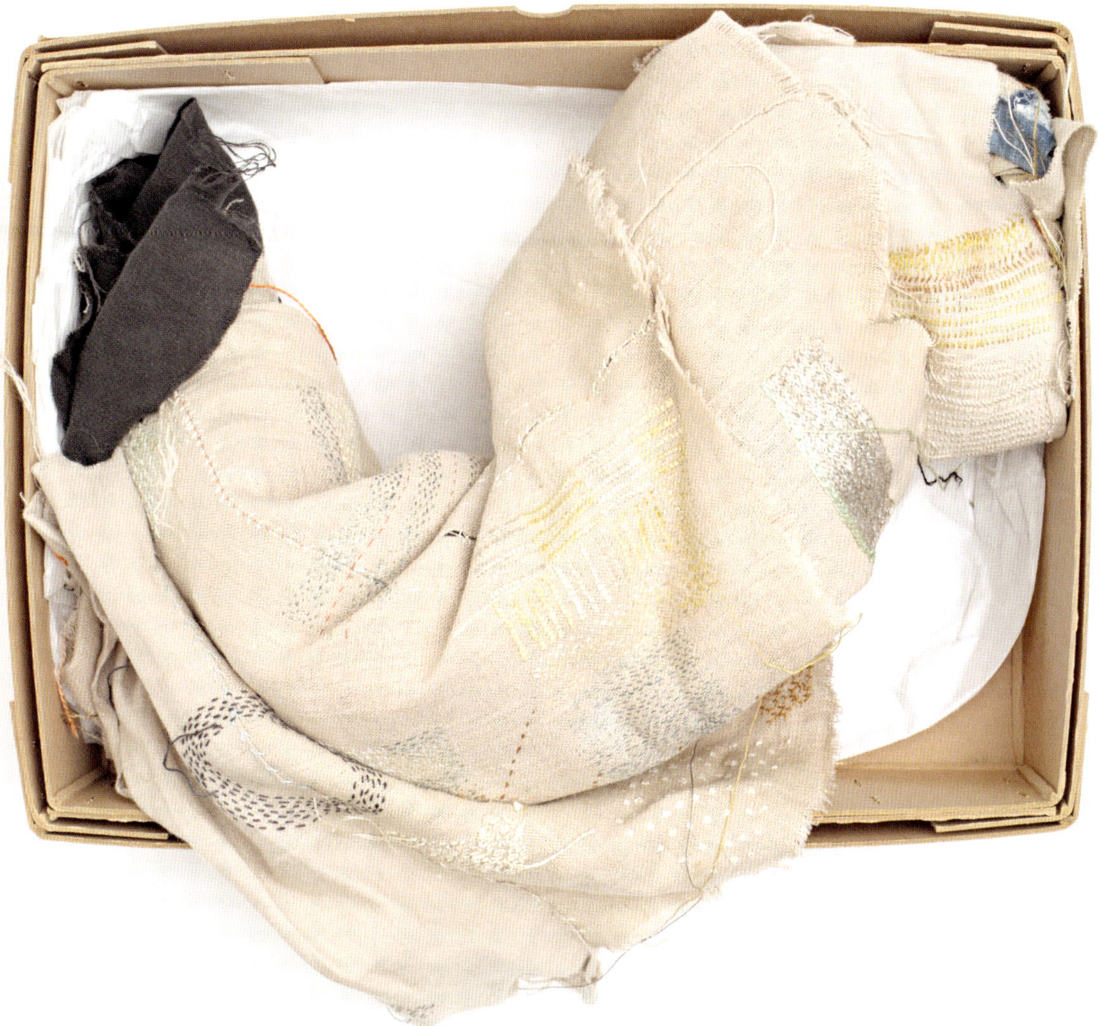

OPPOSITE
Stitch Journal (2013-2023) (detail), final sections made of patched and pieced linen.
ABOVE
Stitch Journal in its archive box.

My stitching at this time also changed and I moved away from multiple blocks of running stitch. Through a long period of writing, editing and rewriting I used a needle-weaving technique to work through my thinking as I wrote. The threads used included neon-bright polyester, very much like the highlighter pen I marked my printed pages with. With a sharp needle the precision of weaving in tiny spaces on cloth gave me the additional focus I needed.

After a decade of creating a space to simply focus on needle pushing through fabric, I decided to archive the work. A lot of life had gone into this piece; it is like a diary that only I can read back. Now stored in a nest of tissue paper in an archive box, I find the layers wrapped together create a safe container for my thinking-through-making over a decade, a repository of all the life held within.

Stitches to measure time

A needle-woven square

I have borrowed this simple needle-weaving technique from my mending and darning practice. This has mainly been used in a practical way, extending the life of clothes and household textiles, darning the odd moth hole in a jumper. Adding needle-woven squares to a backing cloth is a satisfying process, each one complete in itself. Joining multiple needle-woven shapes together can make a small, pleasing composition. The threads I dye are rarely uniform in colour and these slight tonal differences make for a more interesting surface as a decorative technique.

MATERIALS

- Linen base fabric
- A selection of threads
- A sharp and a blunt needle to suit your thread choice

METHOD

1. Stitch a warp in the base fabric by making parallel lines of the width and length you want (1-2 in the diagram). Consider the threads you're using – fine threads will need closer spacing.

2. Using another thread (you could choose a needle with a rounded end for this to prevent the thread splitting) enter the cloth from the back and weave the thread back and forth through the warp stitches (3-4 in the diagram). To maintain the square shape don't pull the thread too hard.

3. Experiment with colour and use different coloured threads for the warp or weft stitches.

4. Stitch your warp threads diagonally across the square from corner to corner.

5. Remember to attach the needle-weaving stitch through the background fabric before beginning each woven row. This anchoring stitch attaches the whole assemblage to the backing fabric.

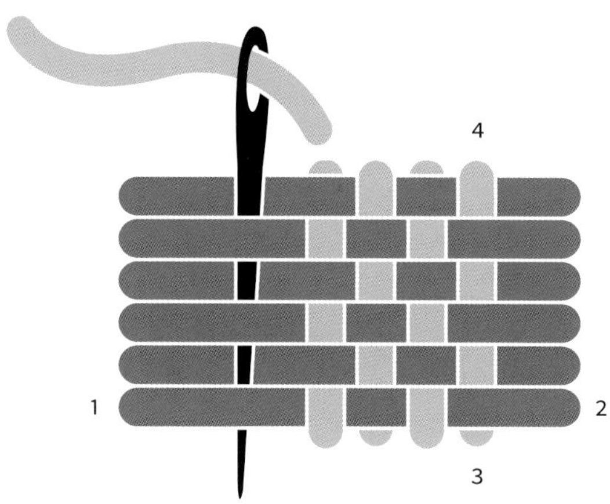

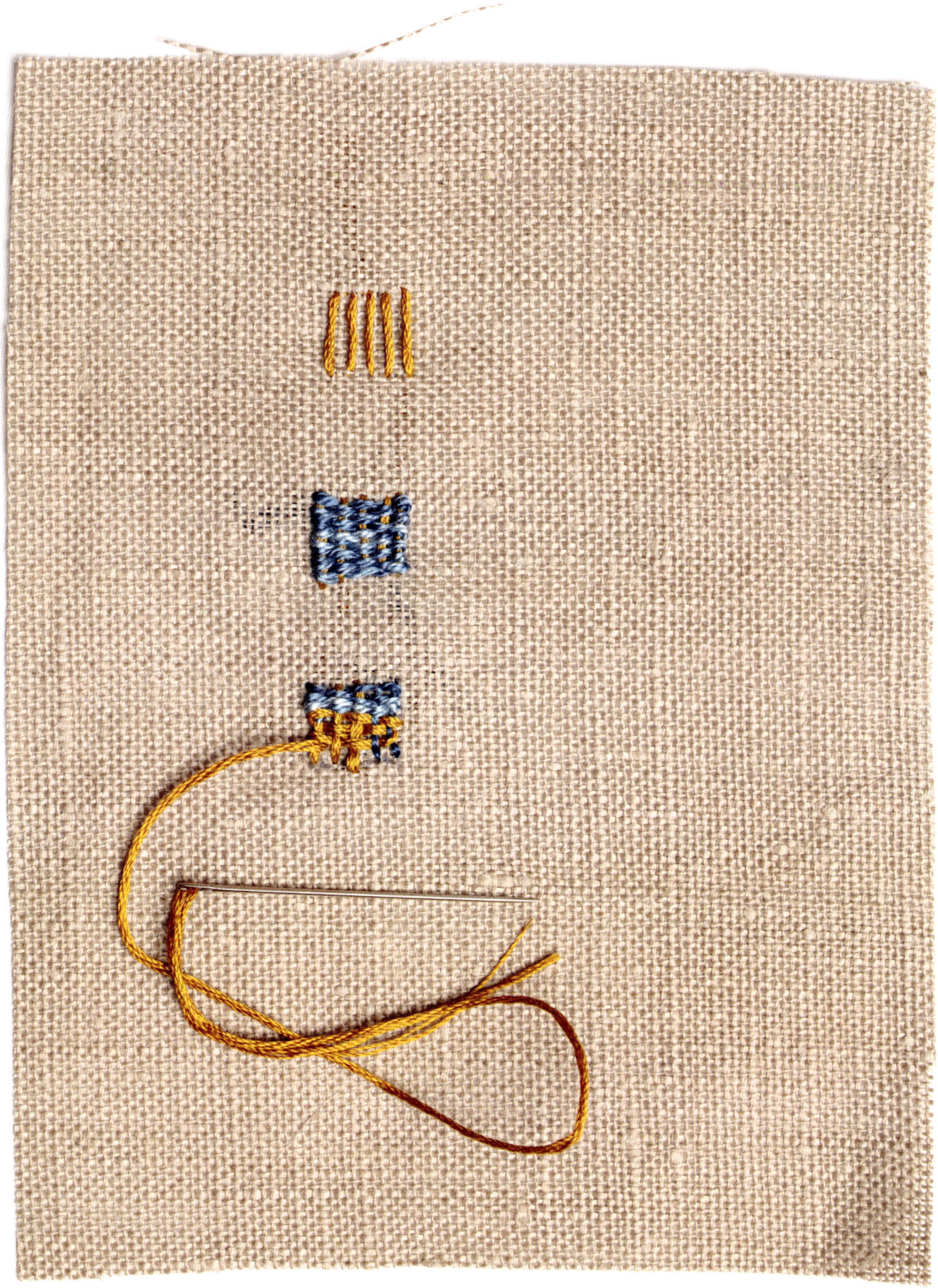

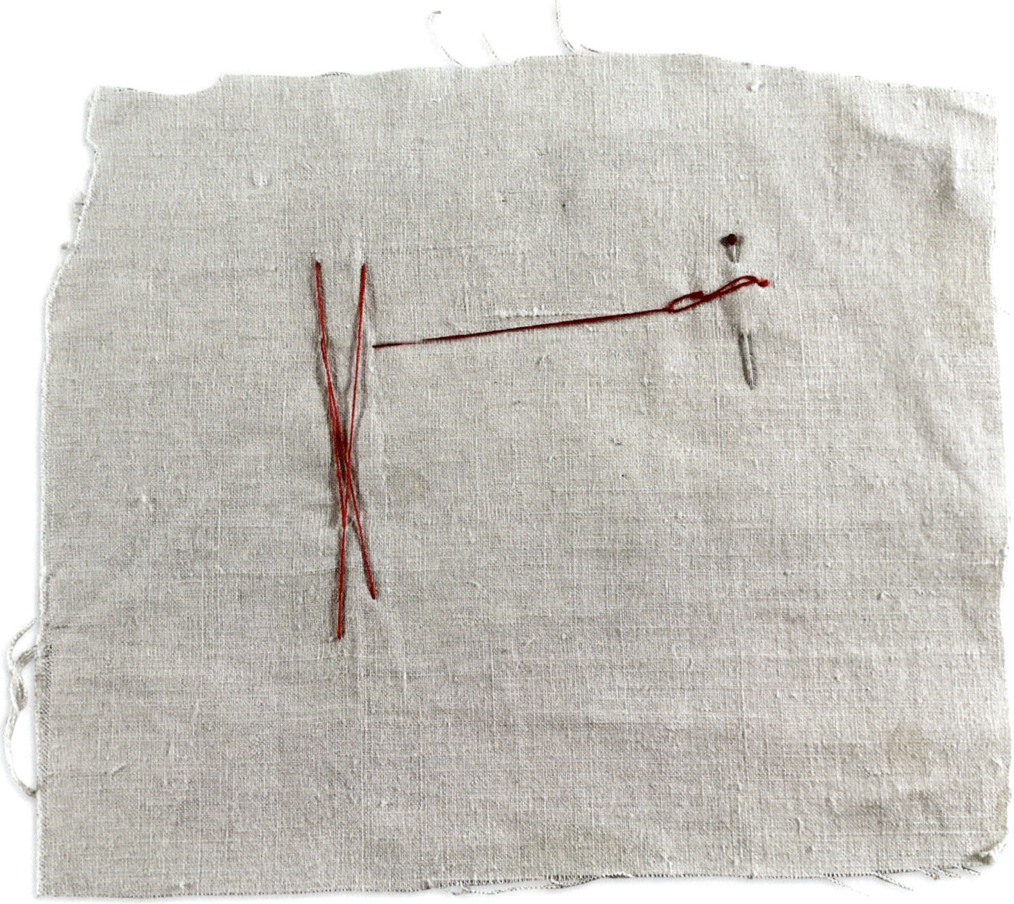

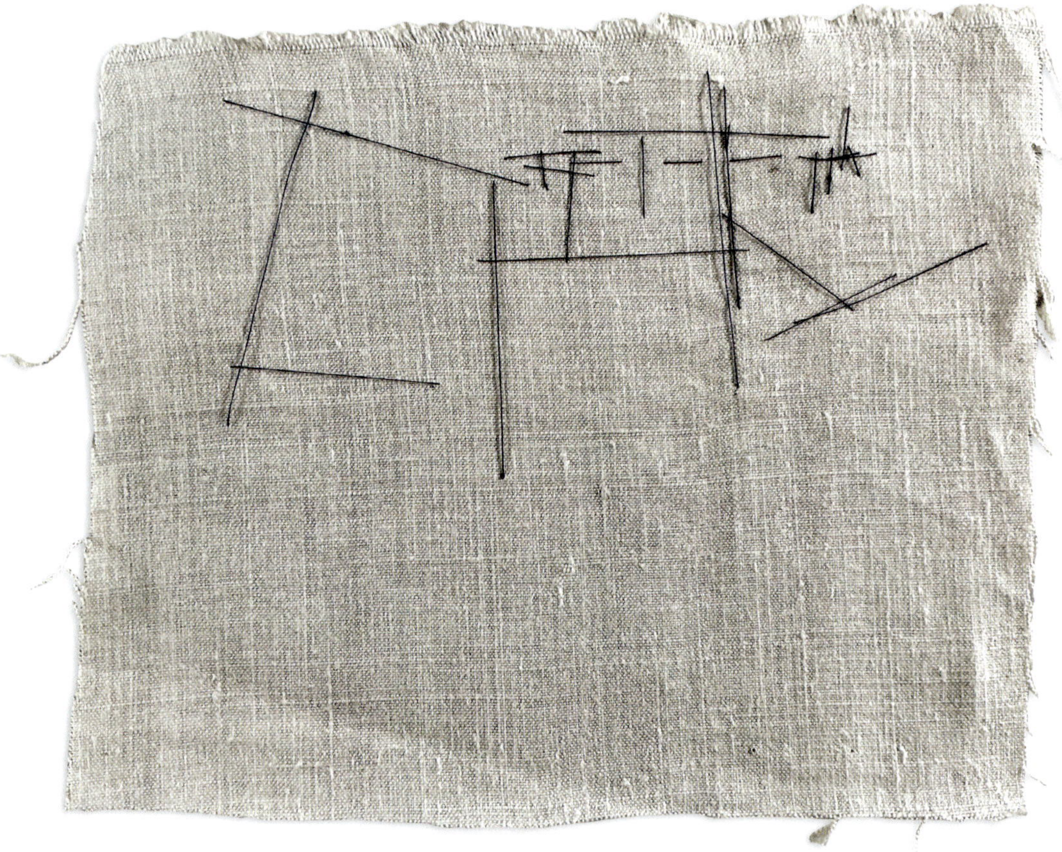

Carol Tulloch

Carol Tulloch is a writer, curator and Professor of Dress, Diaspora and Transnationalism at the University of the Arts London based in the School of Design at Chelsea, Camberwell and Wimbledon. She is an Honorary Senior Research Fellow at the Victoria & Albert Museum.

Morningness

'I was initially inspired by Claire's practice of daily stitching (2015), that I developed into morning stitching, which I refer to as "morningness". This includes stitching produced in the slipstream of writing my morning pages (*The Artists Way*, Julia Cameron, 2005) that helps to diffuse the fog of worries, enabling me to see more clearly.

'This act of morning stitching is driven to be as meditative and intuitive as possible. There is always tea and a candle. The materials include old linen of different weights cut randomly with raw edges. Threads are what I am drawn to; the colour red occurs often. Stitching is done with eyes open and sometimes closed in order to sink into a meditative rhythm and be as intuitive as possible, to translate how I feel at that moment of stitching to guide my hand, the stitches I make, the directions they take. Following the completion of the stitching, which is rarely more than 10 minutes. I write a summary of why I stitched, with the date and time of stitching, when it started and/or ended. This is handwritten in ink directly on to the piece or on a Post-it and pinned to the fragment.

'On one Post-it, dated 10/11/24, I wrote "Finally claimed space to stitch", a reminder of what my morning stitching is also for, to alleviate the regimented tempo of the upcoming working day. Other claimed spaces include the evening train journey from work to home, where I close my eyes and do mental stitches as a meditative process to help transport me from the business of the day to down time.

'These stitched notes are the translation of feelings that, conscious or not, are informed by the slow, snowball practice of living and caring for the self. My morning stitching acts as a mirror of reflection. I process this through my mind-hand-stitching coordination. What emerges is a diary of images, meditative moments that only such a reflective practice can produce.'

OPPOSITE
Carol Tulloch (UK) (2024)
Morningness linen, hand stitch (dimensions vary).

Crafting Resilience

BELOW AND OPPOSITE
Crafting Resilience (2024-2025), linen, recycled fabric, hand stitch. Each piece 17×40cm (6.6×15.7 in).

In October 2023 I started a new textile record, *Crafting Resilience*, a page per week to accompany a research fellowship by the same name. The fellowship offered me time for new research and writing connected to socially engaged textile practices. I decided to use a textile recording method after sitting staring at spreadsheets and Gantt charts, working out my time and schedule and later cutting a stack of 52 small textile pages from recycled linen and placing them on the shelf opposite my desk. Moving a page week-by-week to a shelf on the other side of my desk, I was able to visualise the time used and the time left. This was the great gift of the fellowship – offering me time for writing and thinking through new research.

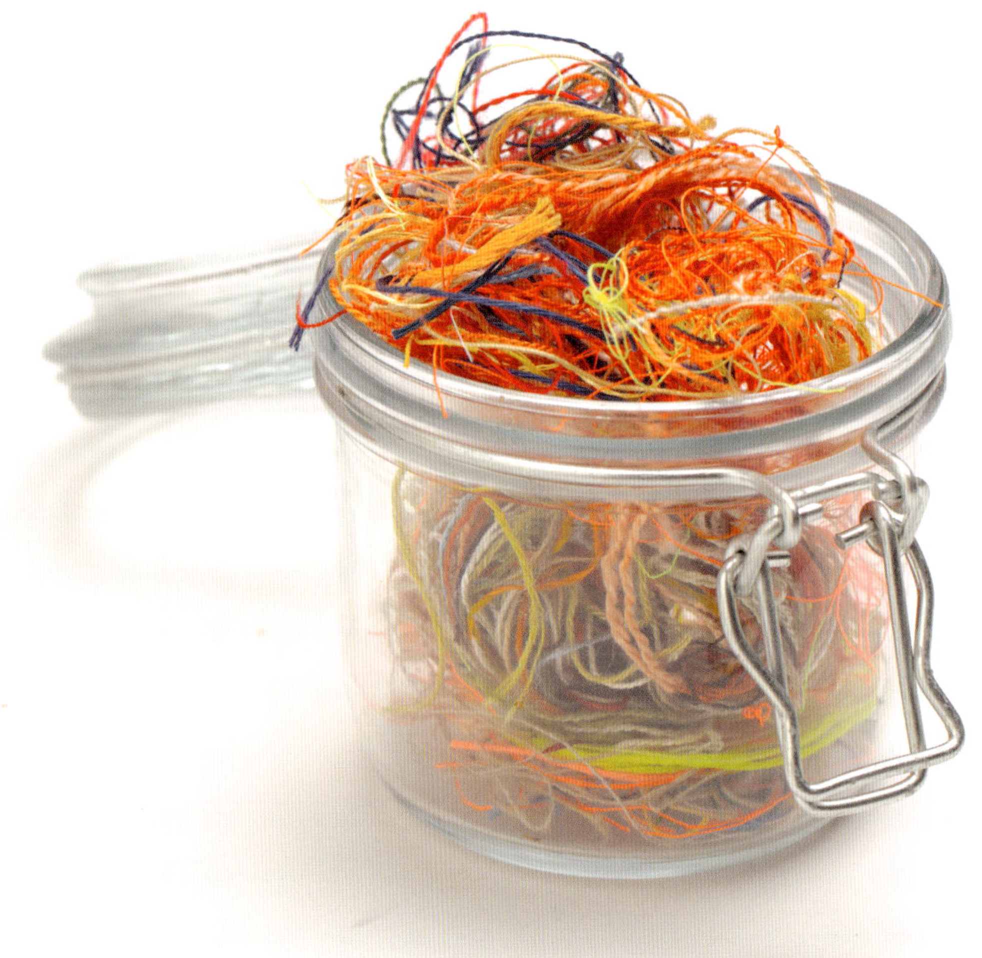

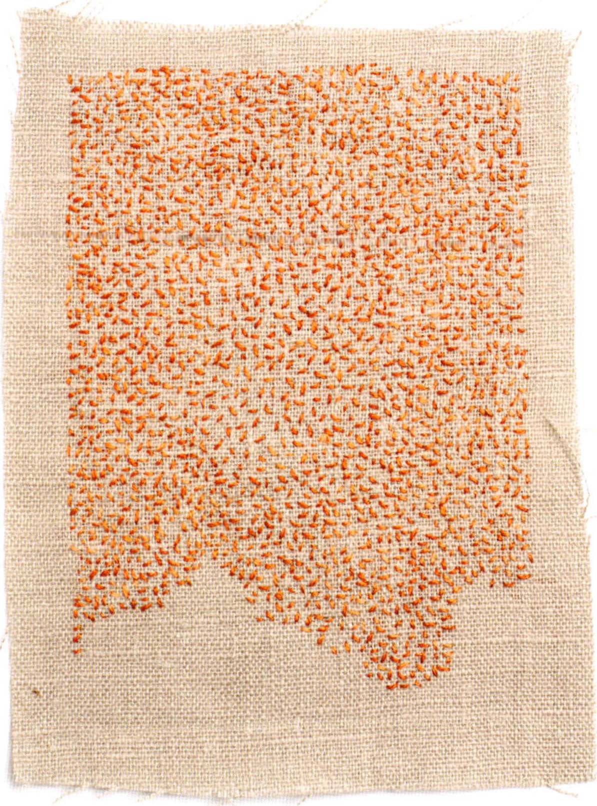

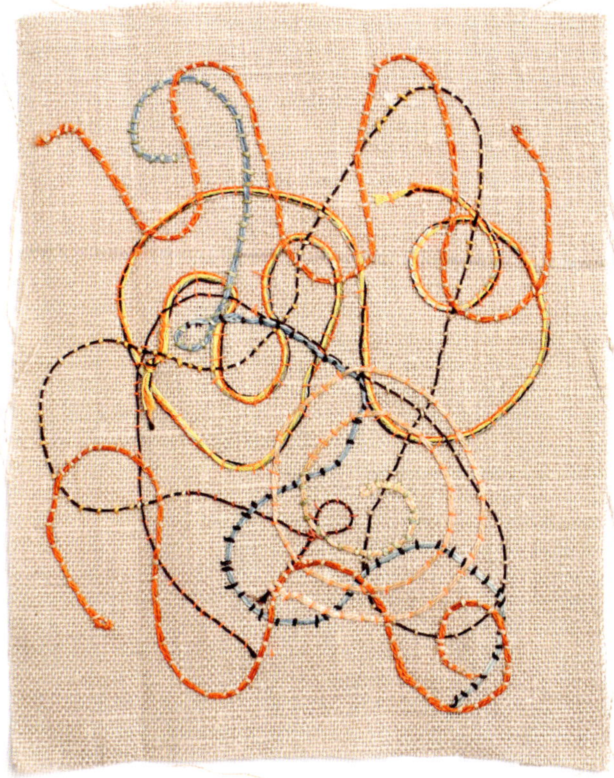

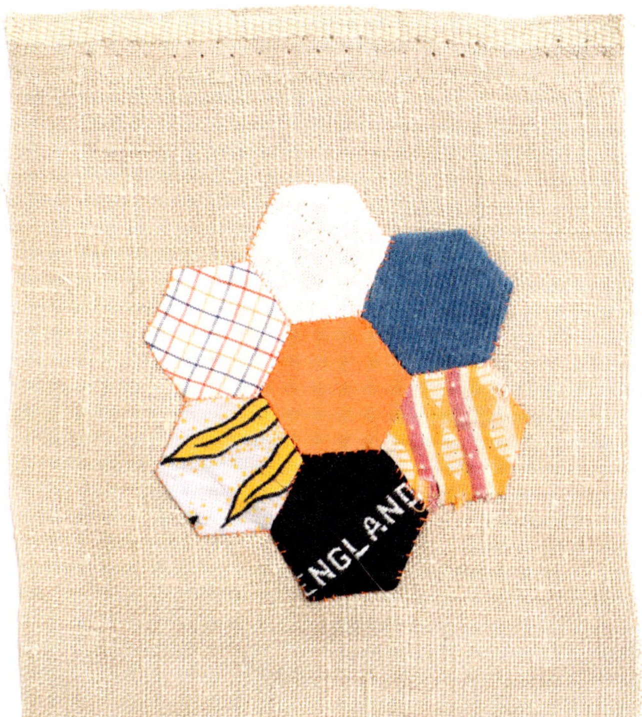
ENGLAND

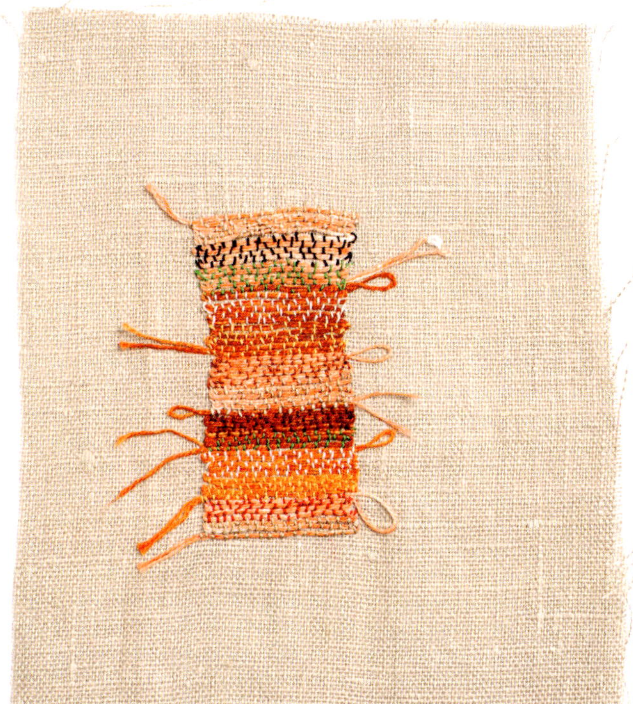

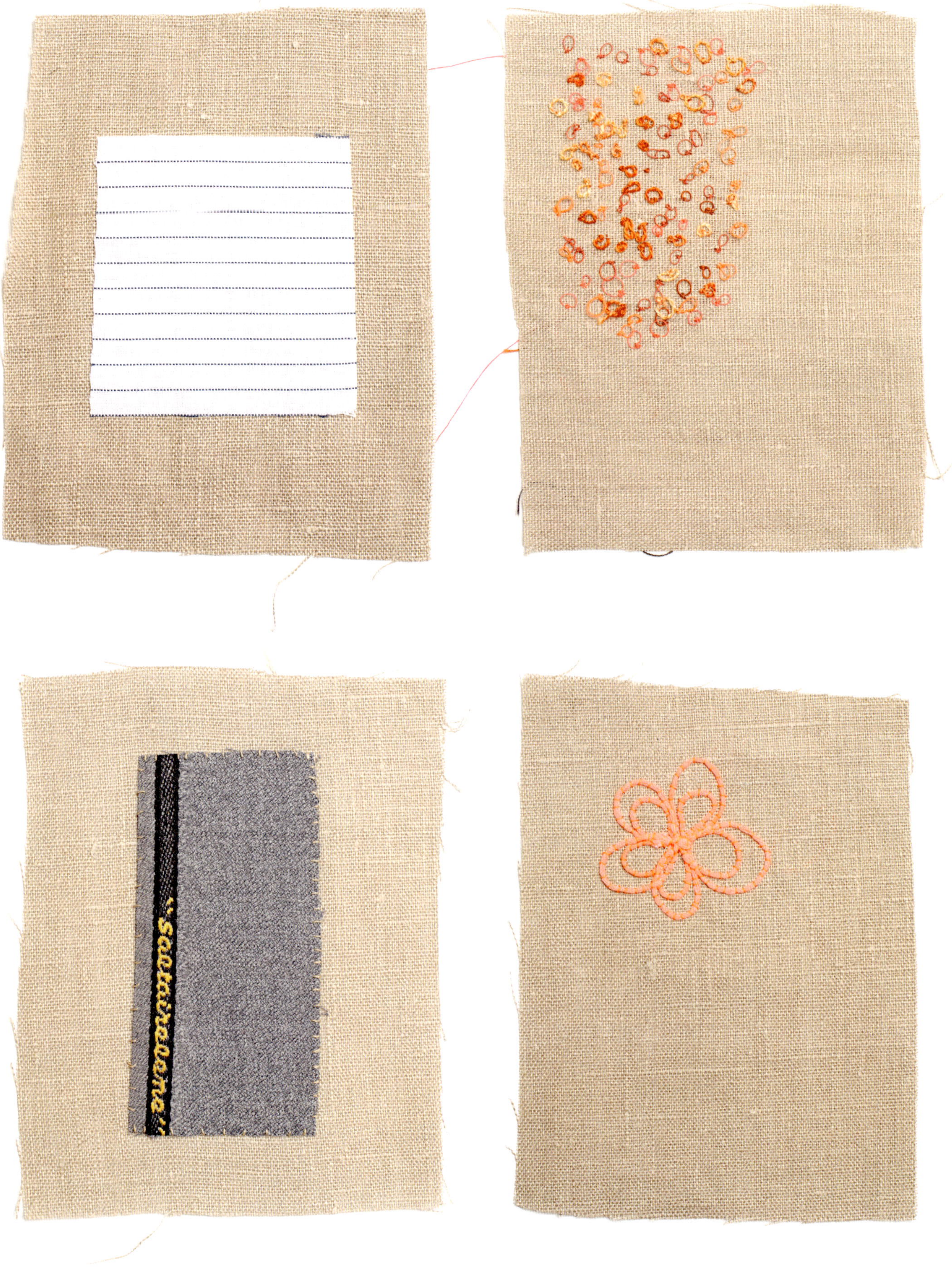

OPPOSITE

Crafting Resilience (2024-2025), linen, recycled fabric, hand stitch. Clockwise from top left – the dreaded blank page; looped French knots and tangled thoughts; couched neon flower in dark times; 'Saltairelene' selvedge on Terylene/Worsted cloth a reminder of a visit to an archive. Each piece 17×40cm (6.6×15.7 in).

The material aspect of my research ideas is visible in these pages. Madder-dyed threads feature heavily, as does neon polyester which had become a shorthand for my editing process in the final stages of my PhD and used in this way again here. I kept all my scraps of leftover thread in a jar, dipping into it and reusing them when I had a particular colour combination in mind.

During my decade of daily stitching my *Stitch Journal* (2013–2023), I developed various ways of interpreting my thinking-through-making in stitch – the forms and marks made with needle and thread, fastening off neatly (or not), the colours I used – and these re-emerged in this new project. Its 52 pages record my thinking through this period and how they connected to my research.

One page, appliquéd with a selvedge edge of a worsted, Terylene men's suiting fabric called 'Saltairelene', was made during a week spent in archives in preparation for a curatorial project about the origin stories of synthetic fibres. The fabric was from the 1950s and made in a local textile mill in Saltaire near Bradford. 'Saltairelene' links its origins with the new polyester fibre Terylene.

Another week, a loop of dried dandelion cordage was couched in a circle connecting local stories of making and growing that I listened to at an allotment project. The chaos of my Christmas ribbons for wrapping gifts appeared in a December week, colourful threads couched down with golden catching stitches.

Life always gets into work though, and I found that my planned textile responses to my research project, more often than not, became about everyday things. The thinking and making I do while growing and tending my allotment was a constant throughout. The flare-up of an illness featured more than I might have hoped: bright neon pinks and oranges became shorthand for the inflammation I was experiencing. For the first time I wrote a small diary page of notes alongside my stitching each week.

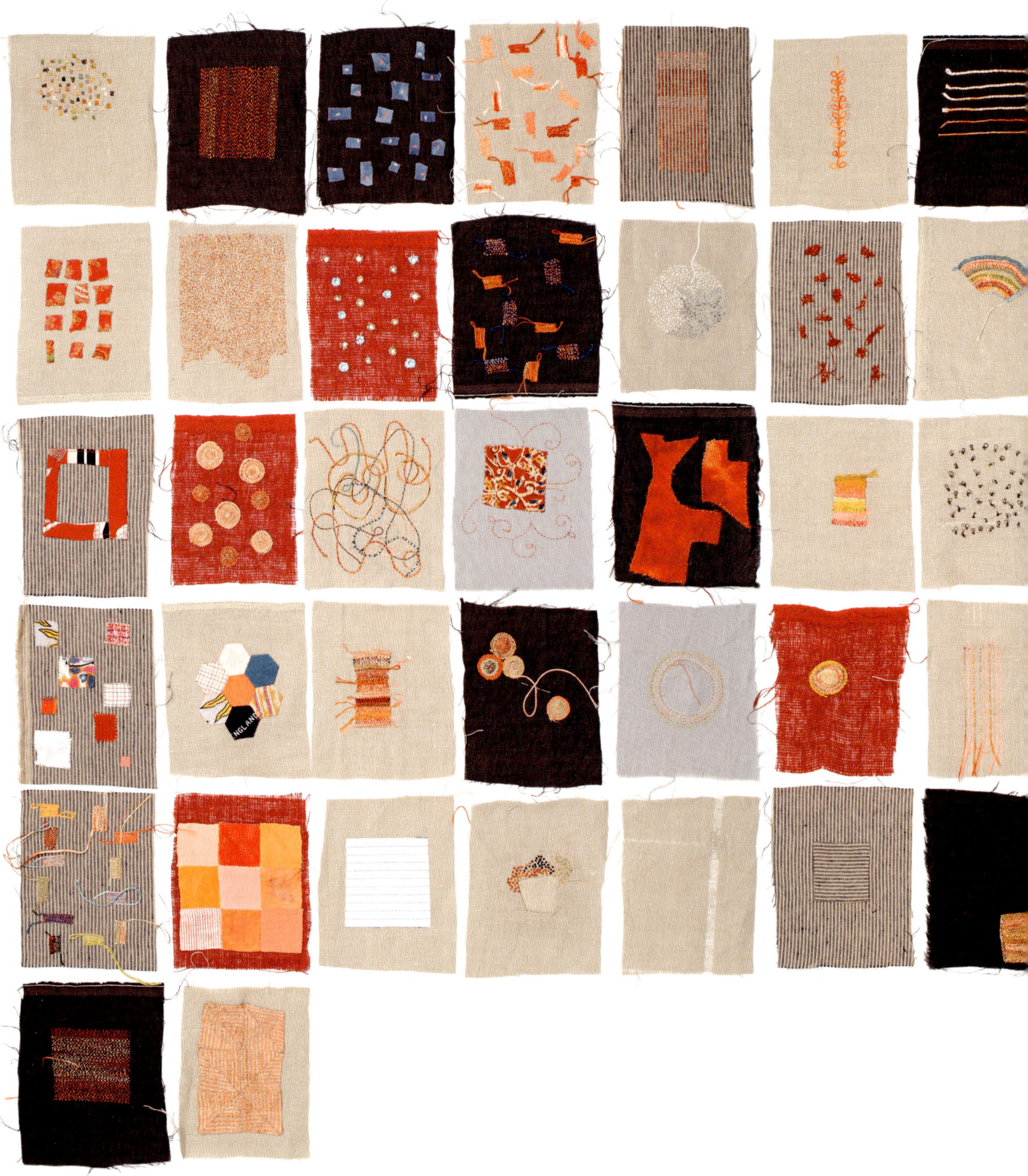
ENGLAND

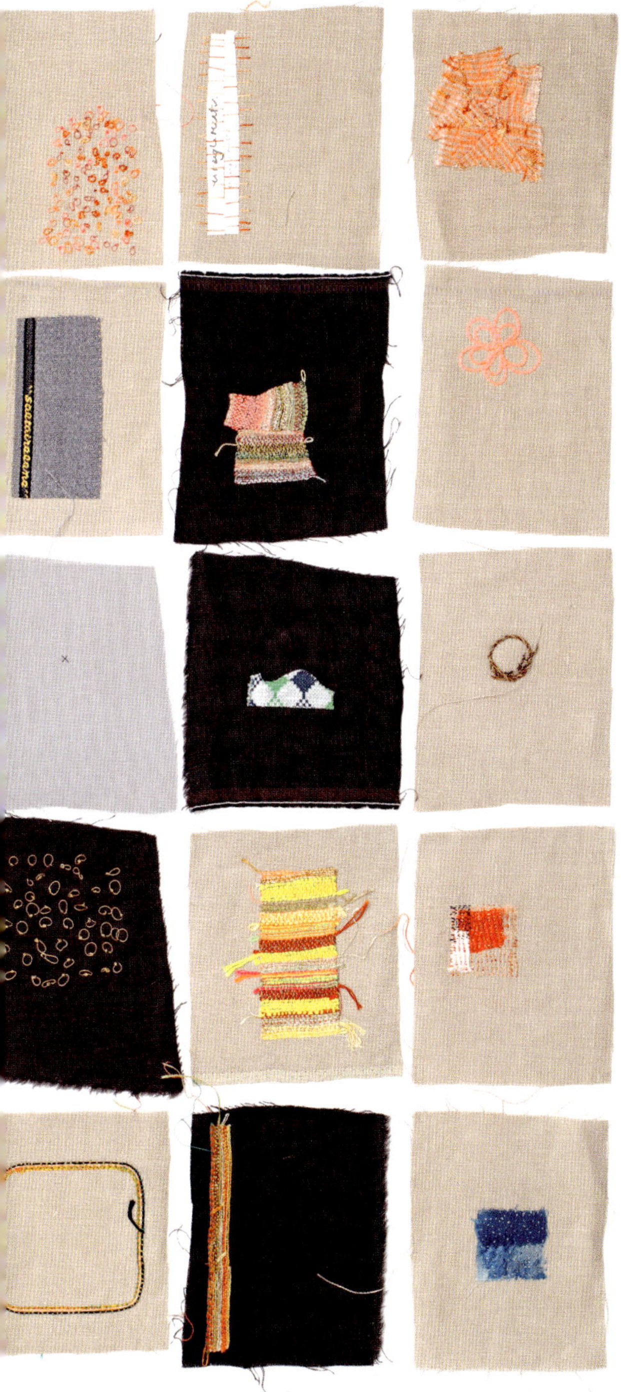

OPPOSITE
Crafting Resilience (2024-2025), linen, recycled fabric, hand stitch. 52 weekly reflections of an academic research fellowship. Each of the 52 pieces 17×40cm (6.6×15.7 in).

A brief reflection on the materials and techniques plus a few sentences reviewing the week. For example:

> **WEEK 4**
> Light linen. Madder scrap thread, overstitched with polycotton, beeswax.
> *Trying to focus/pull in lines of thought. Closely laying threads together, paragraphs, lines of enquiry. Finer thread offers precision – more precision in the stitching than the writing currently. Pulling it together?*
>
> **WEEK 9**
> Dark linen. Madder thread, blue linen thread, couched blocks, neon polyester.
> *A precise mess. Hanging threads. Unwritten, unresolved, open questions. 9-patch block – does this make any sense of it? Freezing cold weather.*
>
> **WEEK 34**
> Light linen. Couched threads in a block.
> *Beeswax glides through the thread – or rather the thread glides through the beeswax. I like knowing I made these things – the colours and the wax (or rather, refining it for use) holds things together.*
>
> **WEEK 40**
> Light linen. Took a neon line for a walk and couched it down.
> *Loops and whorls. Waiting, terrible weather, no sun. Grim news cycle that keeps getting worse. Did stitching a neon flower help in any way? Not really.*

The rhythm of a weekly project provided additional ways of thinking about durational projects. As a contrast to the work of a daily reflective project, I set a period of time at the end of every week to reflect on what I had done. In this way it shaped the working weeks of the fellowship, allowed me to think about what came next, and offered me a complete record of the year.

Ruth Broadway

Ruth's work captures things at the cusp of change – a moon, a moth, the tide. Using the physical acts of stitching, binding, folding, printing, collecting and preserving to tether the ephemeral, she embraces the ritual of daily noticing, recording and making to foster mindfulness and appreciation of the quiet transformation happening around us. Inspired by traditional folk craft, she embraces the prosaic nature of these techniques to create works that are love letters to the passing of time, transformation and the fragility of life.

'In my textile practice, I mark time not with a clock but with a needle. My work often emerges from long, slow acts of noticing – how the moon shifts shape, how the light changes a room, how the tide leaves its salt on cloth. These rhythms

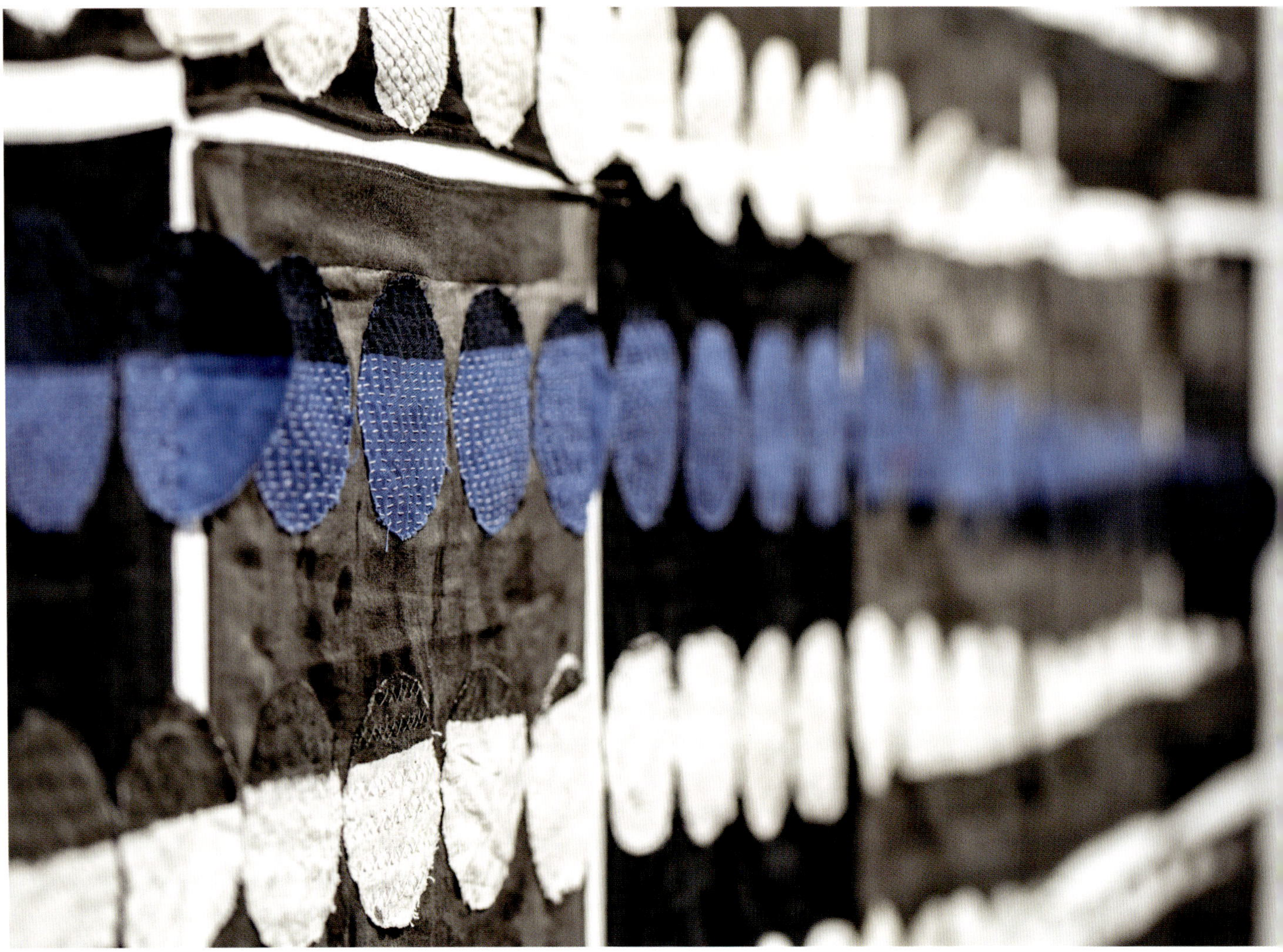

guide me more than any schedule. *By the Light of the Moon* began as an act of daily devotion: I hand-stitched a single fabric moon each night for 384 nights, tracing the lunar cycle not as a calendar but as a companion. This quiet ritual unfolded during a time of upheaval and uncertainty – a way to ground myself through repetition, to anchor experience in material. Each moon is both the same and different. So is each day. The work was stitched in the same chair each night, but the place changed around me – seasons turned, life shifted. Time became something I could hold. The resulting piece is a gentle archive of presence, recording the emotional and environmental tides as much as the astronomical ones.

'Place, for me, is often a collaborator. I return regularly to Mawddach in North Wales – a wild estuarine valley where I've taken artist residencies. There, the land is visibly marked by time: ancient slate scars, moss overtaking walls, tidal rhythms reshaping the same view hour by hour. I walk the same paths again and again, gathering impressions, drawing, stitching. The land teaches patience, slowness and repetition – the same qualities required by hand-stitching. This reciprocity between landscape and practice feels like a form of listening, of being in conversation with a place over time. I'm also interested in "interrupted" places – spaces of flux, decay or renewal. In some works, I've stitched directly into garments that have been damaged or worn, allowing change to become part of the story. I've used brackish tidal water as a dye to physically mark fabric with time, letting nature do its unpredictable work. These processes become metaphors for resilience, impermanence and transformation.

'Technically, my work involves slow, repetitive hand-stitching – acts of devotion more than decoration. I allow time, process and emotional response to guide the outcome. Materials are chosen not just for appearance but for meaning: domestic cloth, things that carry memory. I often leave the reverse side visible, threads trailing, knots exposed – a quiet resistance to perfection, an embrace of the honest backstory. Reflective stitch, for me, is not just about looking back. It's about being present long enough to notice. The materials become a kind of journal. The act of stitching becomes a meditation. And the resulting textile – however quiet – holds a record of that time, that place, that noticing.'

OPPOSITE
Ruth Broadway (2020) (UK) (detail) *By the Light of the Moon*, cotton handkerchiefs and fabric scraps, Indian ink, thread. 210×150cm (82.6×59 in).

OVERLEAF
Ruth Broadway (2020) (UK) *By the Light of the Moon*, cotton handkerchiefs and fabric scraps, Indian ink, thread. 210×150cm (82.6×59 in).

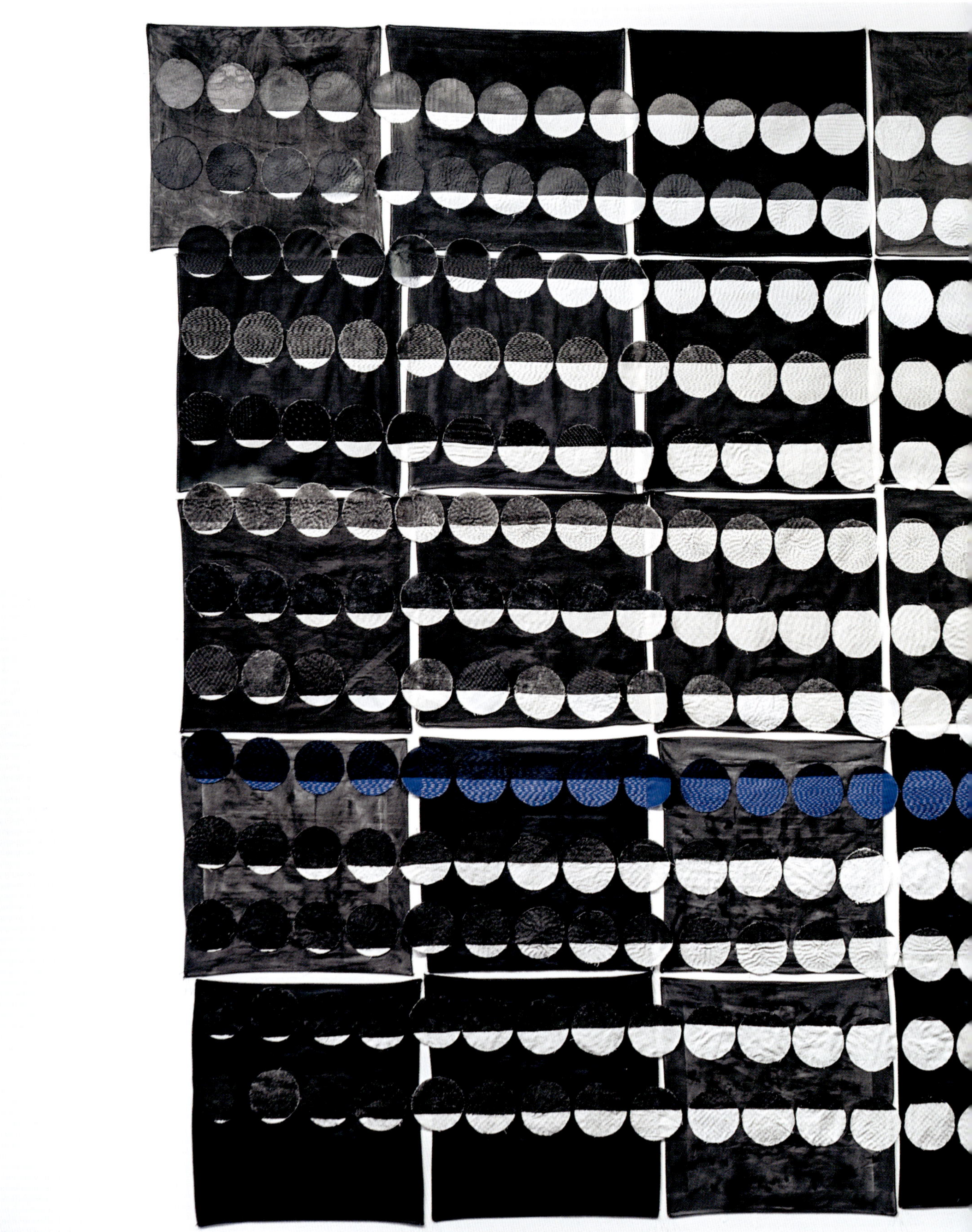

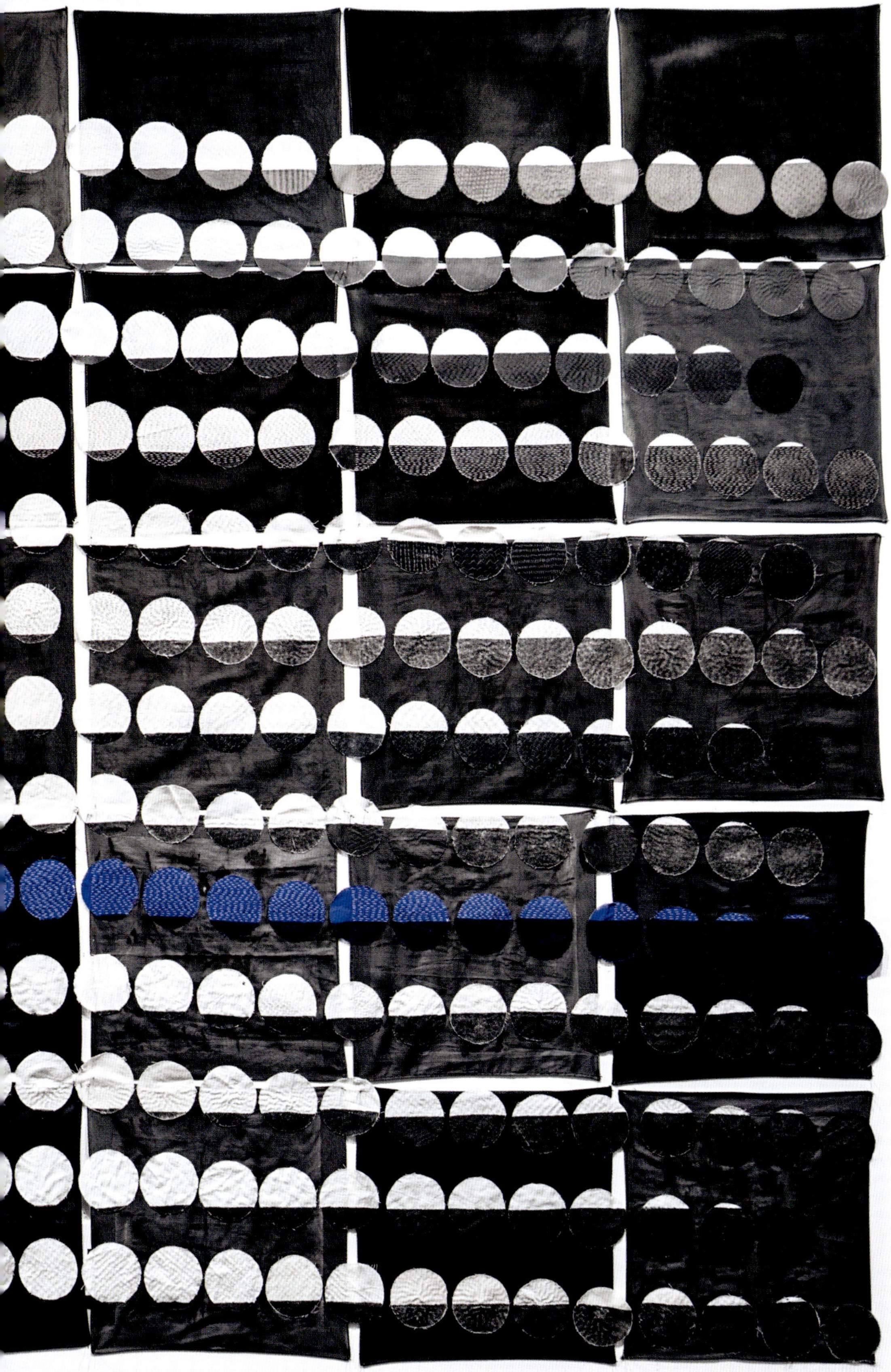

Jordan Cunliffe

Jordan Cunliffe is an embroidery designer and author with a focus on data and storytelling. She takes traditional and historic textile techniques, and pairs them with contemporary concepts.

'I categorise my work as "data visualisation", by which I mean the measuring and documenting of my experiences. Time is a subject that I return to often; not only is the data easily accessible, but it is something everyone can relate to. In the past, I have created embroideries showing "blocks" of time, but looking at the way different cultures and languages express their relationship with time caused me to re-examine this. *Linear Time* was inspired by research into linguistic relativity; exploring how the language we use impacts how we experience the world. Generally, in the English language, we discuss time as being "linear", so we would say something happened a "long" time ago. But other languages use more volume-based vocabulary, describing things lasting a "large" time. To explore this concept, I made a very long and thin piece of embroidery, meticulously measured and counted to create a stitch for every day of my life. The result offered a freedom to display it in different ways. I could see my life

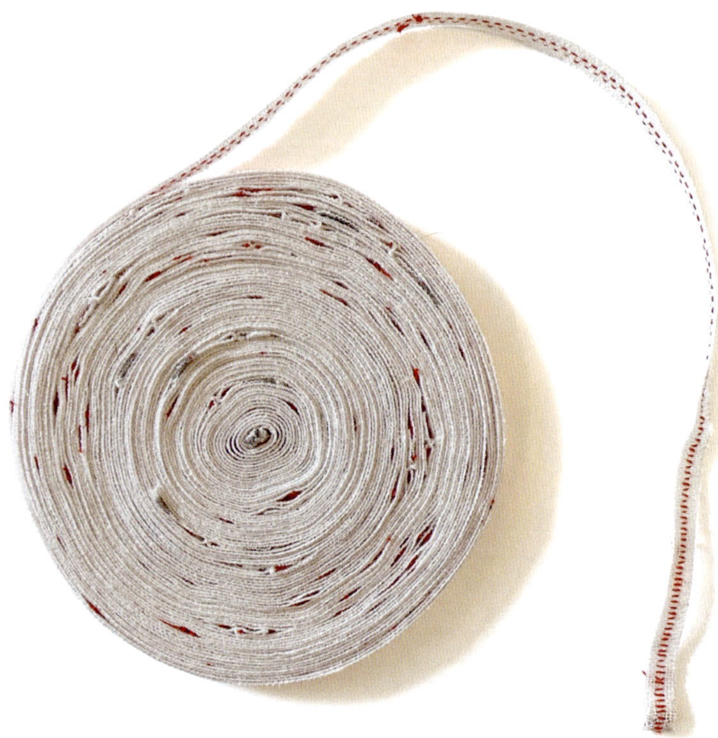

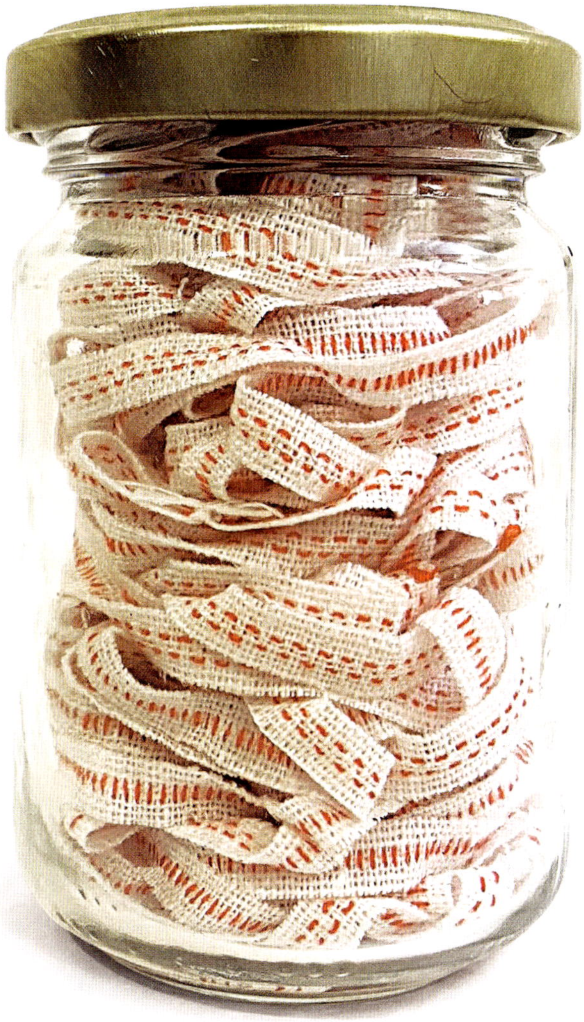

stretched out into the distance or see which vessels it would fill. What size jar will I need to contain my life 50 years from now? The process of creating these stitches was a mindful one. Because each stitch represented a day I had already experienced, it was an opportunity to reflect on a life lived so far. This piece of fabric holds all the places I have seen and all the versions of myself I have been. As with most of my pieces, it is not an ongoing project, it has a definitive end point, and I stopped sewing when I caught up with my present-day self. I like my embroideries to represent moments in time – building my archive of memories.'

OPPOSITE AND ABOVE
Jordan Cunliffe (UK)
Linear Time (2020),
hand embroidered, red
cotton thread on linen.
1201×0.5cm (472×0.19 in).

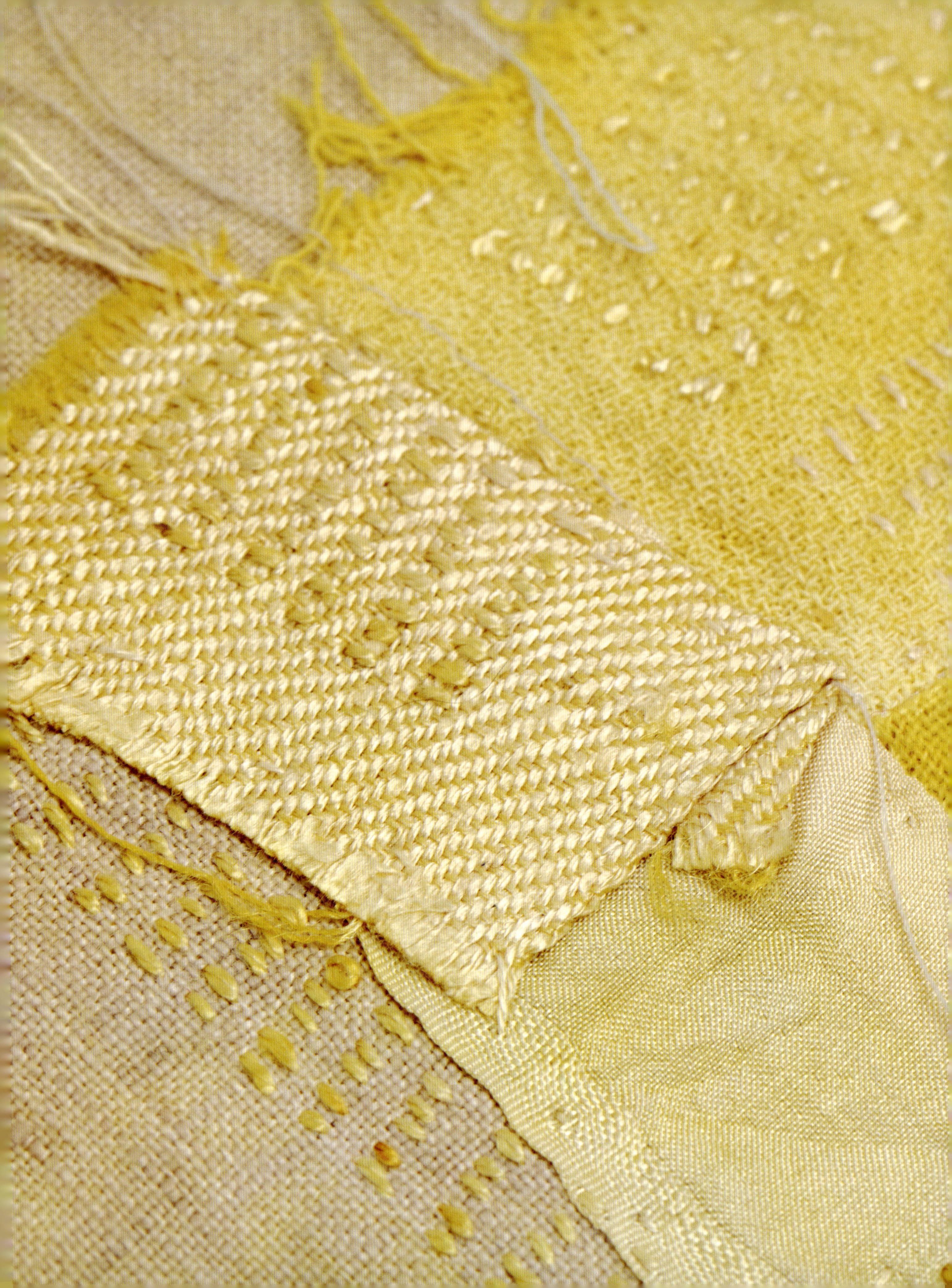

Place

Observing place

Observing the place around you has been part of many community-based projects I've worked on over the years. A simple prompt at the start of a session, 'Tell us about something that you have seen in the last week', brings all kinds of reflection. Project participants offer small stories about the shifting light, things growing, noticing change. It is a way of focusing the members of a group on each other, an opportunity to share experiences and minor details from everyday life.

As an artist-researcher, I've collated hundreds of these observances, everything from 'finding some inner calm painting a radiator' and 'I had a visit to the library', to the more poetic 'I saw seagulls over the landfill in the light like little silver darts' and 'sunrise – pale yellow, flat clouds and dark hills' offering a rich sense of place and landscape.

These observances of the minutiae of daily life serve as a stepping-off point for discussion. They are a gathering moment for groups, settling us back into each other's company and readying us for the real business of the workshop session.

As a practitioner I find these gathering moments mean that I become more observant too. I store up details seen during my week and decide which one I'll share with the group. As projects progress, the observations can sometimes become something tangible in the work of the group with artistic responses to the shared noticing. Urban settings offer an opportunity to look up and look down. Finding ornate stonework above a shop front or a tenacious plant growing through a crack in the pavement can provide new inspiration.

Take a line (or thread) for a walk

One of my favourite aspects of community-based textile work is the idea of taking a line for a walk and 'following the materials'[1] sometimes literally, as a meandering stitched line across a

[1] Ingold, T. (2009) 'The Textility of Making'.

piece of cloth, but also in seeing what happens, a process of empathetic listening to what goes on in the room, including during periods of silence. The ecology of the textile workshop space allows for pauses and quiet among the busyness of making together. Through this listening process I look for clues: through the materials used, the choices made by the group, the requests for information about different techniques. This is how the work becomes a whole.

In a recent conversation with a group there was a discussion about the perception some participants had of what our 'finished' piece of work would look like. They admitted to occasional anxiety that it would never be complete, certainly not in a form ready for exhibition.

But as we worked towards our deadline, the final piece emerged from scraps of cloth and multiple stitchers' hands. One described my role. She said, 'You plant the seeds.' As someone with many years of 'growing' projects, providing inspiration for work from plant forms but also growing materials to work with – dyes, fibres, herbs – this phrase appeals to me immensely. Growing as a process also involves listening, being attuned to the seasonal rhythms of projects, nurturing plants and green spaces and improvising when things don't go according to plan.

Much of my current work has been informed by the idea of journeys. How we get here, arriving, belonging, the interruptions and diversions on the way. In pieces of group work I see very literal interpretations of this theme – the journey to the community centre, the walk down a local canal, an emphasis on very local places. I also see reimagined journeys and those taken through multiple countries, those of displacement and new starts. Taking that thread for a walk can be the beginning of different ways of thinking about place, self and community.

These stitched journeys can be the beginnings of connection too, not just between time and place, but also between participants. In one creative health project, I was powerfully reminded of this and the wellbeing benefits of observing the smallest of journeys: that they can offer a more expansive view of the world around us. In one conversation this was described as lifting one's head from the details that provoke anxiety; something we can all aspire to.

Unpicking place

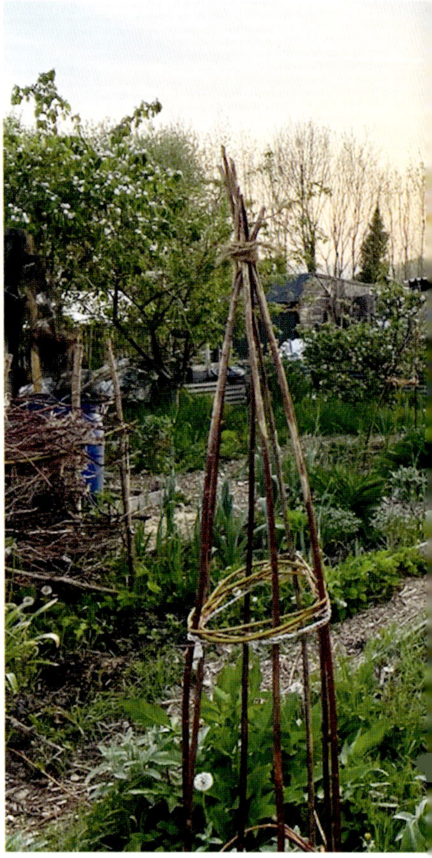

There are endless connections linking growing, textiles and communities. This can be expressed through gardens that produce dye and fibre plants, but also through everyday growing too. Plant forms and behaviour can inspire forms for print blocks; the scents from a herb garden allow space for reminiscing.

Several of the projects in this book connect to my allotment. It is on a site that was once part of the grounds of a nineteenth-century manor house. I think my plot is where the pigs and the chickens were kept (not where the croquet lawn was). The final owner of the Grange was a dyer with a large local dye works. After his death the house was briefly home to some of the thousand Belgian refugees who came to Bradford after being displaced during World War I.

A project I worked on in 2023 explored the work of Bradford-born embroiderer and educator Louisa Pesel who worked with this sanctuary-seeking community, setting up a Belgian Institute with craft workshop spaces in the city centre[1]. My research and community practices link to creative health and wellbeing projects and, as such, I think through the place-based connections that exist everywhere, particularly when these connections link to green spaces and textiles.

Geographer Caitlin DeSilvey in her book *Curated Decay: Heritage beyond Saving* writes about 'perforated places', locating her analysis of place in the 'fine grain of materials'. As I'm often found with needle and thread in hand, the idea of a perforated place immediately brings to mind stitching: the patterned ground sketched out in madder stitches connected to my colour-growing practices, the work of keeping an allotment and the architecture of former industry that surrounds the place where I live. I have known these allotments for over 15 years, beginning with a community plot where I developed my first dye garden.

In less than a square mile of urban land I find connections to textile heritage, changes of use and complex layers of history. This allows me ways of unpicking place, working alongside people and making the stories matter.

[1] *Together with Needle and Thread: Legacies of Louisa Pesel*, Claire Wellesley-Smith (ed) 2023.

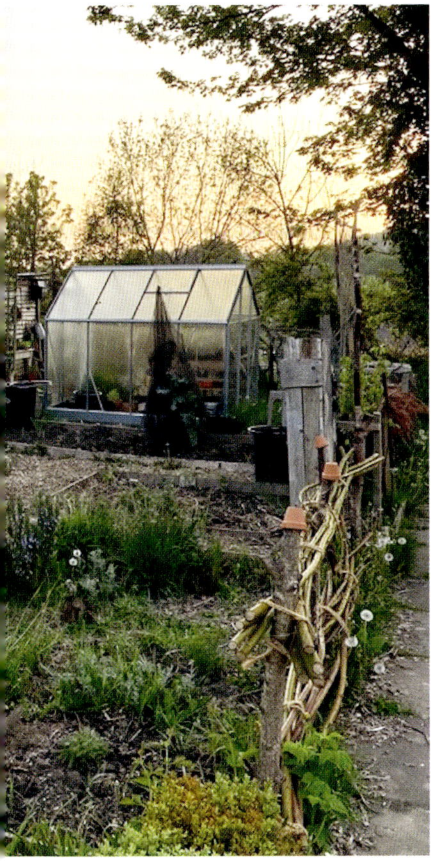

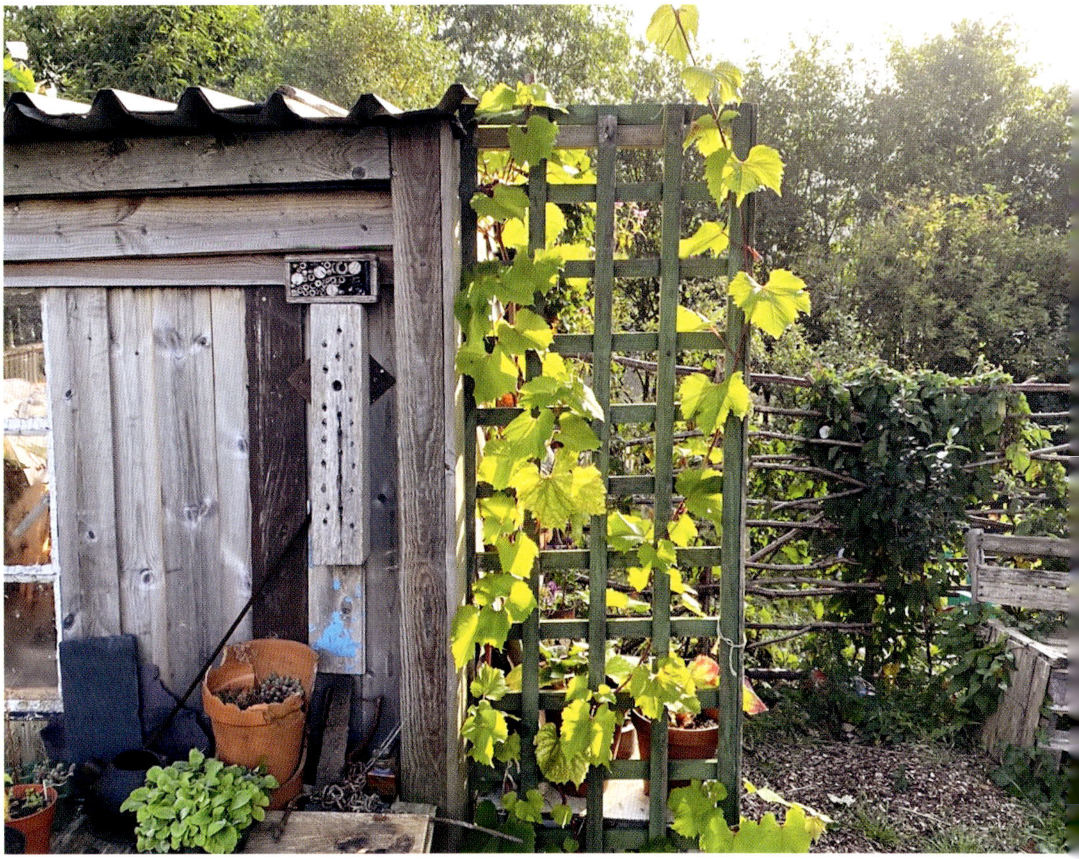

In my allotment notebook I find this reflection:

'The gaps between visits to the allotment start to lengthen in September as the season shifts. Growing seasons here in Yorkshire can be tricky – damp springs often followed by grey summers. Cold clay soil and the lack of sun combined mean that much of my dye and herb beds need replanting and, in some cases, sowing again from seed. For me, it's been a season to look at other details around the allotment. A cutting from a grape vine that grows in multiple plots around the site is being encouraged up and over the front of the shed. I layered up part-broken terracotta pots to make whole ones to plant my mint in. A line of calendula is growing around the base of the greenhouse. The on and off piece of stitching that I work on in the shed hasn't had much attention. The basket where it is kept with my small batches of solar-dyed thread has become wreathed in spiderwebs, as have the allium and cardoon heads I'm drying. I've been observing the lack of activity as much as the successes.'

ABOVE
Author's allotment plot in Shipley, West Yorkshire, 2025.

Grounding

Collecting materials from a specific place and gathering them together can be a good way to 'ground' a new project. This centres your focus, providing you with an archive of a place and inspirations for your work. You could collect items from the natural environment: leaves, seed heads, colour samples. You could also look for collections of objects, perhaps in your home, but I've also found local second-hand shops to offer a wealth of inspiration. In developing a project about a small town in West Yorkshire my local archive included the following:

- A postcard of the local marketplace from the early 1960s when it was being modernised
- Playing cards produced for a local dyeworks
- Clay pipes dug from my allotment
- Oak galls collected on a walk down my street
- A commemorative plate (1897) from a now demolished chapel
- A reel of buttonhole silk twist from Lister Mills (once the largest silk mill in the world)
- Pins from a primary school fundraiser

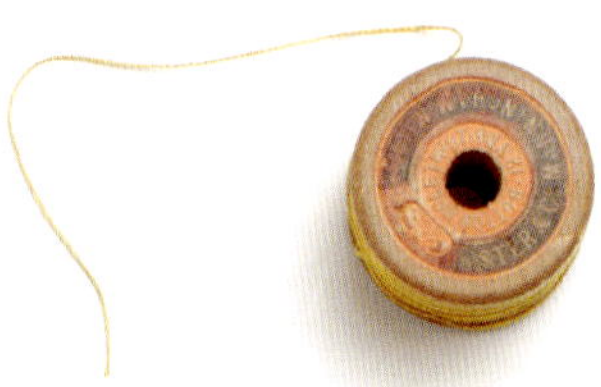

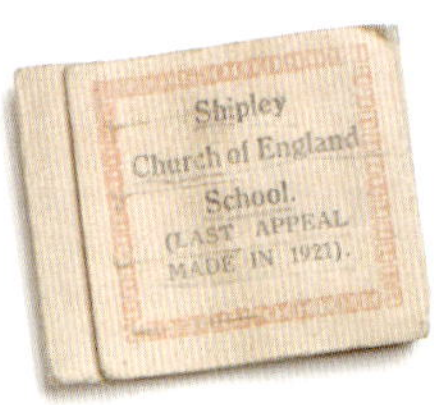

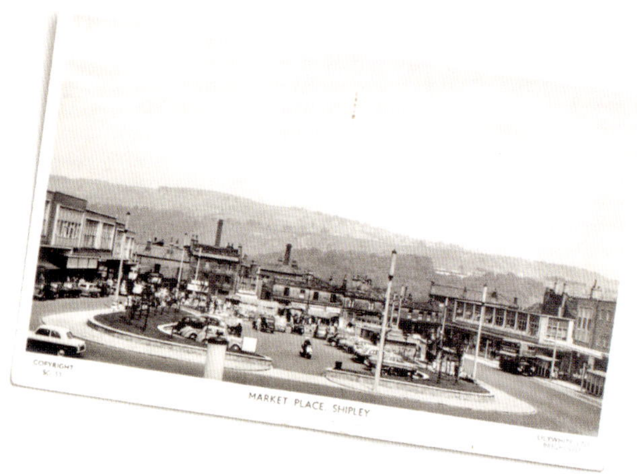

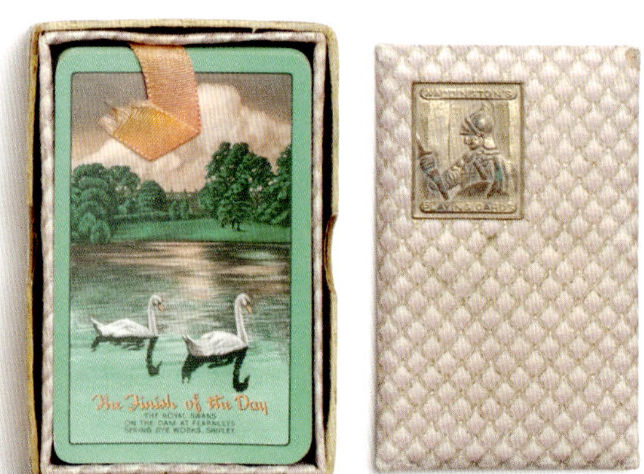

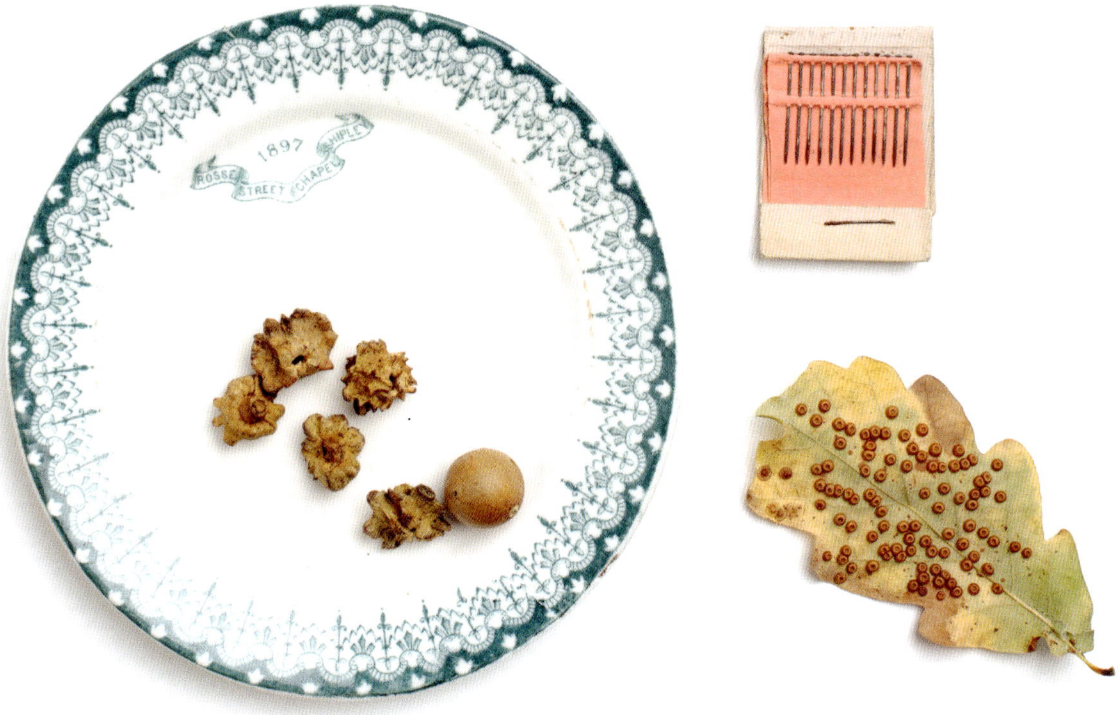

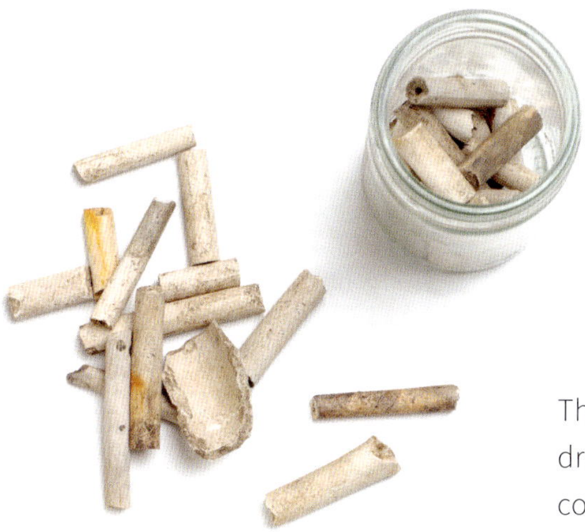

OPPOSITE AND ABOVE
Collected materials for site-specific projects around an allotment site in Shipley, West Yorkshire including broken clay smokers' pipes, oak galls, thread from a local mill, pins and playing cards.

This eclectic collection offers me a sense of a place over time. It draws links between the urban environment, the industrial and community heritage of the area and the growing spaces around it. In her book *The Creative Habit*, dancer and choreographer Twyla Tharp describes her working habits and creative project-management methods. She calls this system 'The Box': each new project is given a new file box and she puts everything related to the idea together.

'The box makes me feel connected to the project. It is my soil. I feel this even when I've back-burnered a project: I may have put the box away on a shelf, but I know it's there. The project name on the box is a constant reminder that I had an idea once and may come back to it very soon.'

Tharp's box technique has been a useful reminder of collected ideas. My own archive boxes hold visual clues and inspiration that can develop into more realised and complete work.

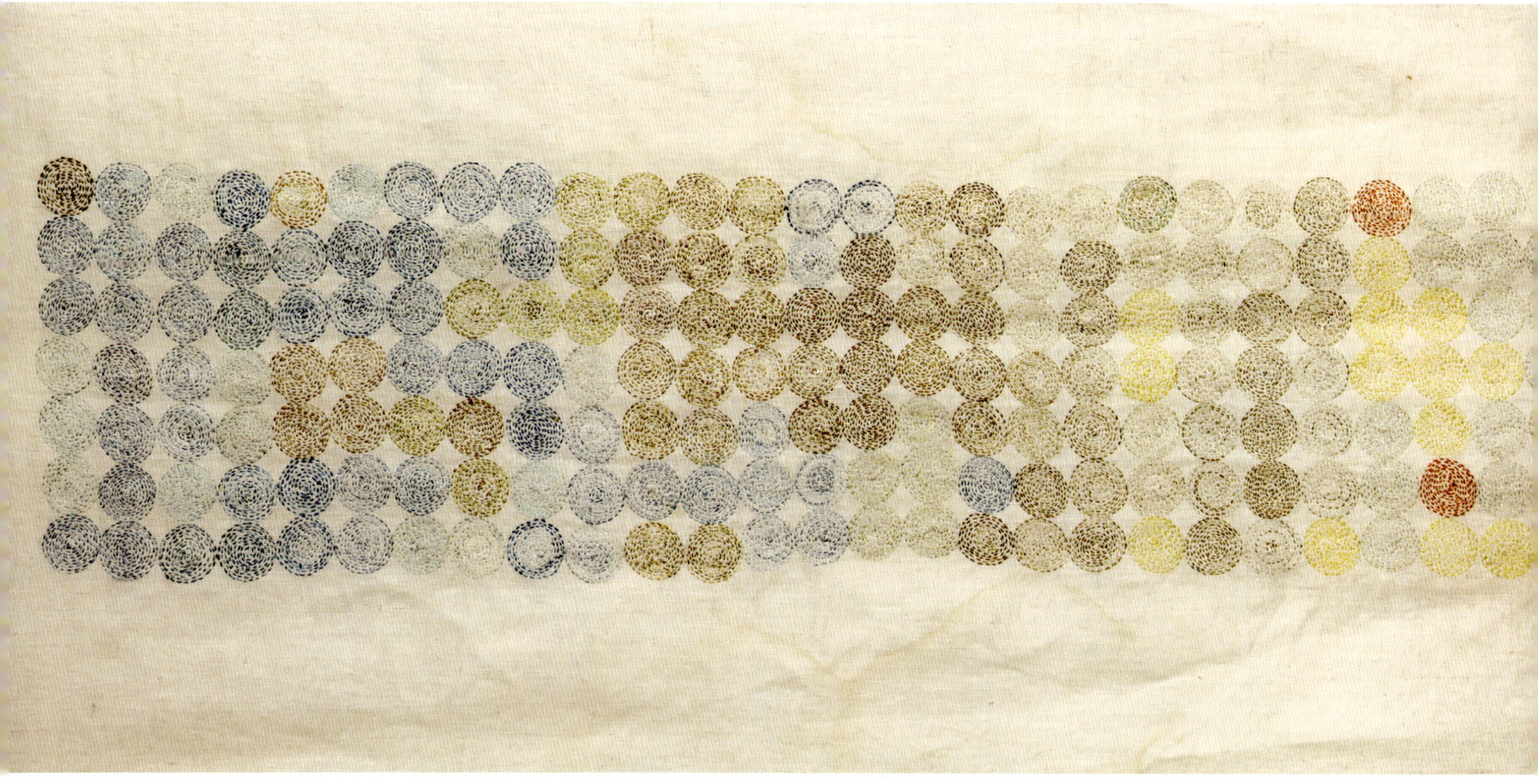

Shift

Shift is a durational piece of work recording 2022 day-by-day to mark ten years of growing food and colour at my urban allotment. The daily average temperature at the nearest weather station decided the colour and I used silk thread dyed in small batches with the plants I grow there. The colours shifted through the year as different plants came into season and included indigo, madder, dyer's chamomile, cosmos and onion.

Some were modified with scrap iron dug up on site, shifting the colour. In the traditional dyers' lexicon this is known as 'saddening', a way of muting and darkening a shade. Using this method, bright yellow becomes dull olive green. I stitched a circle each day onto recycled linen. It was a different kind of observation, a reminder of the minutiae of the everyday and a record of a place that is important to me.

I planned the year by creating a colour-based temperature key: each five-degree increment was a different shade. An unforeseen outcome was a period in high summer that featured

OPPOSITE AND ABOVE
Shift (2022), naturally dyed thread, recycled linen. 225×76cm (88.5×29.9in).

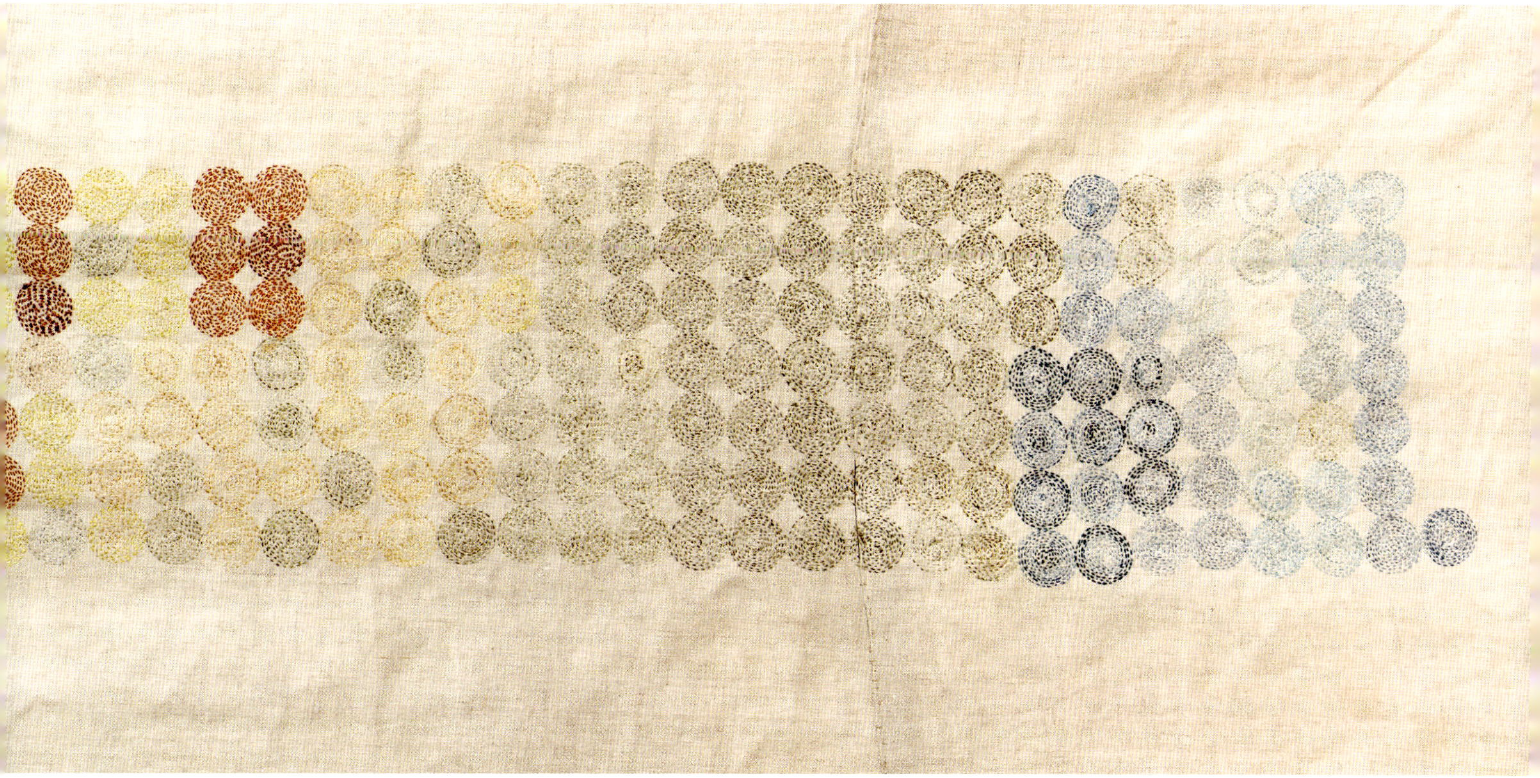

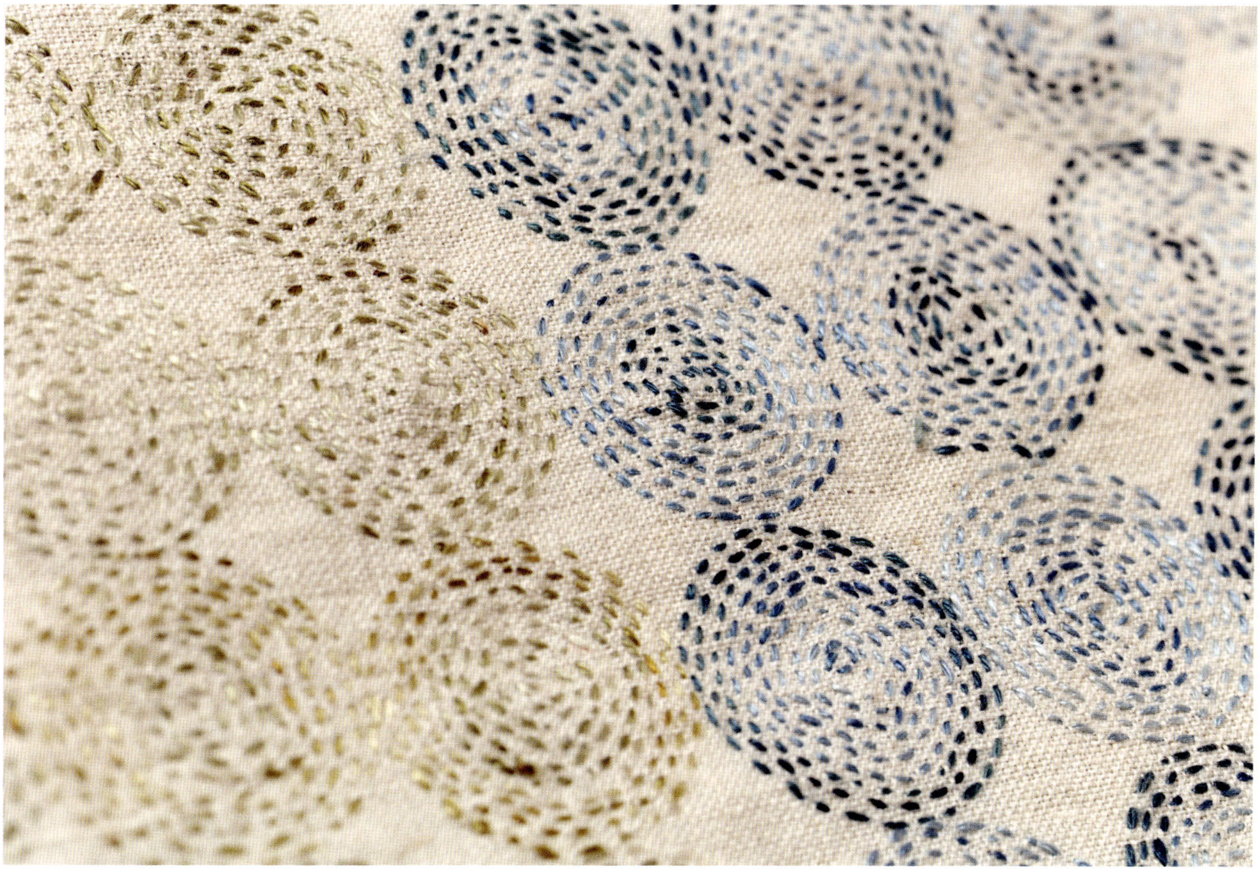

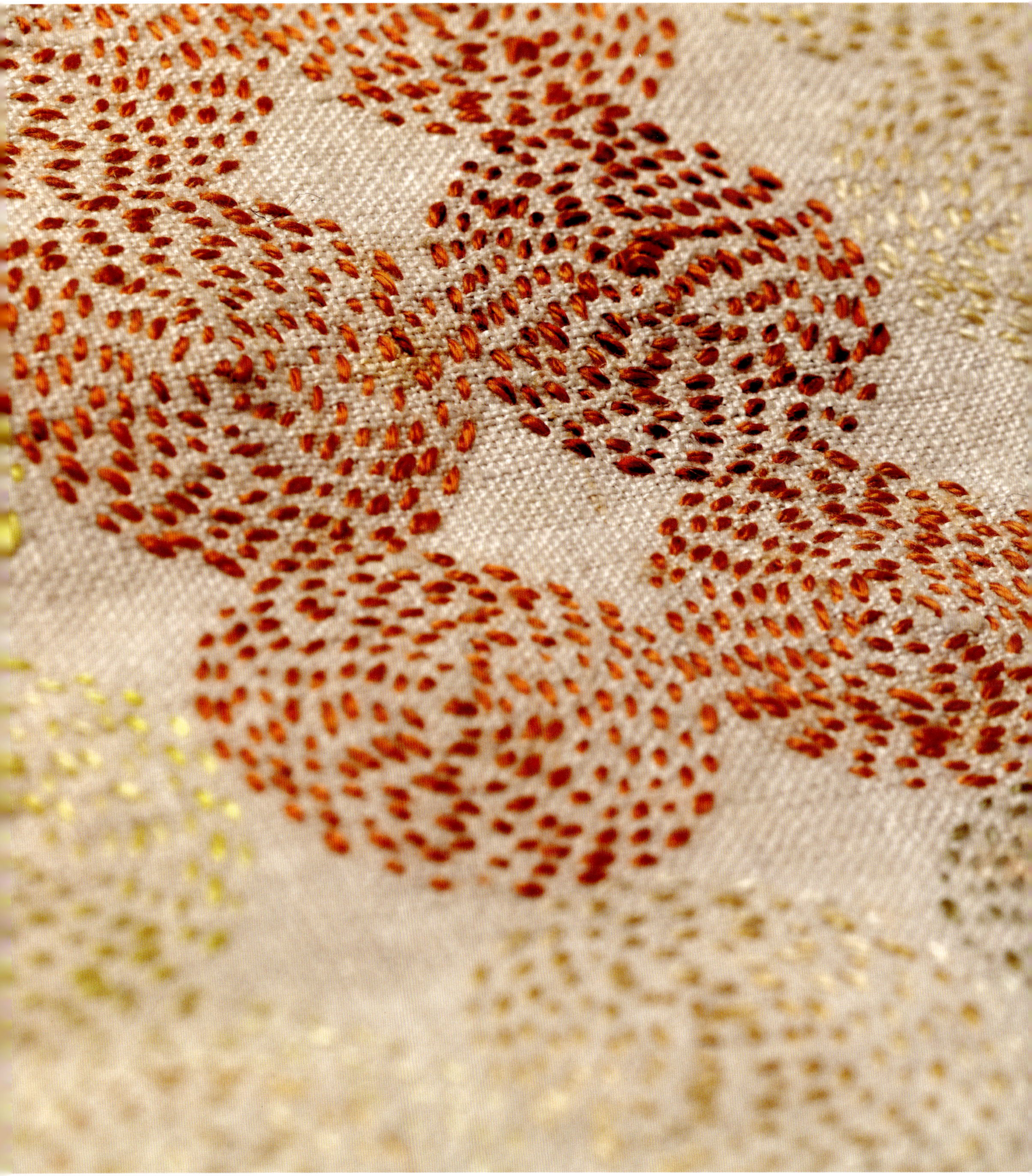

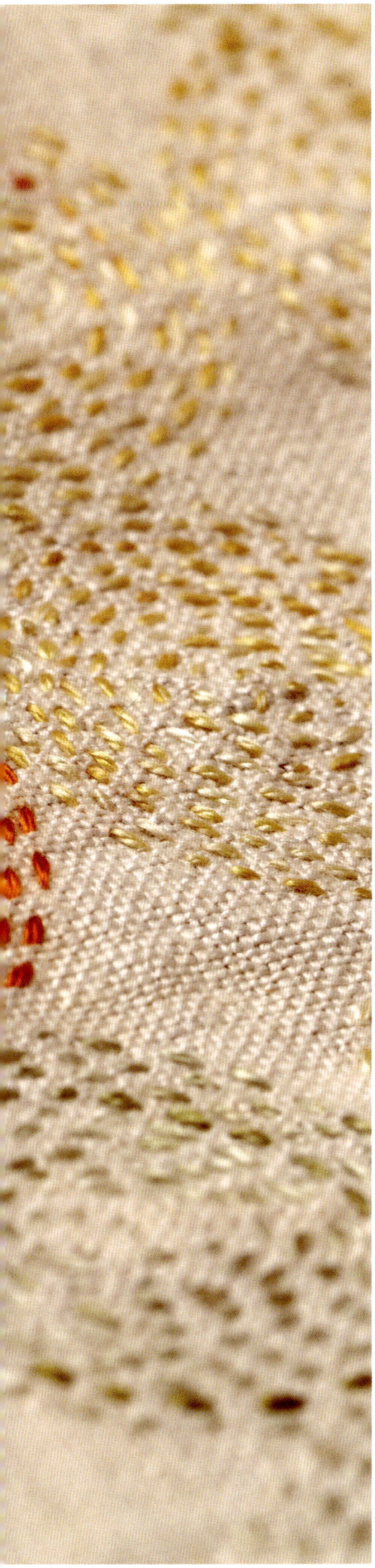

OPPOSITE
Shift (2022) detail from August 2022, the hottest time of the year thread dyed with madder root and dyer's chamomile.

extreme temperatures for the UK. I needed to find additional plants to create a new colour. I chose cosmos, which initially produced a bright pink, but as a fugitive dye this quickly faded to a pinkish grey.

I drew around an old cotton reel each day to create the space for me to stitch in. Using a simple device such as a circle allowed me to monitor the activity. It took approximately eight minutes, and two lengths of embroidery silk to complete a circle, filling the interior with running stitch – not a huge amount of time or energy. However, on one occasion due to illness I missed stitching for a week and had to catch up. It felt less of an observation, less connected to the day in hand, more of a chore. When stitching once a day on this piece, the pleasure of a growing, generative piece of work emerged gradually and became an essential marker of time.

My allotment remains my place-based practice, a site of ordinary growing and the vagaries of the weather, the carrots that don't germinate, the kale eaten by pigeons. However, alongside these mundane observations the site gives up other things. I've collected a jarful of broken pieces of smokers' clay pipes that rise to the surface of the beds, evidence of gardeners at work at least 120 years ago.

The heavy clay soil that I curse as it becomes waterlogged in winter, and parched, cracked and dried in summer, also offers me a medium to make a resist for indigo dyeing. The work of the other gardeners I share a site with gives colour inspiration through displays of sunflowers and dahlias. We share blackberry harvests in the boundary hedges with the birds and leave with fingers stained purple.

Having an observational relationship with a place can work in many ways. Alongside many community-based projects I have devised that engage with green spaces and built heritage, I am also interested in ordinary spaces and the care that is afforded to them, or not.

Stitching the City

Stitching the City took place in Bradford, West Yorkshire, in 2023 as part of pilot work for Bradford as the 2025 UK City of Culture. In this project, lines made by walking, wandering and wheeling through different parts of the district were made visible through simple textile maps. I am interested in wayfinding, making sense of our surroundings through the daily interactions we have, how we cross paths with others. To me, these offer new ways of connecting geographies of making, materials and communities in the city and beyond. The project offered an opportunity for community-based spaces of care – community centres, church halls, health hubs – to host sessions that explored the lived experience of people in the district through everyday physical engagements with it. Urban theorist Kevin Lynch in his 1960 book *The Image of the City* writes 'people observe the city by moving through it'.

Using textile in this context can be seen as gathering, a way of using the threads we stitch with to join together the stories of communities' arrivals, how they belong in the city today

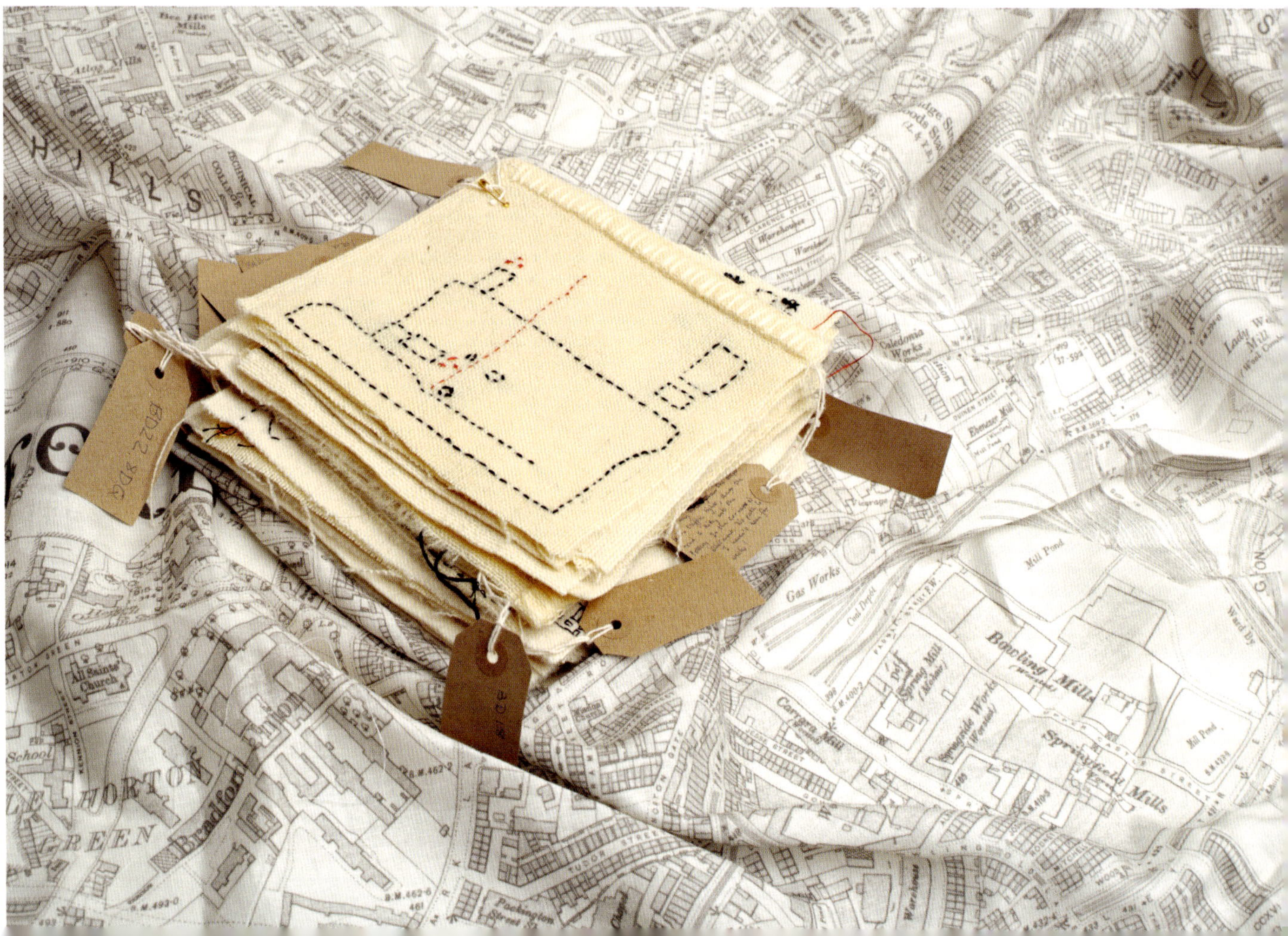

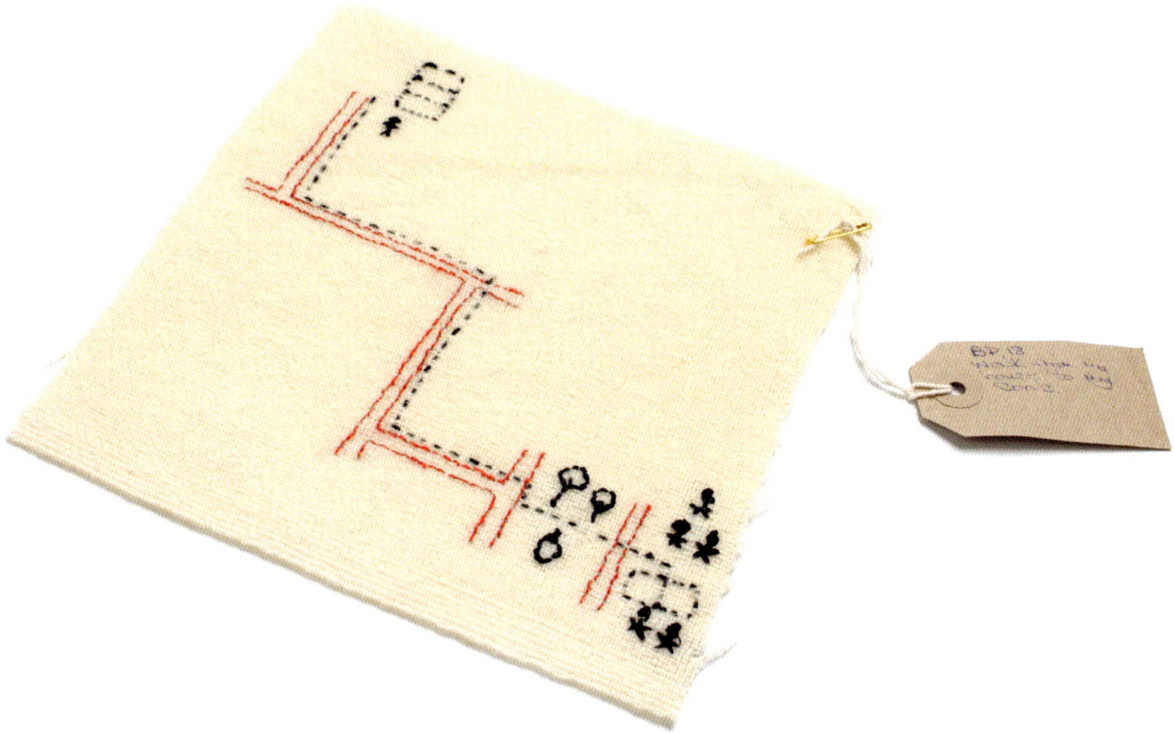

and how they relate to the global mobilities of the textile industry over the last two centuries. Geographer Doreen Massey describes multiple senses of place, and this offers me maps as a 'completed present' with a textile metaphor of 'loose ends' and the 'thrown togetherness' of stories.

The use of textile as medium within this project ties it to the geographic location. Artist and academic Alice Kettle describes the way that cloth can be socially engaged or socially enacted, embedded and entwined in community making and in recording histories. Textiles can speak in myriad ways. In their making we can find common language. They offer traces, in the lines taken for a walk, or the length of a piece of thread measured from tip of forefinger to elbow. In these sessions, storytelling emerged through the spatial and geographical routes that were plotted through the district.

Anthropologist Tim Ingold describes maps *as* storytelling, suggesting that 'drawing a line on a sketched map is much like telling a story'. In their simplest form a description of a journey with directions can involve commonalities of experience and different kinds of spatial understanding. You can make a gestural map using your hands to point and show directions.

OPPOSITE AND ABOVE
Stitching the City (2023-2024), community participant personal maps of Bradford with a digitally printed map of the city from 1908. Each map 20×20cm (7.8×7.8 in).

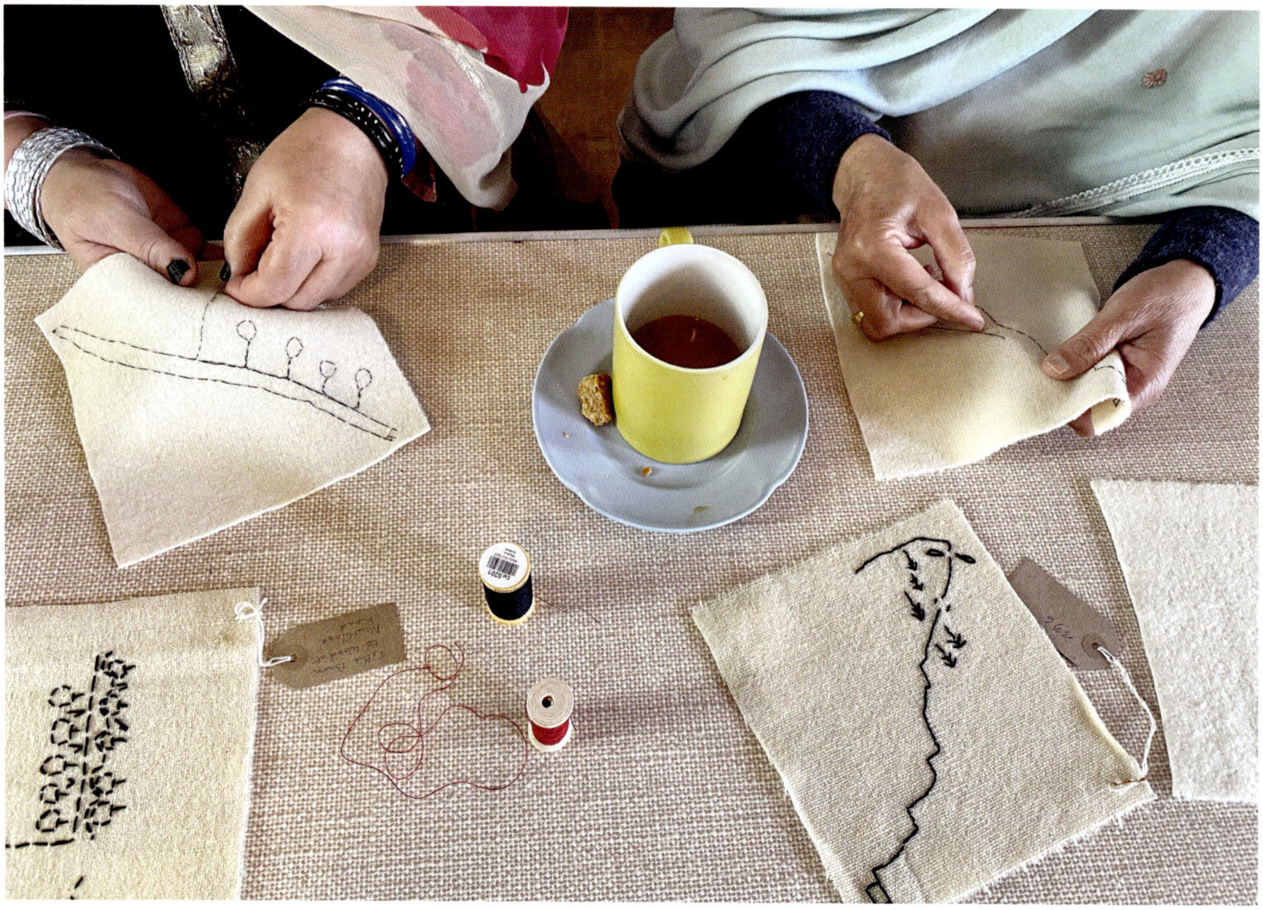

In the *Stitching the City* workshop sessions, participants were encouraged to think of a regular route taken and describe it to the person sitting next to them. Scrap paper was offered to sketch a journey, the stitching was with limited materials and only black and red cotton could be used on a white recycled-wool fabric background – a nod to the local heritage, Bradford as 'Woolopolis', or simply 'Wool City' as it was known during the nineteenth century.

The workshops used projected maps of the area surrounding our meeting place, historic and current layered together. Tabletops had old *A-Z*s, Ordnance Survey and other maps of the area for perusal, and some participants made a route on their mobile phone map for reference. Typography and map symbols were reflected on, and some participants used them in their personal maps. Nearly everyone focused on a hyper-local story: home was usually the starting point with routes to significant community buildings: health centres, libraries, churches and mosques, green spaces, shops, friends and family – three elderly sisters in one group all stitched the same street, marking each other's houses as stopping points.

ABOVE
Stitching the City participants from Keighley Association for Women and Children, 2024.

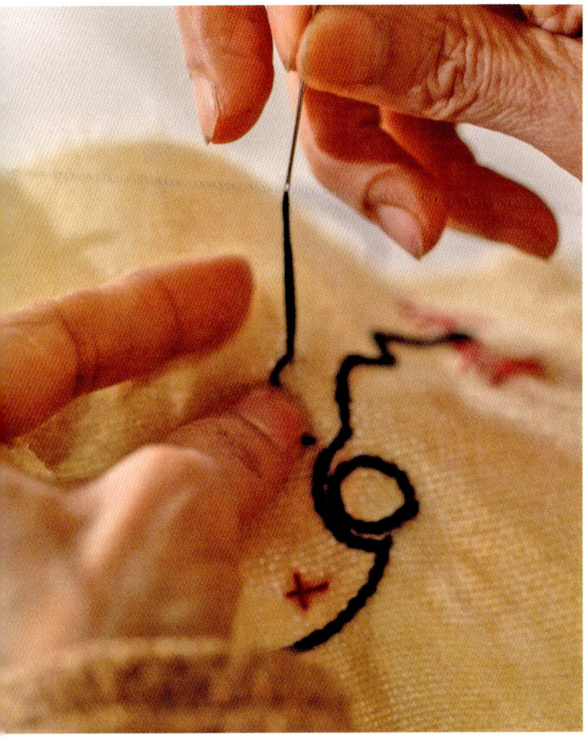

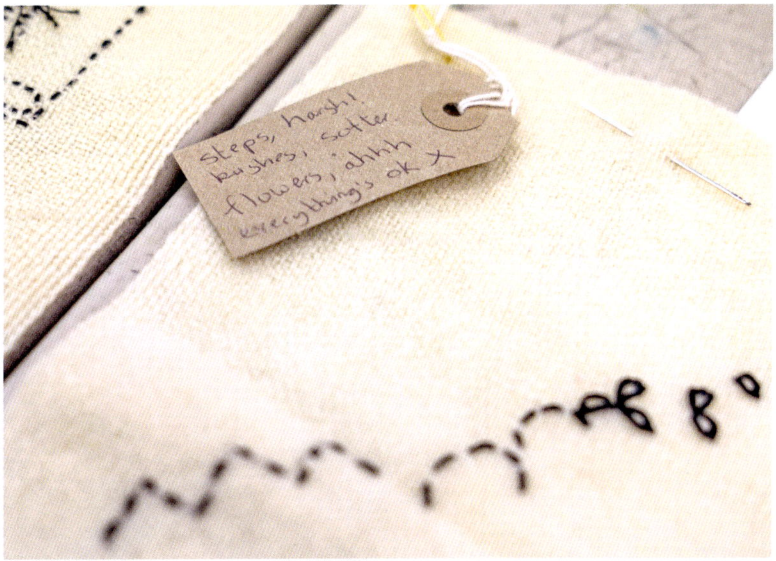

Participants were supplied with a luggage label to capture two things – the first part of the postcode depicted in the map and a one-sentence description of the journey. Some read like poetry: a walk to the supermarket past an allotment described thus:

'Steps: harsh!
Bushes: softer
Flowers: ahhh
Everything's ok x'

In the process of seeing what would happen if I asked people to plot everyday journeys, several things emerged that were less expected. Health featured strongly as a theme. This comment from a participant offered a reflection on walking, drawing and stitching:

'If you'd asked me to draw a journey I wouldn't have come to this workshop. Stitching it feels different, I am stitching like I walk: slowly. I put one stitch in front of the other, like I do with my feet.'

Other maps showed walks to health centres and the swimming pool – described as a relief after a period of illness. A map that included a roundabout depicted a journey taken by car due due to mobility issues. A walk along the canal at Keighley was described as being a space for mental wellbeing out in the new green of springtime.

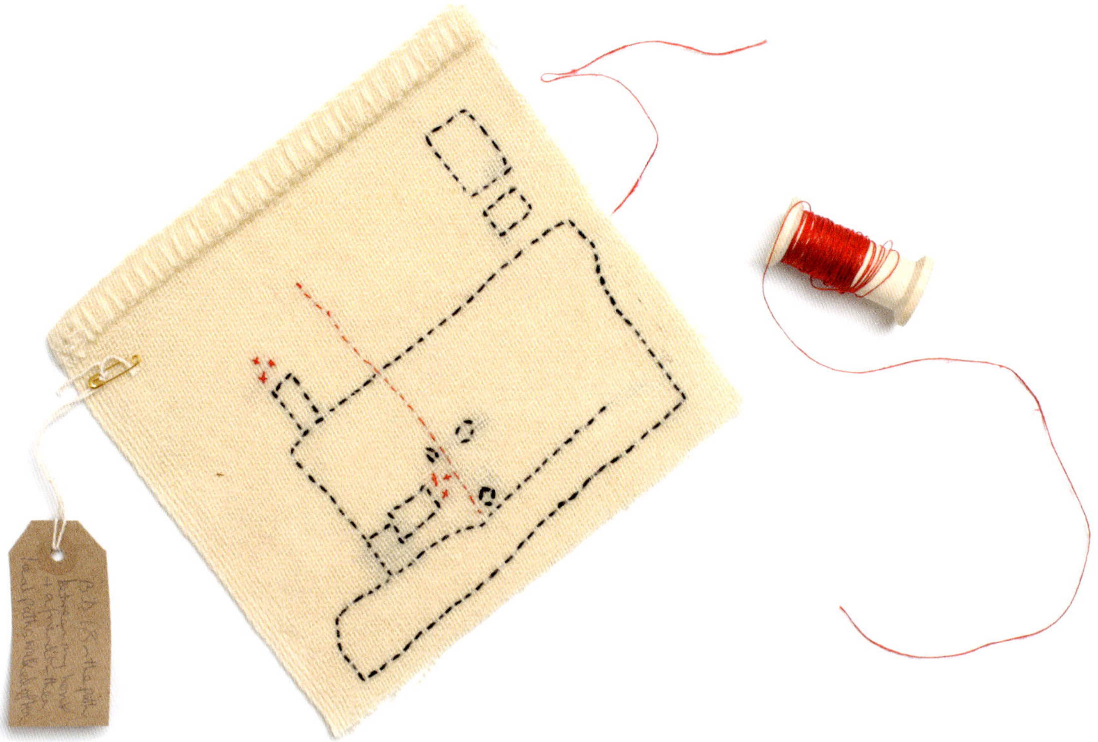

The depictions of routes taken were very specific to parts of the city, bordering areas or villages rarely featured. A number of maps became reimagined, significant journeys and featured stories from childhood, or locations that are now very different in the post-industrial city: a journey from an aunt's house in Manningham, past the Polish shops on the way back from mass; a journey home from school, picking up mum from her shift at Drummond Mill on the way, where production ceased in 2001, and the building was destroyed by fire in 2016. Other maps told stories of dreams for the future. A map of a garden in Pakistan: 'I'll build my dream house in the corner one day.' One map was the journey upstairs, on the way to bed.

A desire emerged in each session for participants to put their maps together, these not-to-scale improvised marks, looking for overlapping places, borders and experiences. A fabric map of Bradford in 1908 left over from a previous project exhibition became the focus of this collective mapping with the textile pieces overlaid, showing common locations, streets, footpaths, the canal. The textile landscape and architecture of industry connected other maps – the zig-zag shape of north-light mill

ABOVE AND OPPOSITE
Stitching the City map of a local park, 2023.

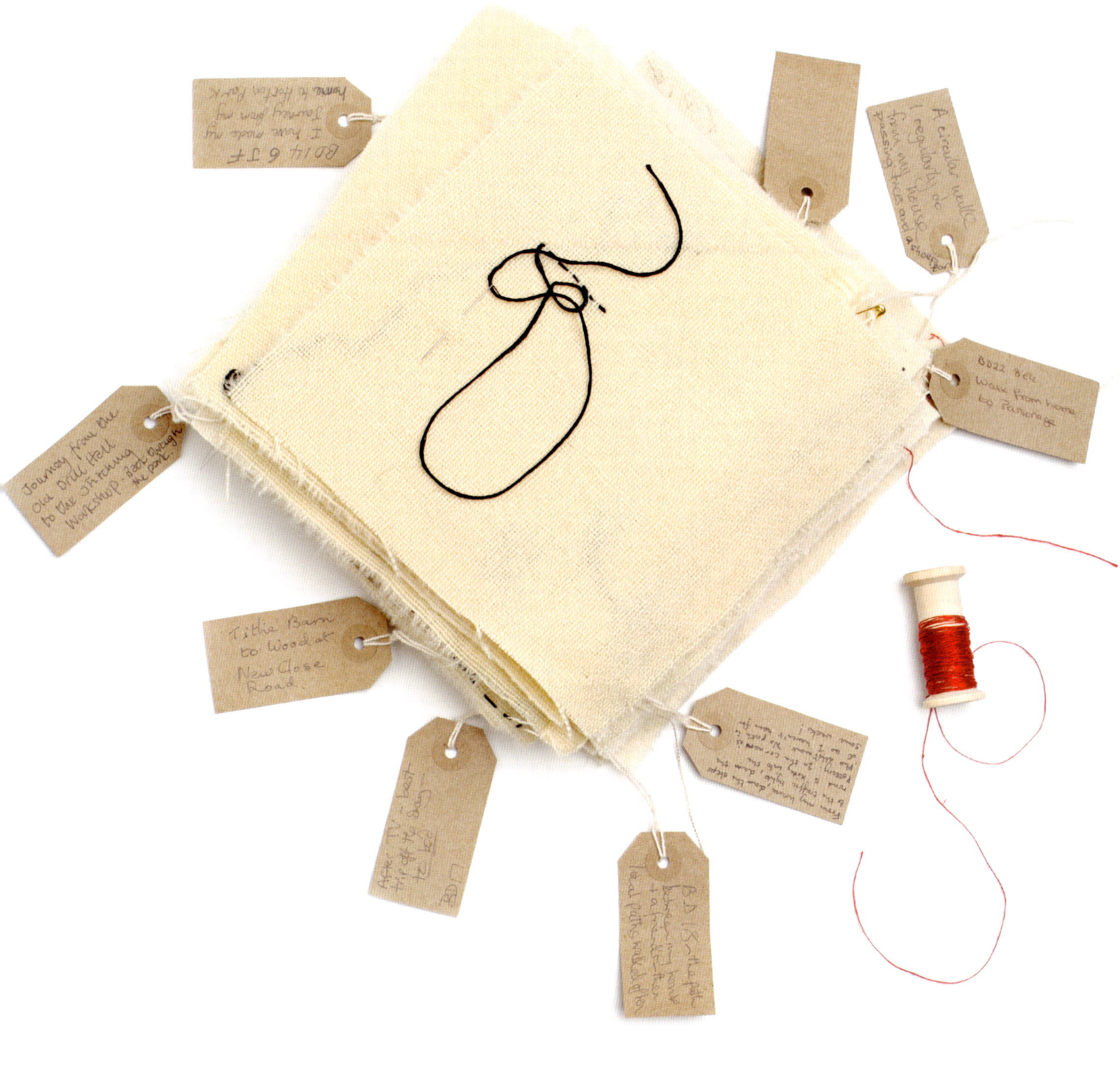

roofs appeared in several. The boundaries and edges of the maps and areas of the city depicted also come into play – whose city is it? Is it open to all?

Using textile-based methods in a city where textile continues to inform the architecture, landscape and memory of many citizens offered rich opportunity to depict, and then expand on, life in the post-industrial city today. Collective creative activity can be instrumental in reducing social isolation and offering spaces for small, less-heard stories to emerge.

Needle and thread as medium

What of the needle and thread as the medium for these small stories? Through my many years of community based textile engagements, I've become very attuned to the pace of textile activity and the impact on group settings. The vibrant, steamy, colourful world of the dye workshop is fast paced and noisy. There is little room for reflection in those spaces. The work of the community garden is paced differently, always working towards something, always impacted by the weather that day, looking for flourishing and becoming attuned to small differences in growth.

The stitching workshop, needle passing easily through wool, offers an ease for participants. It took me many years to recognise the silence that often descends during workshops as a gift. Younger and less experienced, I rushed to fill the space with questions and new conversation starters, but now I see the slow-paced recollections and storytelling in projects such as these as precious – the squares of fabric frame new spaces to tell stories of the city.

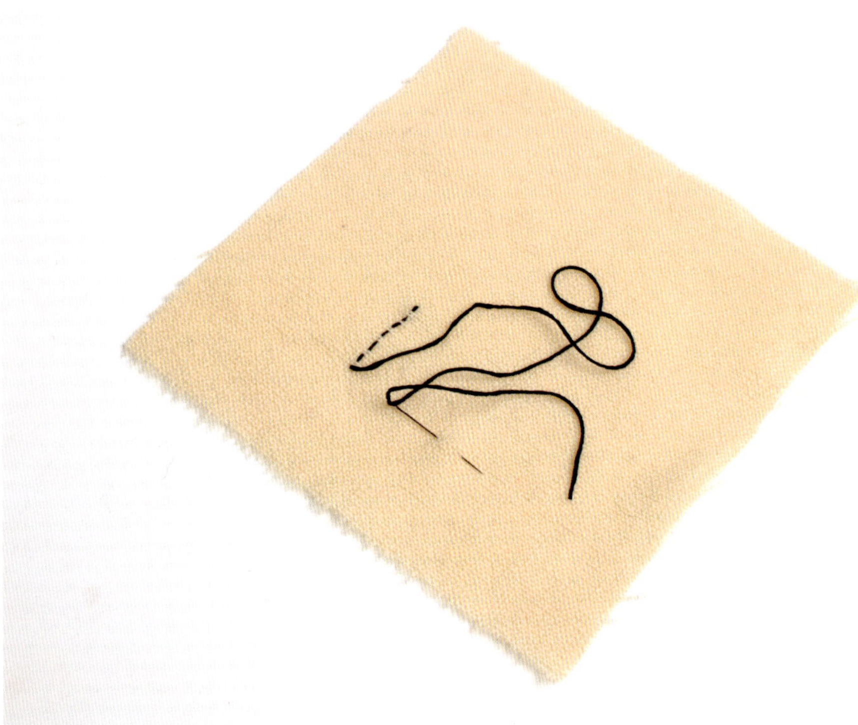

Stitch your own journey

This project worked on mapping ordinary journeys in a city and the wider district through stitch. Using textile to make improvised maps gave a material connection to the geography and architecture of a former textile city. The rhythms and patterns of everyday life offer ways to think about place, how we cross paths with others, how those stories connect us. You can stitch your own journey whether you are based in an urban or rural environment.

MATERIALS

- A plain piece of fabric
- Fine black cotton or silk thread – sewing machine thread would be ideal
- A sharp needle
- Embroidery hoop (if you like)

METHOD

1. Use a plain piece of base fabric and black thread as a starting point.

2. You can use an embroidery hoop to keep your base fabric taut, if you like.

3. Start by taking your line for a walk using simple running stitch. Think of the stitches as you might pace your steps while walking. At this stage you could limit yourself to a single strand of thread and see where it leads you. Don't worry about accuracy – this is a journey as you see it.

To extend this idea, think about regular journeys you make. The journey doesn't need to be to an exciting destination – think local and small. You could draw out the journey, using paper or an online map to plot it. You could choose to fill in the detail with map symbols, or add buildings and green spaces. Creating a series of maps can offer the potential for sharing with others in a group or adding multiple maps of a place lived in or visited to create a personal narrative.

Sue Green

Sue Green's practice is situated at the margins of sculpture, installation and narrative, with an emerging performative element for future exploration through film, audio and site-specific responses. Most significantly it is rooted in process, with the experimental nature of textiles her preferred medium. She is interested in how this manifests within a contemporary fine-art context and enjoys pushing the boundaries of expectation and materiality. Textiles have gained recognition as a valid and significant medium for sculptural expression. Their flexibility, tactile qualities and historical associations provide rich opportunities to explore form, space and meaning in innovative ways. Textiles occupy an influential position within the field of art as a mode of gender, culture and environmental significance.

Sue's work explores material with agency – the capacity to emanate a powerful presence for the viewer. She is interested in fusing this thinking with invested hours of labour, disrespecting the hierarchy of materials and giving status to the unseen repetitive actions of so-called 'domestic' work; she recognises the value of textiles and repositions it within art spaces.

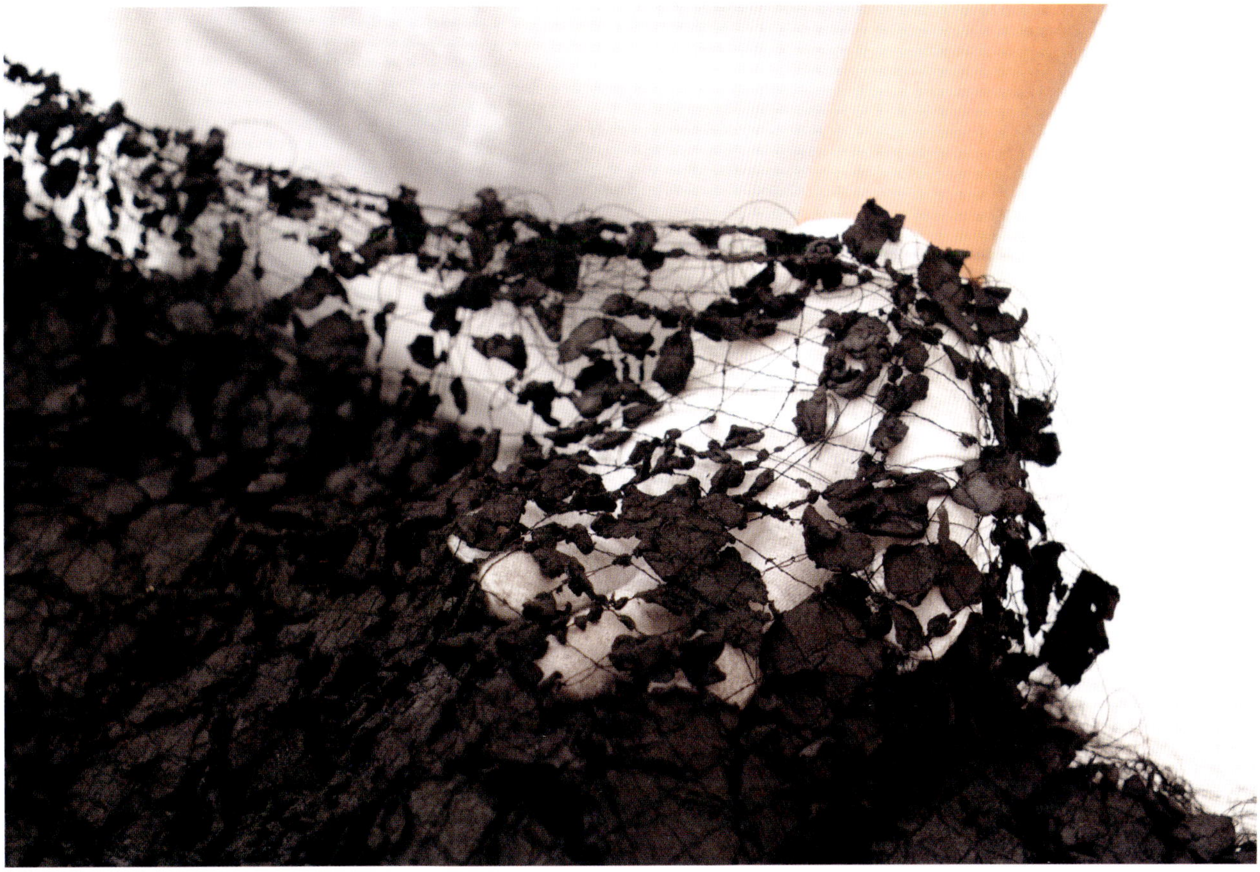

16 Hours

'*16 Hours* refers to the punishing daily schedule of textile mill workers, many of whom were women and children. Metaphorically, the memory of past labour, in this context of a semi-derelict woollen mill and the demise of its industrial output, it is visualised and manifested in the stitched structure of the work. It is the transference of the workload to something less able to cope that I attempt to depict. In this iteration I stitch and dye paper, a fragile substrate imbued with tensile strength through the haptic act of stitching. I set to work as a declaration of solidarity with the workers, stitching repetitive grids into the paper for 16 hours per day. I invested over 1000 hours and stitched 29 metres (32 yards) of substrate, extrapolating the work schedule incrementally as the work itself grew. This is a kind of meditation, a physical and mental addiction of sorts. I feel irritated and twitchy when not stitching. Additionally, the structure is infused with handmade charred pigment, temporarily

ABOVE
Sue Green (UK), *16 Hours* (2024), khadi (cotton rag) paper, thread, handmade biochar, organic binders, lanolin, beeswax 2926×91 cm (1152×36 in).

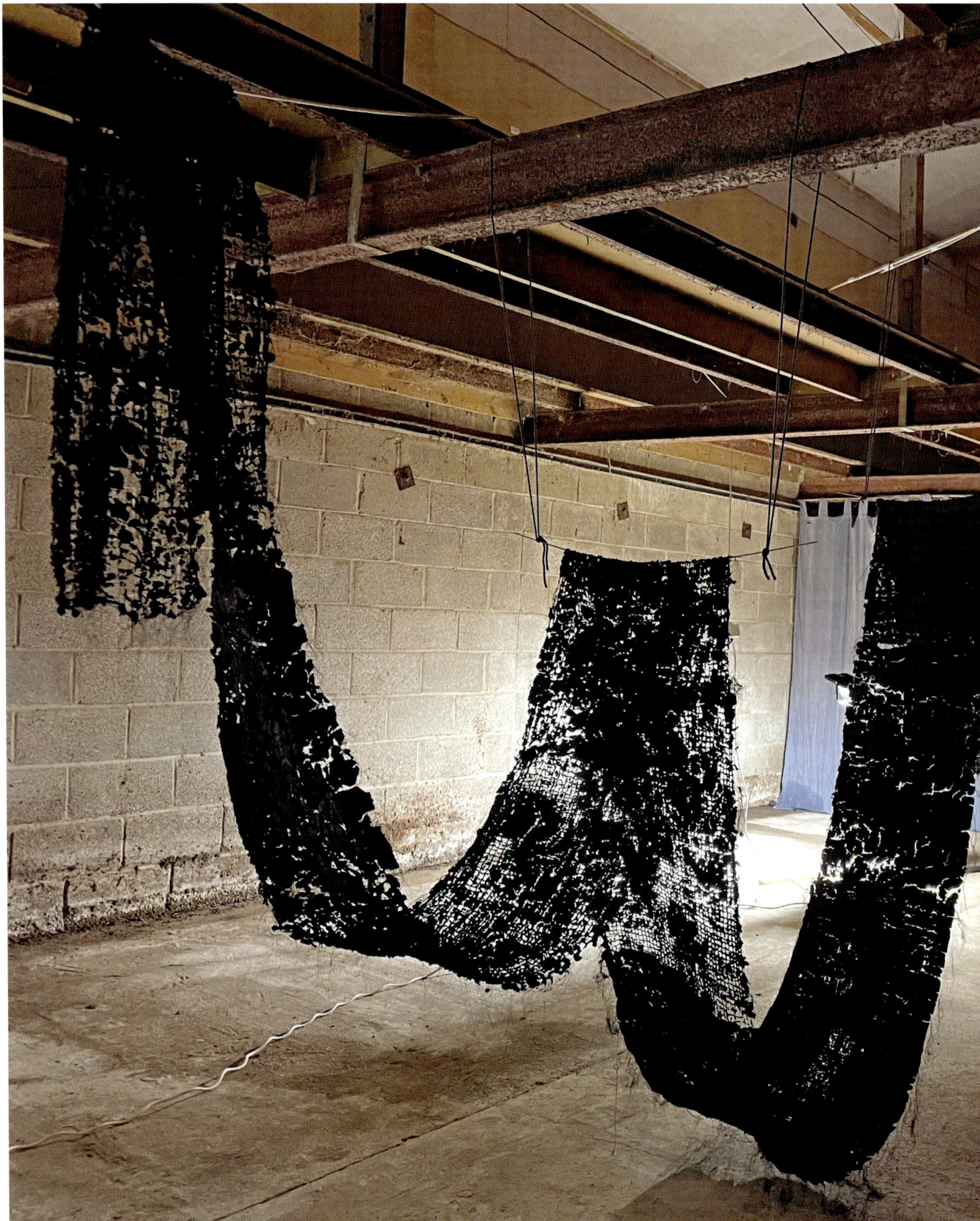

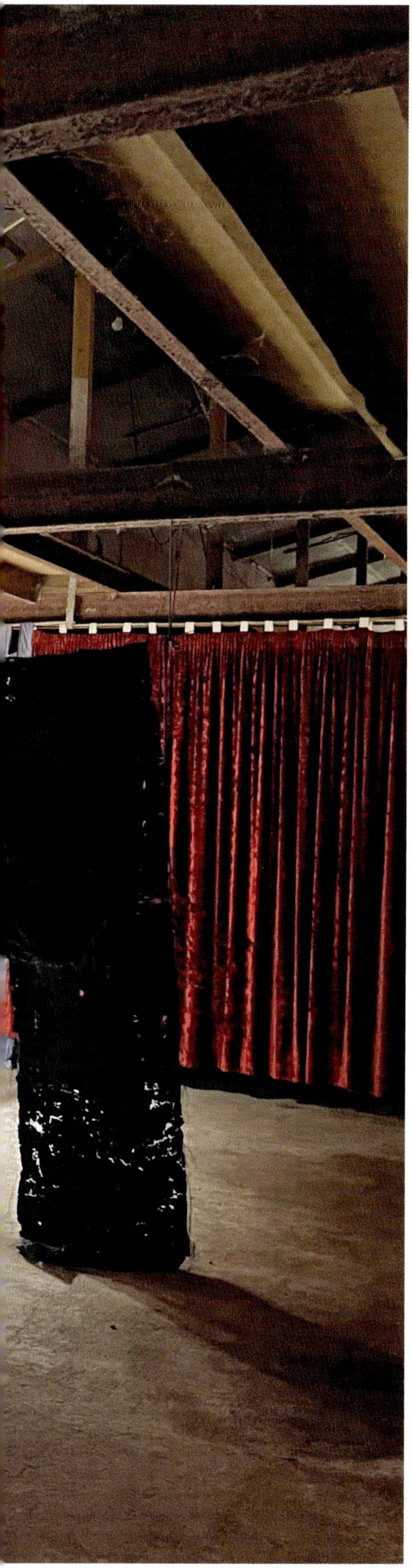

and only loosely fixed so an oily residue is transferred on contact, as an active and agential reminder of the toxicity and waste of the global textile industry, a powdery sediment reflecting a familial tale of a burning mill in 1909.

'My great grandfather was a worsted manufacturer, my grandfather a woven cloth designer, a later family business bought cloth from mills and sold it on a West Yorkshire market stall and my grandmother was a seamstress. There is a linear thread that connects them to my textile work. Broader echoes of past labour and the filthy conditions of our industrial heritage as a nation built on coal, cloth and clay also leave an indelible trace on all who interact with the work. The concept of matter having agency is explored in depth by Jane Bennett (*Vibrant Matter*, 2010) and a kind of democratising and classless structure is discussed through the use of materials.

'Textile "meanings" are unpicked within this narrative as a ubiquitous and wholly relatable material for all, regardless of class or gender, but the work also holds its own materiality and matter that is specific and brings agency to palpably affect the audience. My authorial intention as the artist, is that the deep respect I have for history (or herstory) becomes a material embodiment that is quite literally soaked into the substrate and that this is respectfully shared in celebration of all those women who have gone before me, breaking down hierarchies and reclaiming space for textiles to excel. *16 Hours* stands as a testimony to this.'

OPPOSITE
Sue Green (UK), *16 Hours* (2024), khadi (cotton rag) paper, thread, handmade biochar, organic binders, lanolin, beeswax
2926×91 cm (1152×36 in).

Capturing colour and place

BELOW AND OPPOSITE
Paper pieced samples of allotment dyed silk and wool 17×40cm (6.6×15.7 in).

Working at my allotment I keep a collection of textile materials in my shed, including pre mordanted fabrics and fibres that can transform with the plants I grow there. Here, also, is the result of a simple bundle dye technique where I scattered the last colour from petals, leaves and roots on a piece of old silk to provide a snapshot of the end of a season. Rolled up and tightly tied, I left it on the shed windowsill in a jar of rainwater, the gentle heat of early autumn sun allowing the colour to leach into the cloth.

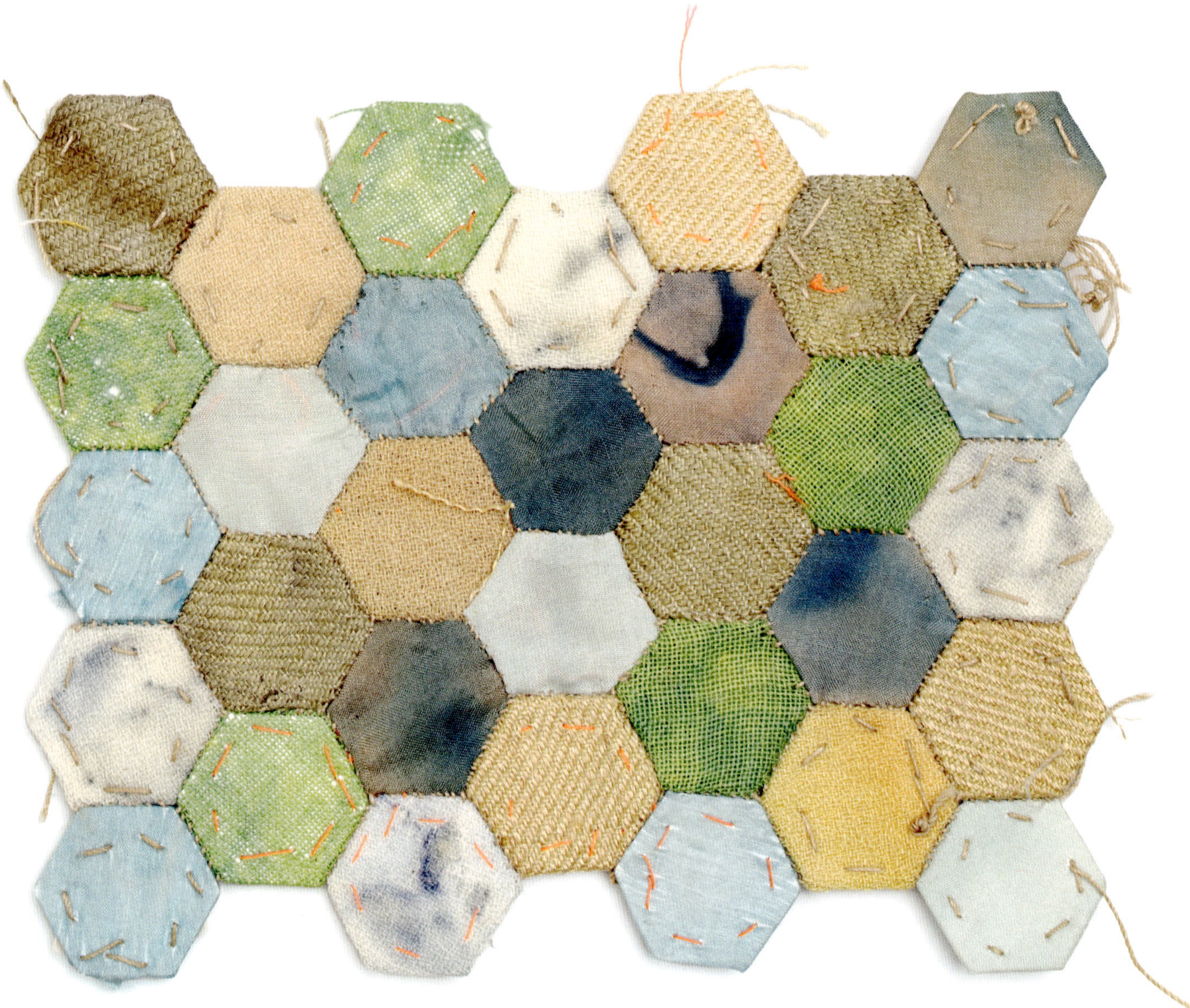

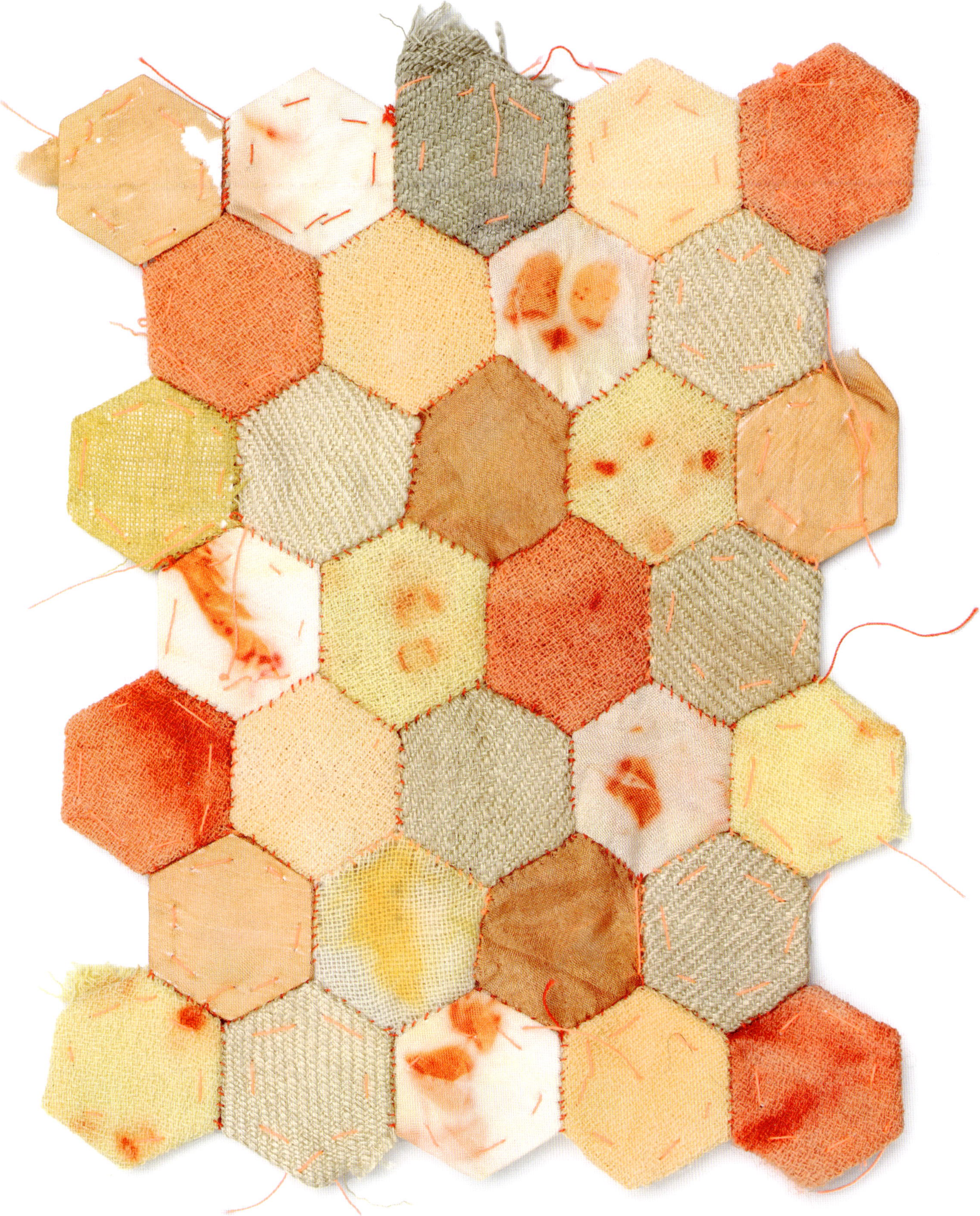

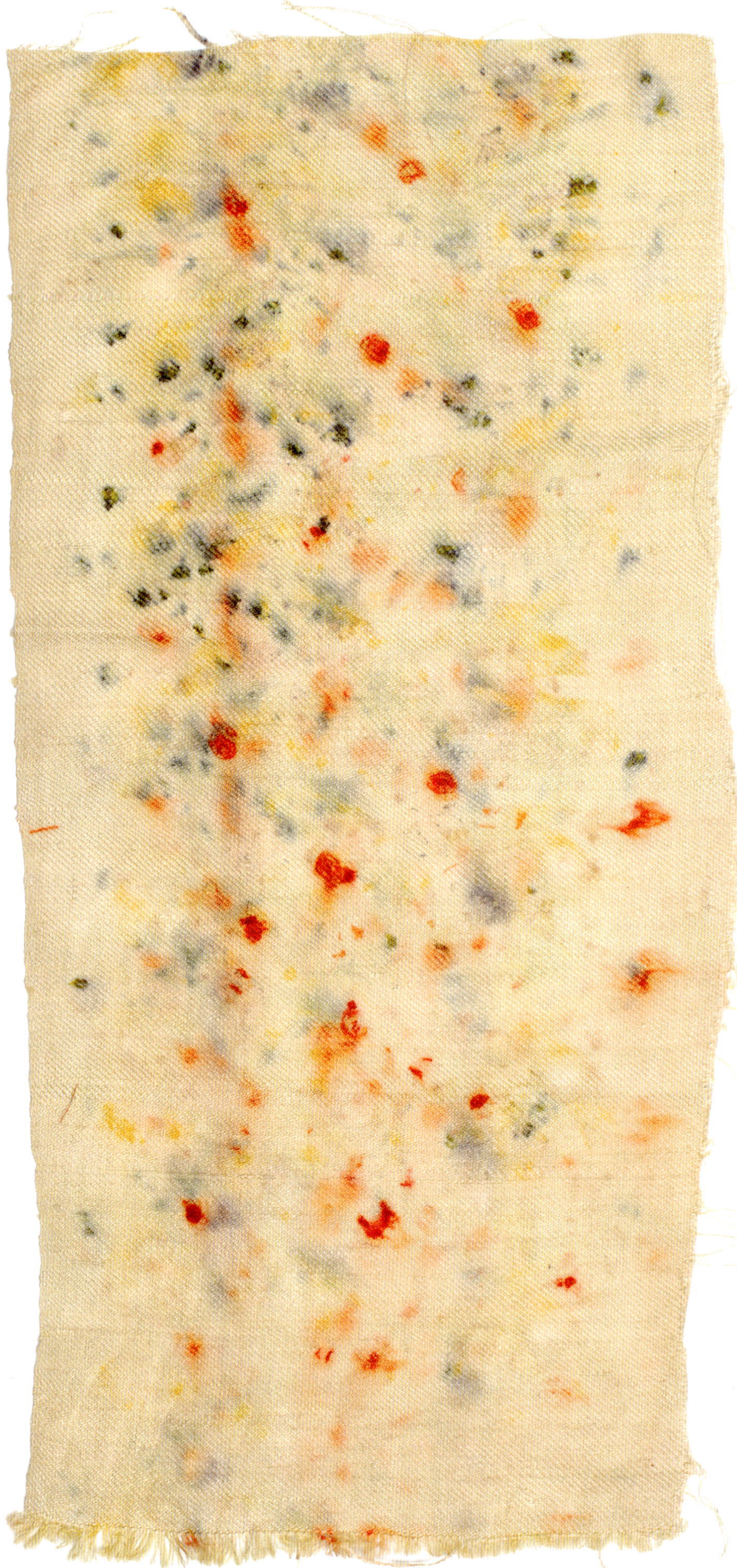

Capturing colour on wool

OPPOSITE AND BELOW
End of Season (2022), bundle-dyed dead headed flowers and foliage on recycled silk 44×21cm (17.3×8.2 in).

Collecting a sampler of colour from the surrounding green space is something I've used as a workshop exercise for many years. The surface of industrial wool felt works as an excellent carrier for colour when leaves or petals are rubbed on the surface. This palette acts like a sketchbook page for the workshop and sometimes has stitched sketches of details in the built or natural environment added to the surface. Swatches of colour from dyebaths can also be added as a record.

METHOD

1. Find a small piece of undyed industrial wool felt (or tightly woven wool fabric) and observe the plants around you.
2. Collect leaves and petals, rubbing them briskly on the surface until the colour is picked up.
3. Take a photo of the plant of origin if you also want to record this information.
4. Extend the activity by collecting additional leaves and petals from the same plants. These can be pressed and added to a sketchbook.
5. Stitching marks from the landscape onto the wool can offer you another reflection on the place you have chosen to work with.

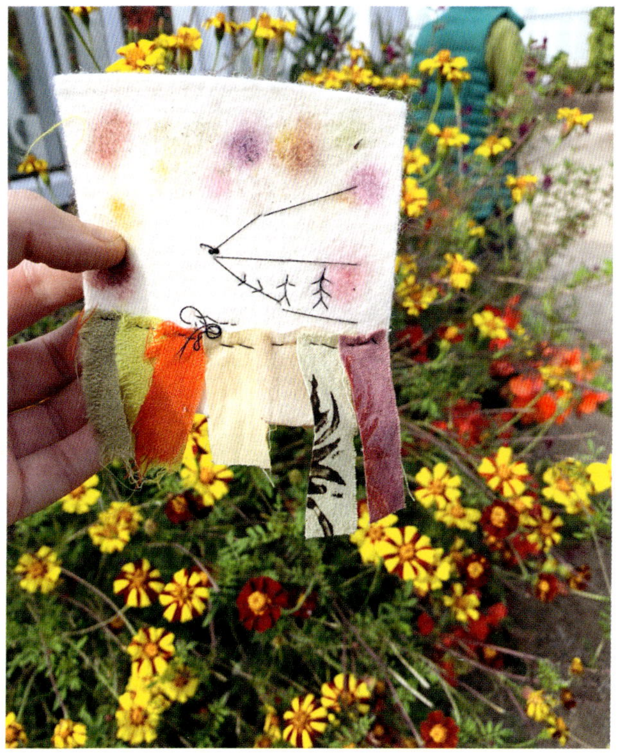

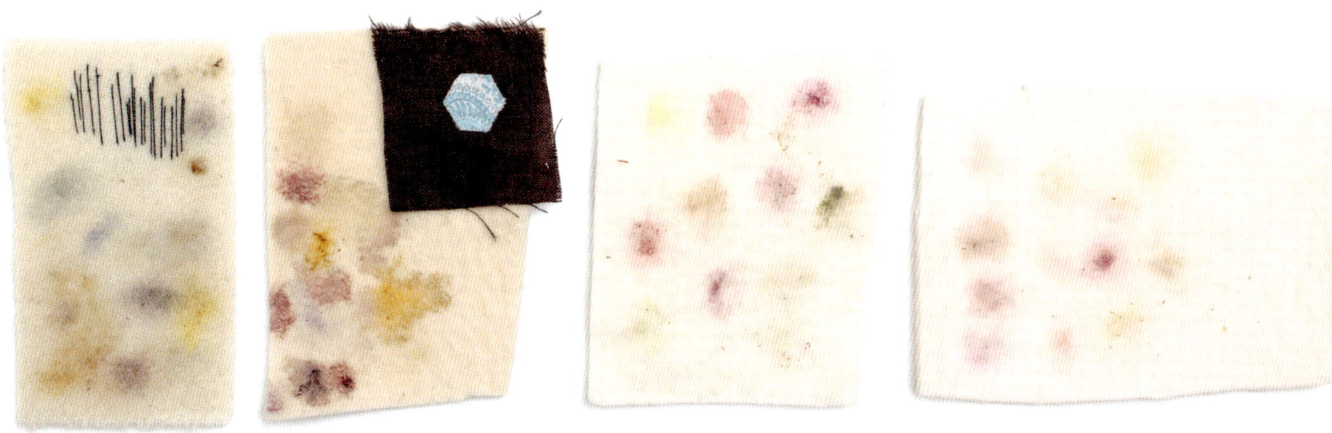

Almanac (12 pieces from a shed)

Alongside growing plants on site for colour and fibre, I record the season using 'blanks' – one for each month of the year. These blanks are small patched and pieced squares, constructed using a variety of natural fabrics, wools, silks and cottons roughly stitched to a linen background.

These are fabrics left over from teaching sessions; some are treated with mordants, others not. This means that the colour on the fibre will appear in different strengths and brightnesses. I was keen to have a record through the growing season by working on these with colour. I did the dyeing on-site in solar dye jars and sometimes by rubbing petals and leaves into the fibre of the cloth. I often dye silk threads using the same plants and then add these to the monthly record with additional stitches. This collection from 2023 gives me a sense of a year of growing and a record of this very local place.

Collections such as these can be a good starting point for longer and more resolved projects. They provide a snapshot of the growing year, the successes and failures of certain plant varieties. On dark winter days they give me inspiration and remind me that places are always in motion, even when they appear fallow. This gives me energy to prepare the soil for a new season of growth and discovery.

OPPOSITE AND OVERLEAF
Almanac (12 pieces from a shed) (2023), wool and silk fabric and thread on linen solar dyed with allotment plants (method shared in *Slow Stitch*, Batsford, 2015) each piece 14×15cm (5.5×5.9 in).

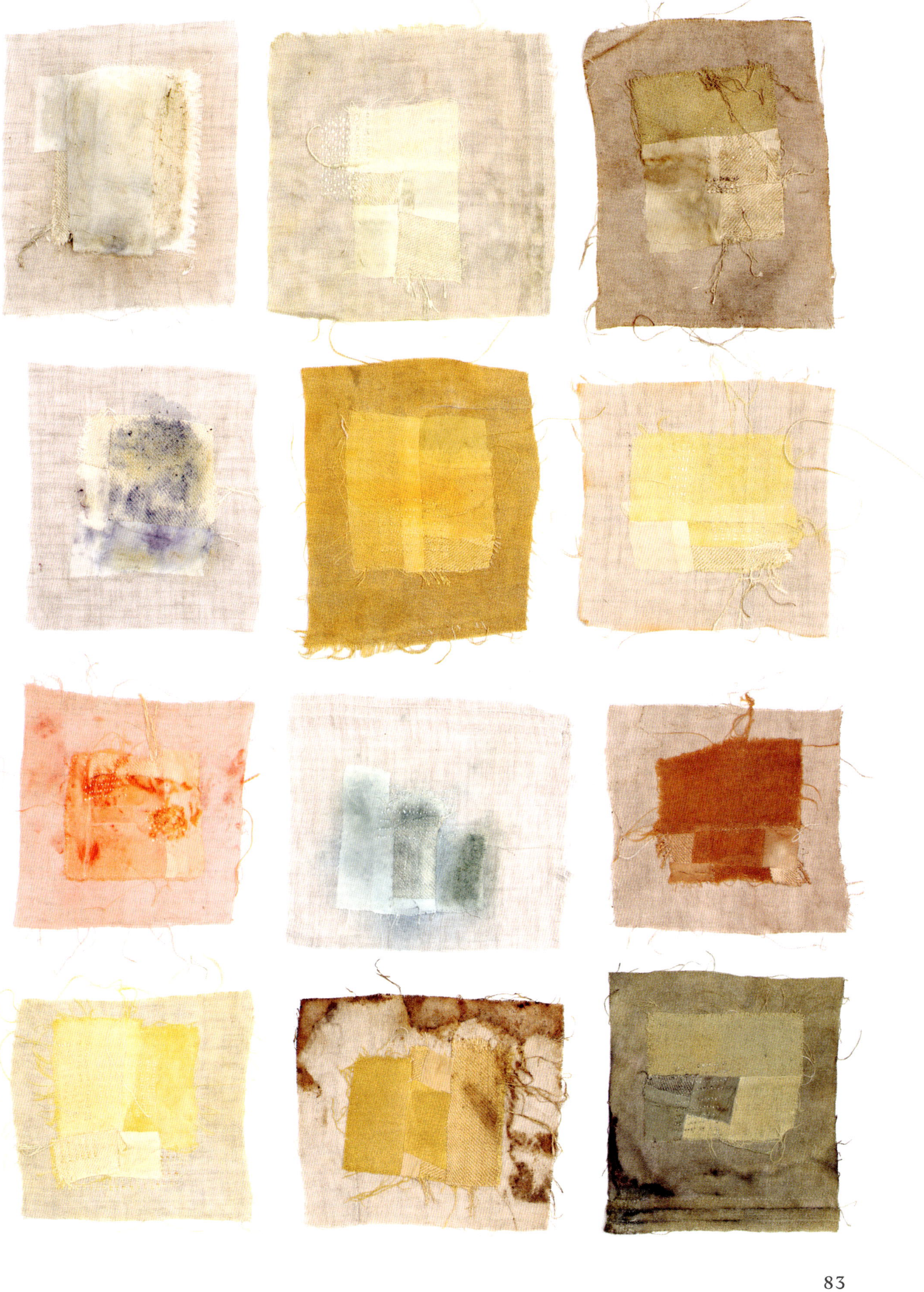

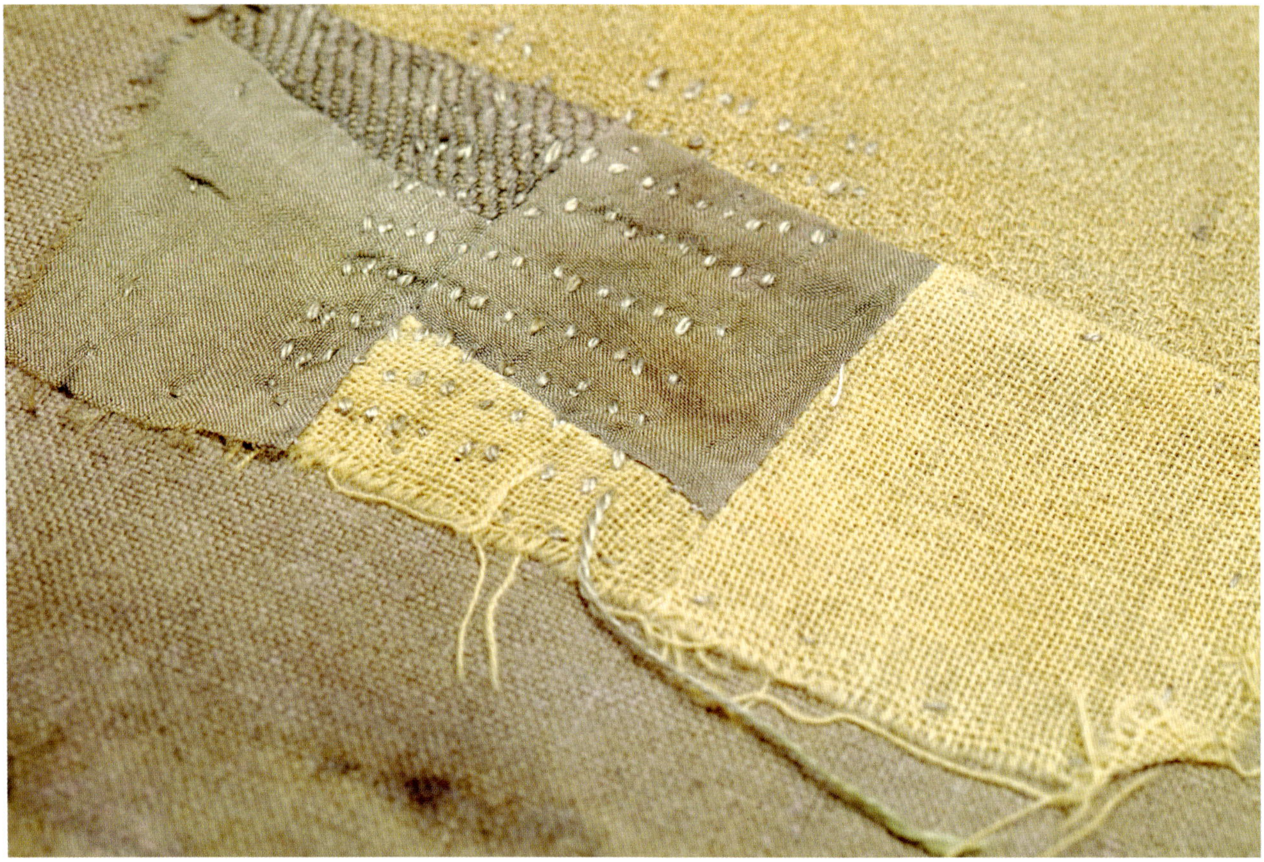

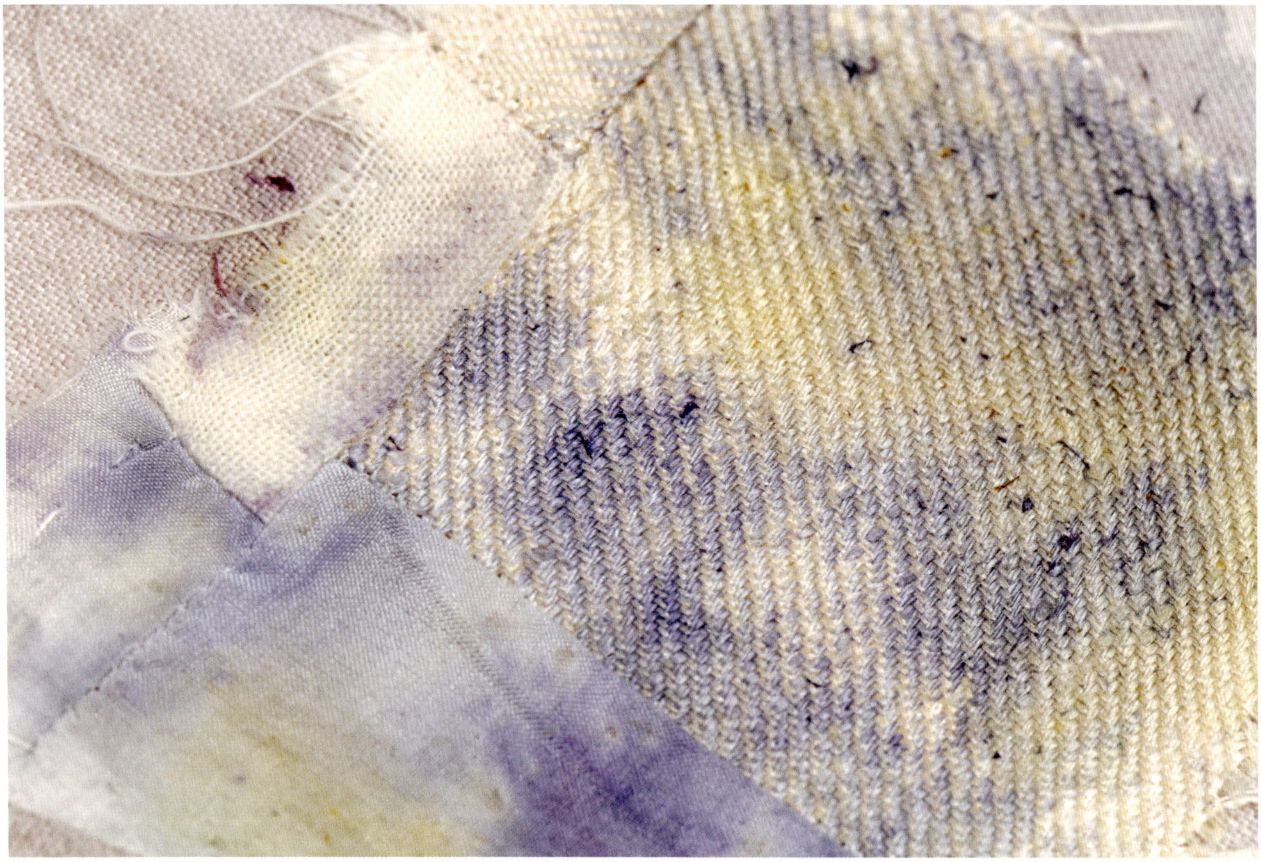

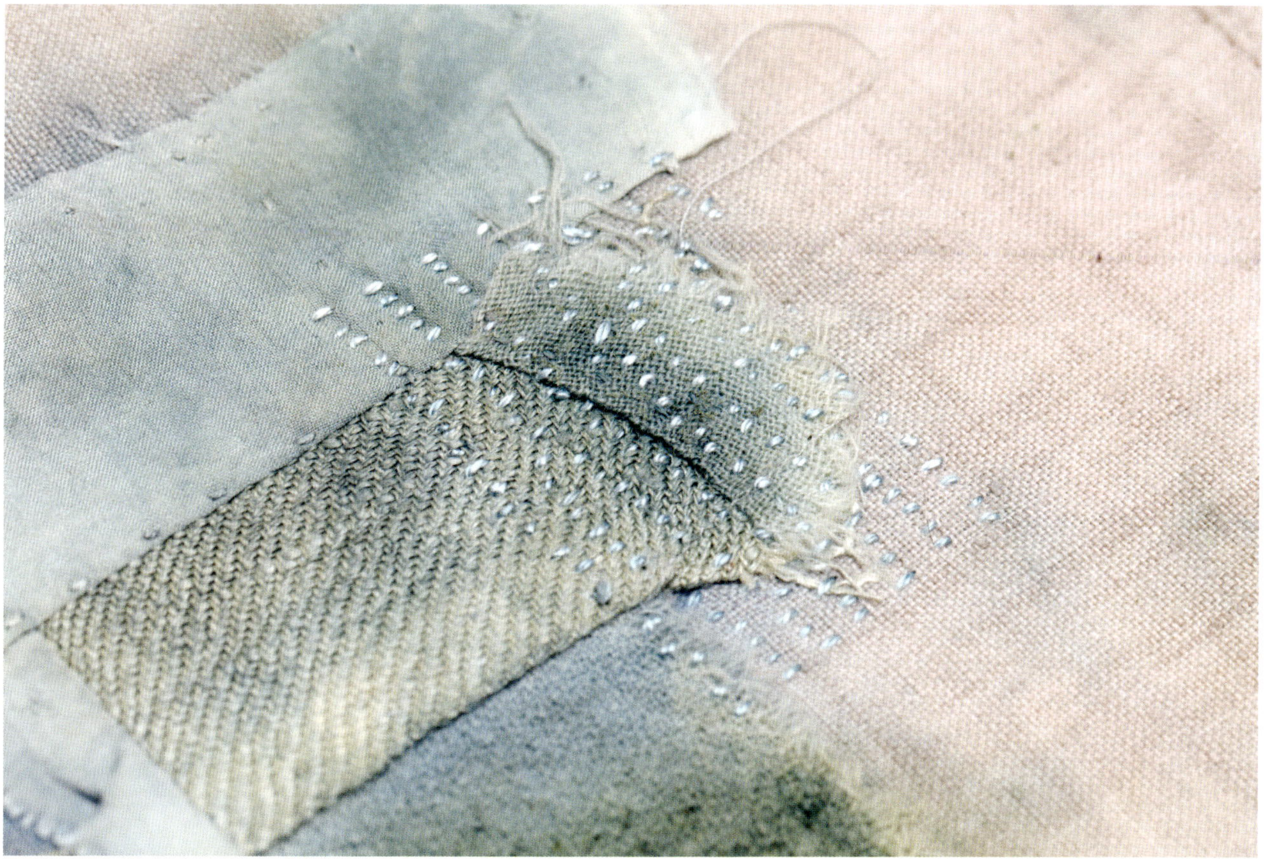

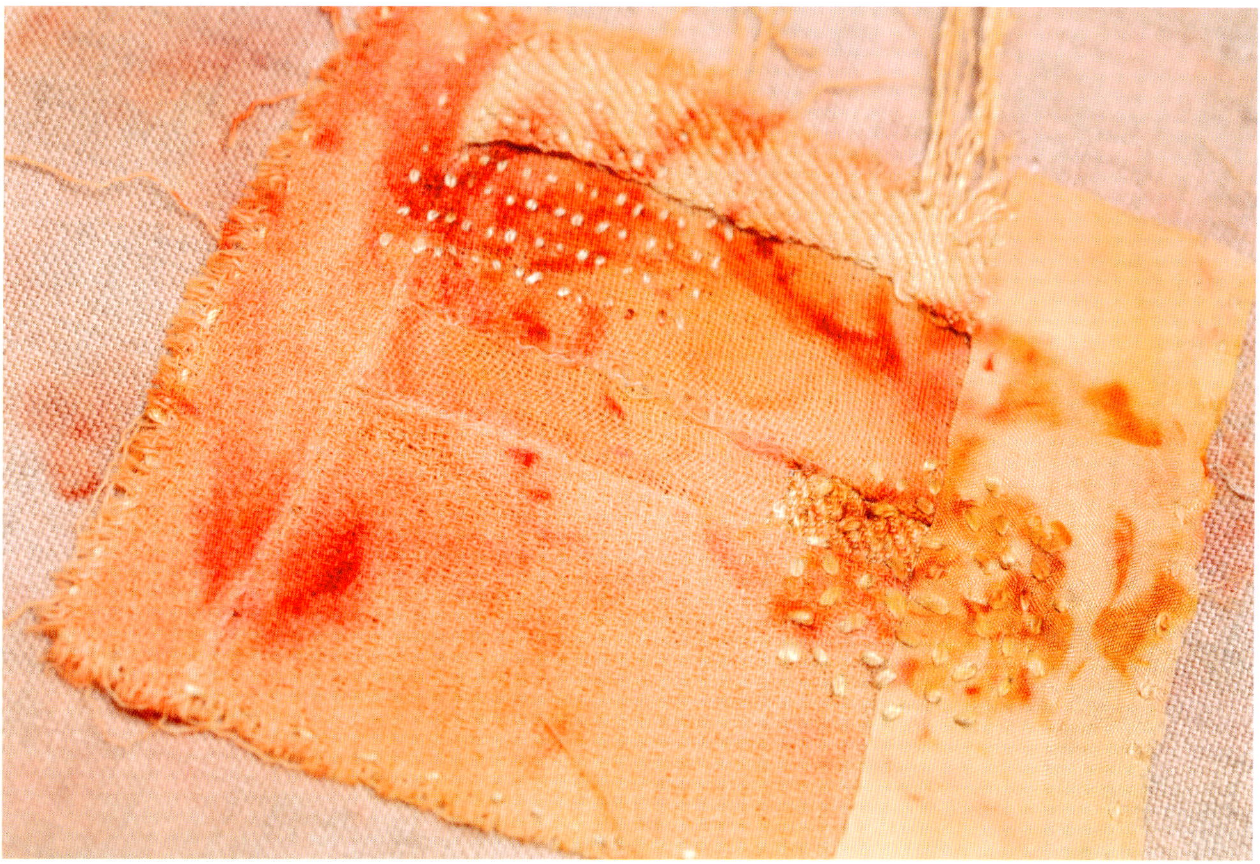

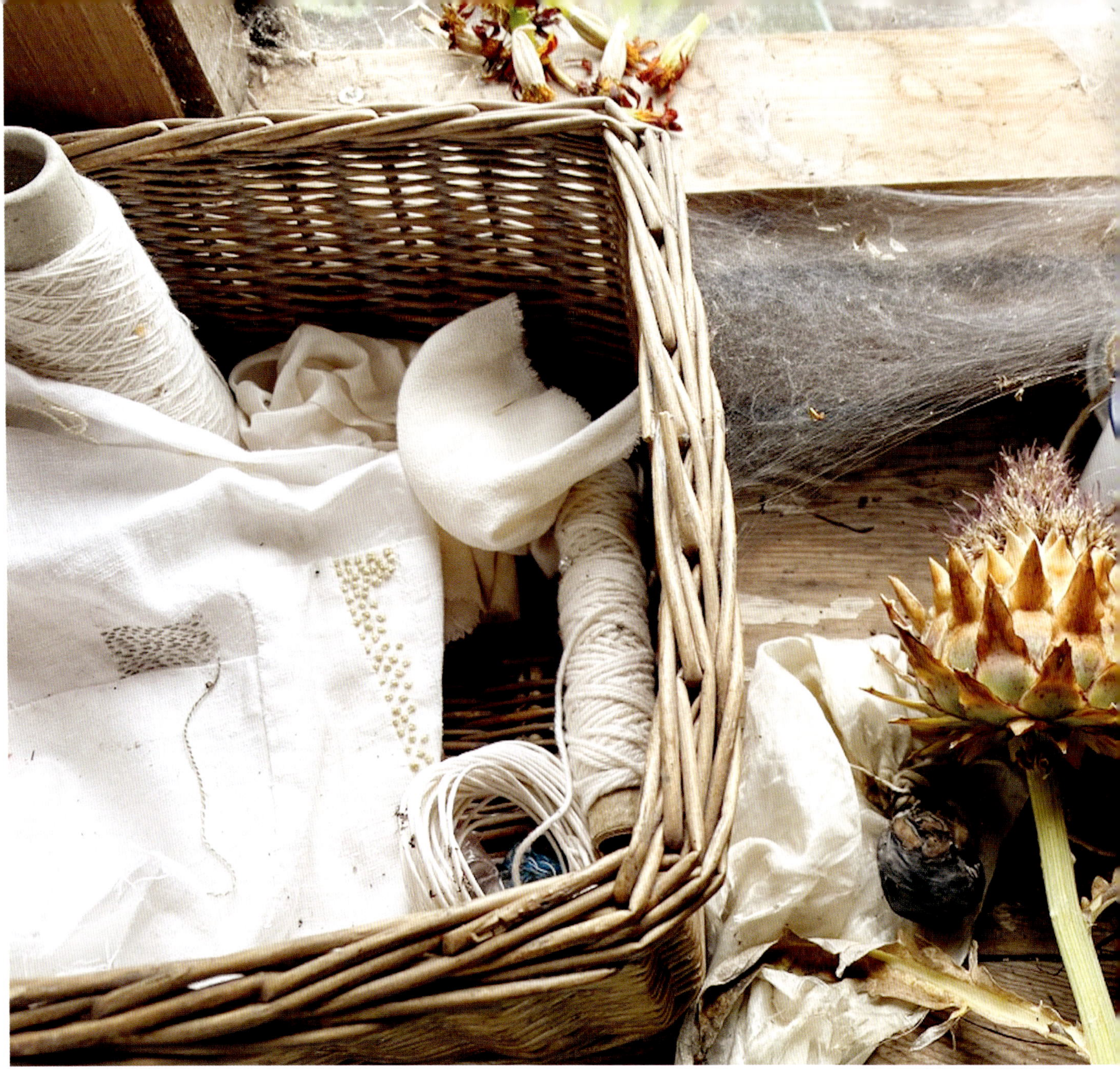

Geographies of making

Connections to place can be found in many ways. In my practice this has often been found through growing projects based in community gardens and allotment sites. These projects grow plants with multiple purposes, from culinary outcomes and herb beds with health and wellbeing benefits, to fibre and colour gardens.

Over the years as an artist based in areas of former industrial textile production in northern England, I have set up many projects growing colour. Working in allotments and shared

ABOVE
Author's allotment shed in Shipley, West Yorkshire including on site stitching materials.

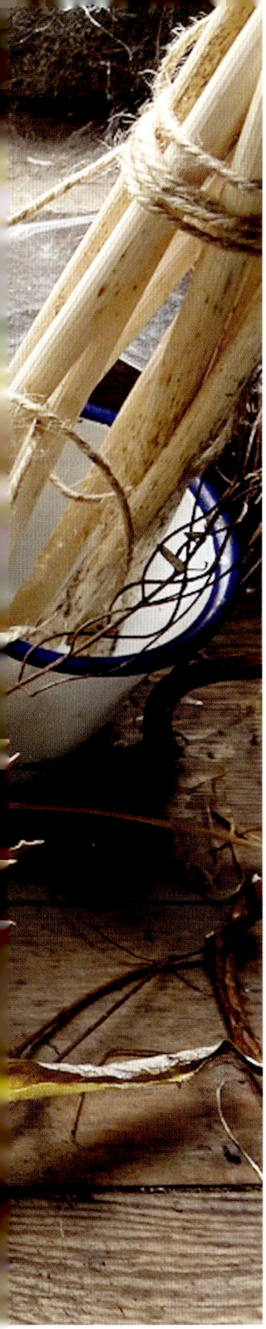

gardens, groups grow traditional dye plants – indigo, woad and weld – and less traditional sources of colour, such as onions for their skins and French marigolds. Starting with a handful of seeds and seeing the plants through to fibre, yarn and fabric offered a whole process.

The vagaries of the Pennine weather mean that not all crops survive, and sessions are often spent sheltering from the rain or drinking tea in a garden shed. However, the process-based seasonal work of these projects was popular, in autumn and winter workshops processing the colour harvest, and led to community quilting, knitting and weaving projects and an opportunity to discuss the connections between craft, care and health.

Connecting colour and place

In my first creative-growing project, I had an experience with indigo dyeing and its transformative work. When the dyed fibre or fabric is brought out of an indigo vat and exposed to the air, the oxidising process changes the colour from vivid green to the characteristic indigo blue. It literally changes as you watch. Participants in a hospital courtyard garden project were excited and inspired, some making connections between mental health and visible and invisible change.

Years later, in a market-hall project in Brussels for newcomers to Belgium, a crushed piece of discarded pomegranate skin created colour at a pop-up workshop where we improvised with the materials we found around us. The capacity of textile, its multiple registers and processes, to connect and transform over time led in part to my stepping into research life. Something as ordinary as a pair of jeans, indigo the connection again, can offer multiple routes into conversation, about fashion, global trade, colonial powers and their extractive work, craft, skill, industry and everyday wear and care.

Madder stories

The heritage and use of one dye plant, madder (*Rubia tinctorum*) has featured significantly in my work over many years through various projects, particularly in east Lancashire. This project strongly connected both time and place. The temporalities of plants are described by Lawrence as 'peculiar and multiple' (2022, p.631). Here they came together in the growing process, creative work with project participants and the economic history of a plant that was formerly grown in huge volumes and imported from Europe for the UK textile industry.

The agency of the madder plant was explored during 'Local Colour', an artist residency in Church, near Accrington, connected

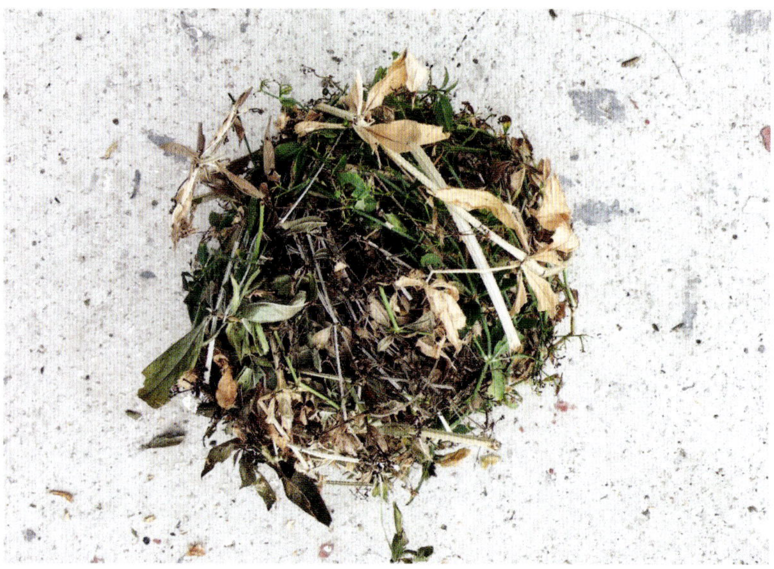

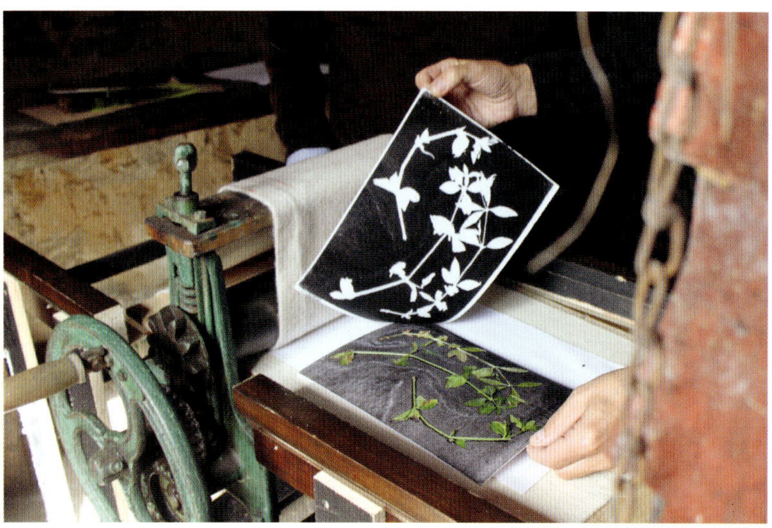

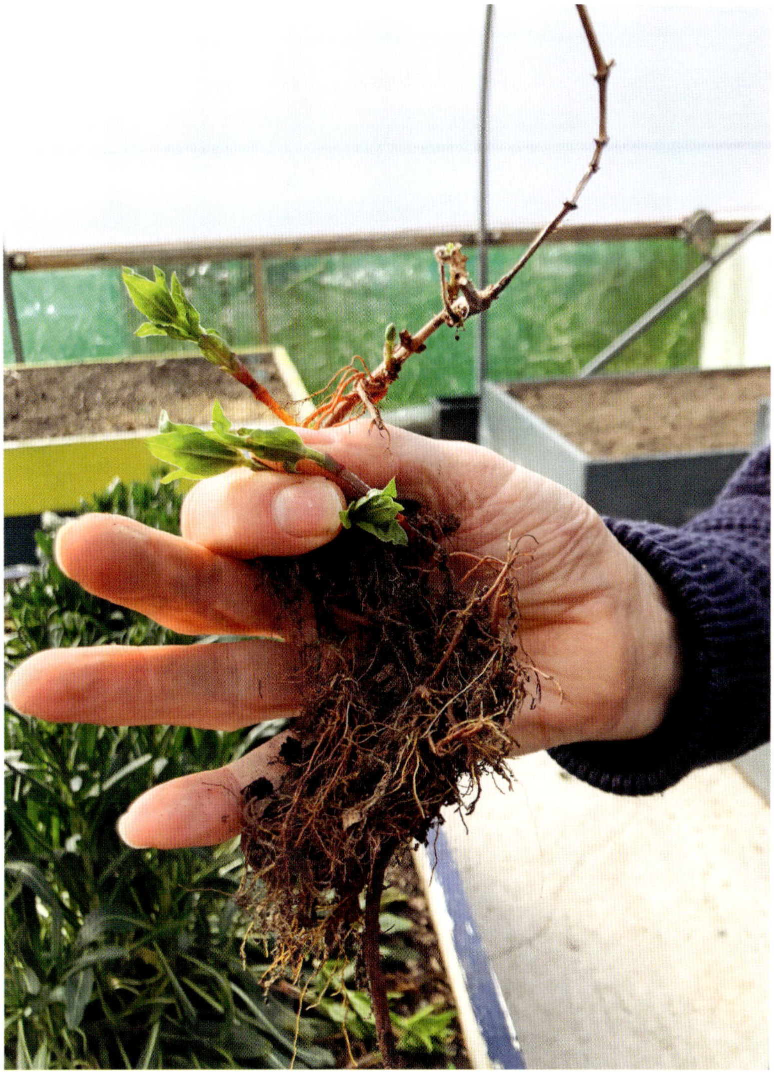

OPPOSITE ABOVE
Dried madder plant tops, Elmfield Hall, 2018.

OPPOSITE BELOW
Laundry mangle converted into a printing press, contact print of madder plant in progress, Elmfield Hall, 2019.

RIGHT
Growing madder in the polytunnel at Elmfield Hall, 2020.

to a nineteenth-century industrialist called Frederick Albert Gatty (1819–1888). His small, now semi-derelict, personal dye laboratory was the focus of the project. I used the tangible, fragile heritage of this building, the development of a textile garden and local walks as part of a socially engaged arts programme with participants who attended the community organisation.

The area had an industrial heritage connected to madder and its use as a dyestuff in the calico printing and dyeing industry from the late-eighteenth century onwards. The immersive process of growing madder over four seasons and making and connecting with its harvest formed part of the residency's slow work. The heritage work of the madder project offered a story of industry and life in a community over two centuries, and the growing offered other ways to connect to local experiences today. With the community group I walked routes that included the remaining traces of industrial buildings, and streets named for business partners and countries of export. We talked about making and connecting and how this made us feel.

The common madder plant (*Rubia tinctorum*) is a hardy herbaceous perennial indigenous to Western Asia and has been used as a dyestuff for millennia: samples have been found on cloth in Egyptian tombs; it was referenced by Pliny; cultivated in Europe from the seventh century.

The maturation of the plant so it becomes suitable for dyeing takes up to three years from sowing the seed. Depending on the material and mordant (or fixative) used and the strength of dye, the shades produced from madder range from pink, red and purple to black. The textile dye is produced from the roots of the plant. As part of a vegetal economy the madder plant connects us to Turkey red, a red dye that was bright and reliably colourfast – the recipe was introduced to France from Greece in the mid-eighteenth century and increased demand for the raw material.

The process of dyeing was complicated, involving multiple-steps and additives to the dye bath that included animal blood, dung and bile, rancid olive oil and hydrochloric acid. The washable printed fabric was popular and accessible to the wider population, and so Turkey red processing became the most profitable of the cotton-finishing sectors in the nineteenth-century textile industry in the UK.

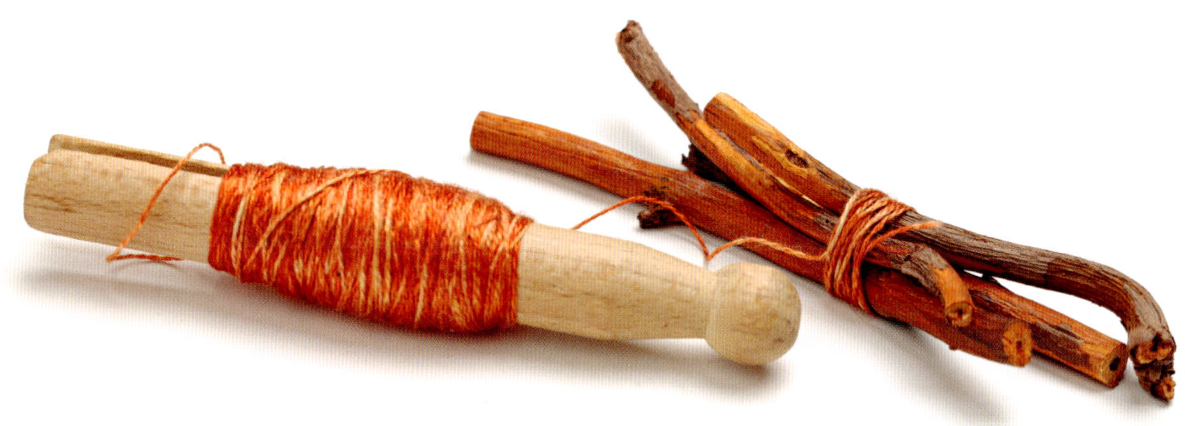

OPPOSITE ABD BELOW
Madder outputs: dyed thread, dried roots, nineteenth-century Turkey red dyed and printed cotton.

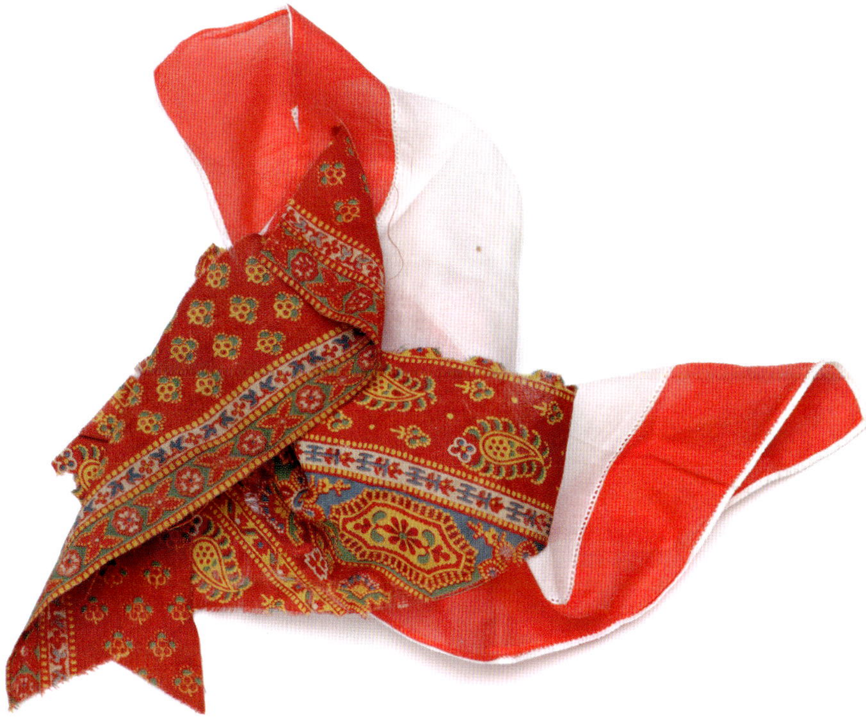

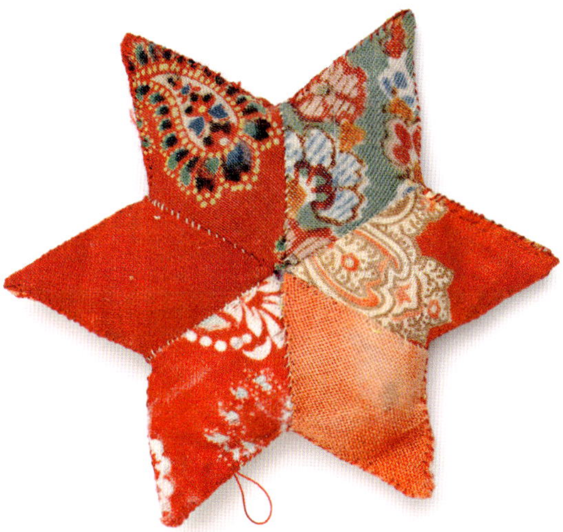

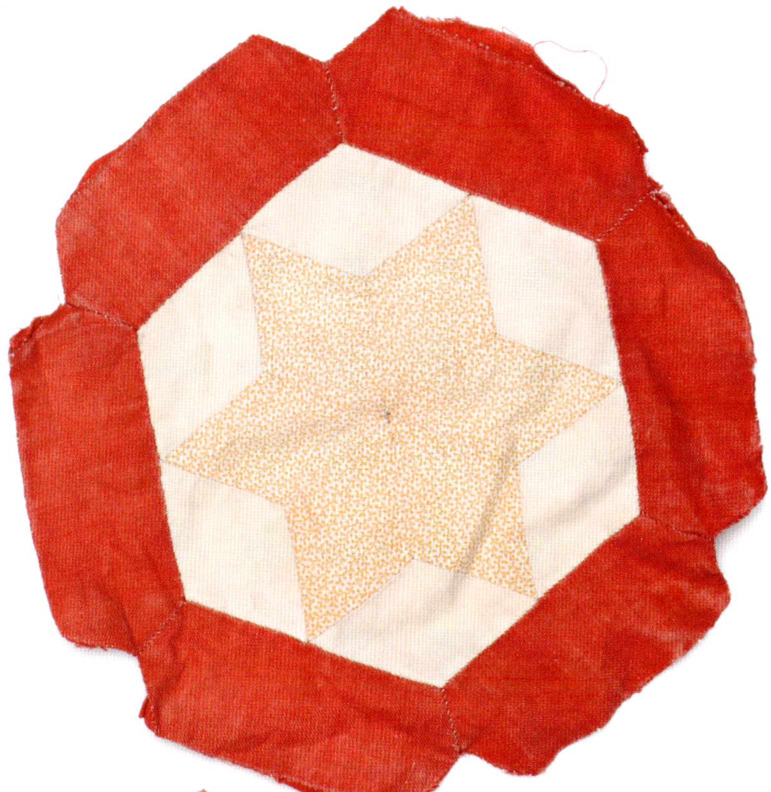

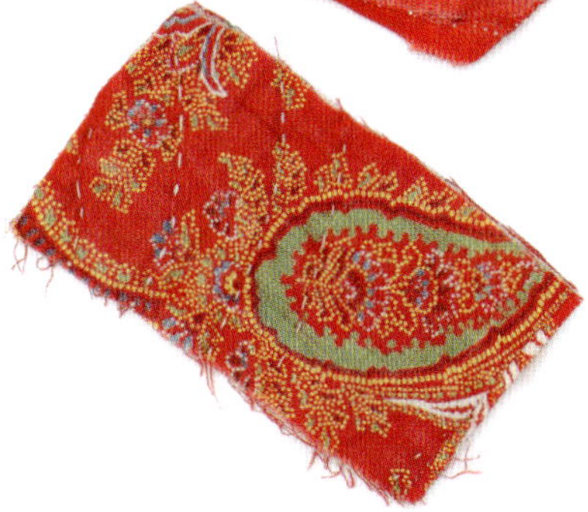

Turkey-red colour samples

BELOW AND OPPOSITE
Pieced and stitched samples using Turkey red cotton fragments, indigo printed conversation prints and naturally dyed wool and thread on a linen background, 2024.

These samples were created with scraps of Turkey-red cotton retrieved from the interior of a much-worn nineteenth-century patchwork quilt. Very fragile and threadbare in places, they were assembled with scraps of contemporaneous indigo-printed cotton and naturally dyed fabrics produced with plants I grew. The additional stitching was closely done on a backing piece of wool blanket. This stabilises the fragile fabric, with madder-dyed thread the prominent surface colour.

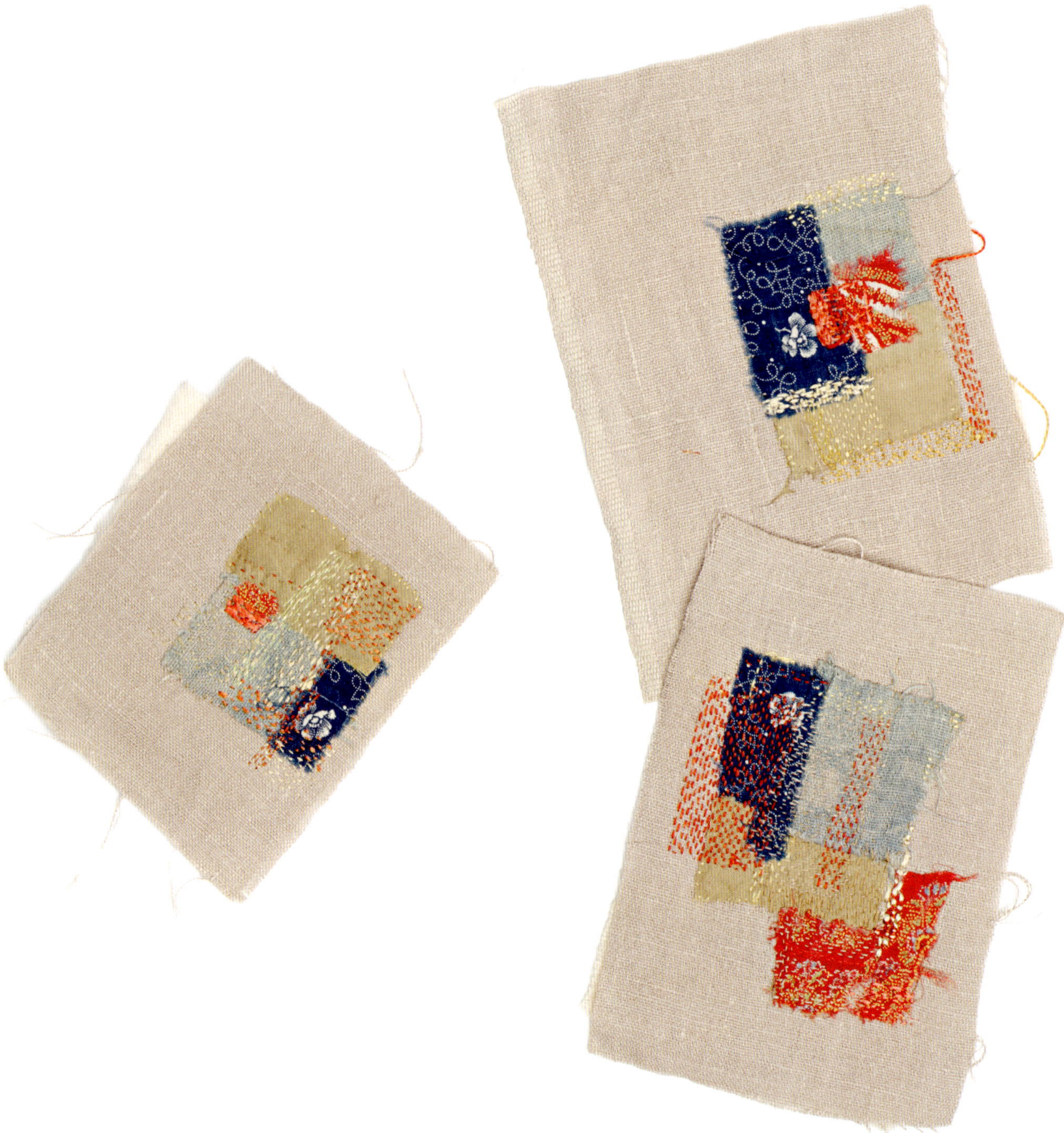

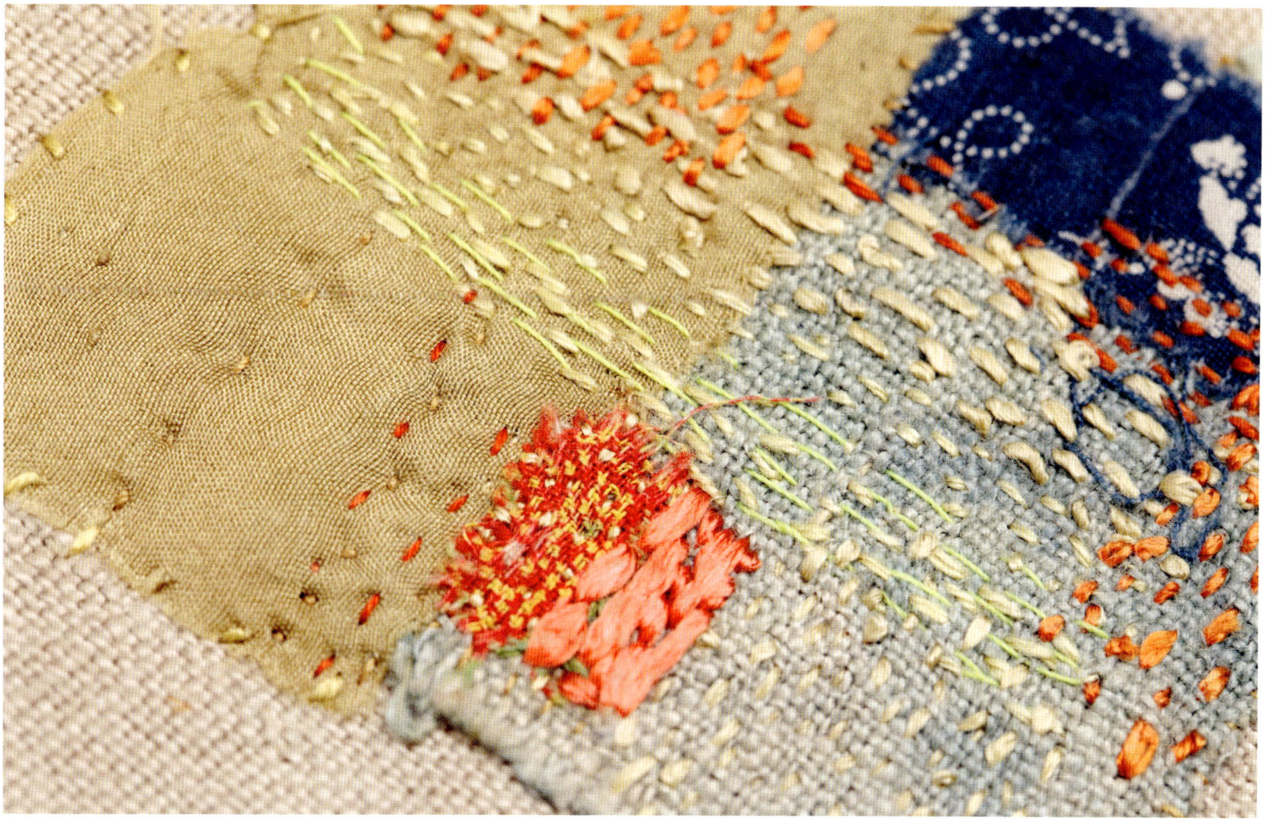

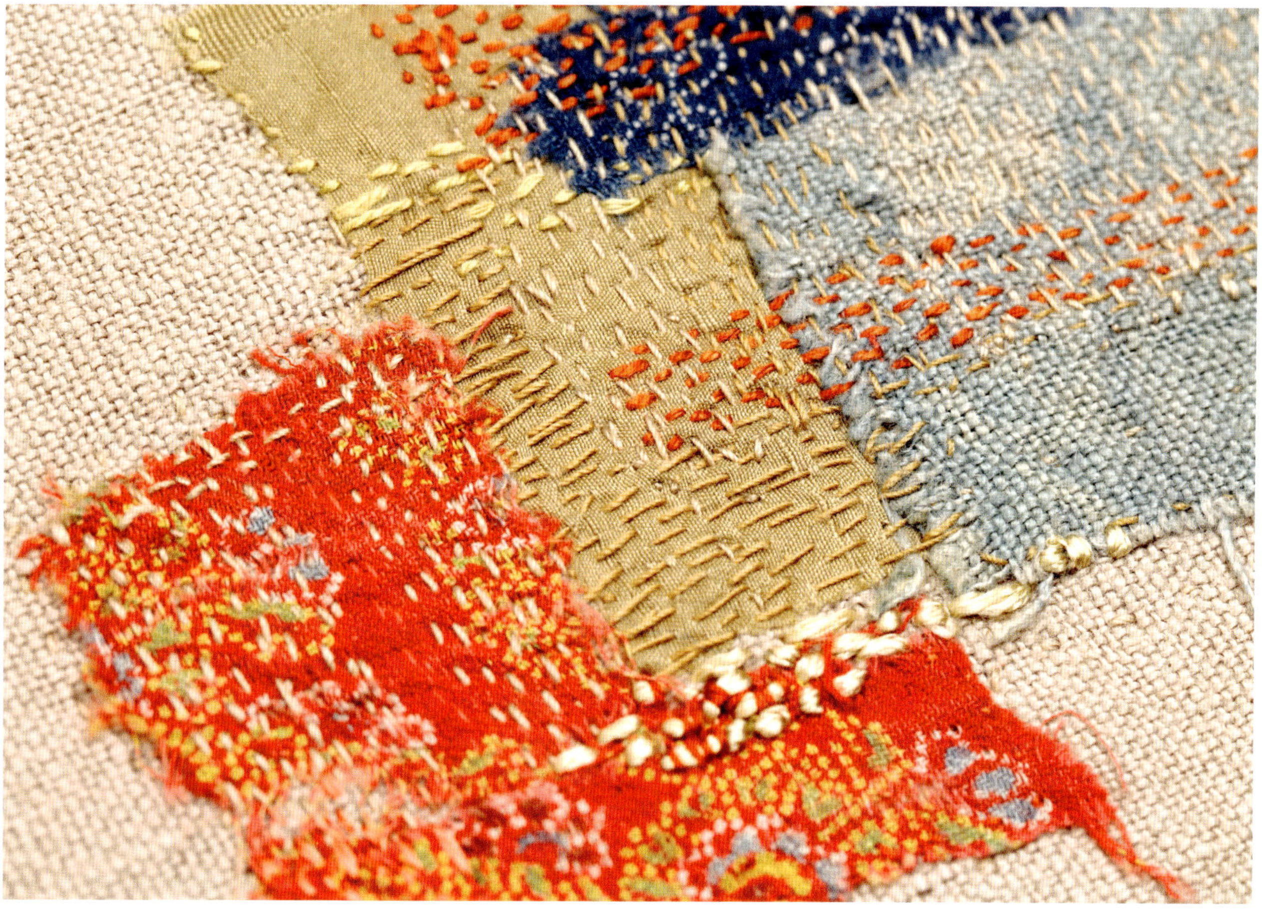

Growing colour

The 'Local Colour' project grew a madder crop in a polytunnel in a large, raised garden bed with red-painted sides. An improvised workshop space was made among the growing beds so we could harvest the freshly dug roots of the plant, wash them and work with them in the same space. In the workshops we transformed locally woven cotton with a soft red colour that deepened as it stayed in the dye pot.

From early meetings and community conversations, a project bringing growing and making together to explore historical connections using a whole process – from seed to fabric – emerged. The roots of the madder plant, tangled, slow growing, embedded in the place, were the starting point. Connections to madder began to be made and shared. We discovered references to madder on maps of the area: Madder Mill Wood, The Old Madder House and a contemporary industrial estate named after Turkey red. A 1910 newspaper advertisement for a local roller rink carnival had a prize for 'the largest calico hat trimmed with Turkey red'.

The seasonality of the work of growing offered different ways of engaging with the madder. We saw shifts and changes in the colours produced in the dye bath, the condition of the plants ever changing. These transformations include the bleached-out straw-like tops left in the bed over winter after the plants die back and multiple sticky green shoots emerging in spring and rapidly covering the surface. In the spaces between plants, you could brush the soil to the side and the bright red roots were visible, knotty and tangled.

Our garden, to an outsider, offered little enchantment at first glance. The potential transformations were lying just beneath the surface, requiring a set of skills to coax them out. The temporalities of the project – working over a number of growing seasons – meant that for the participants, the colour potential of the madder plants built anticipation and evoked memories of the previous years' work.

Among this, the ordinary work of a community garden wandered in and surprised us. Tomato seedlings sprang up in the madder bed, seeds blown in from the food-bank growing project that worked alongside our project. Potted up, they were taken home to grow in back gardens and on kitchen windowsills.

RIGHT
Mr Gatty's Experiment Shed (2019), installation view of madder root suspension in the personal laboratory of Frederick Albert Gatty (1819-1888).

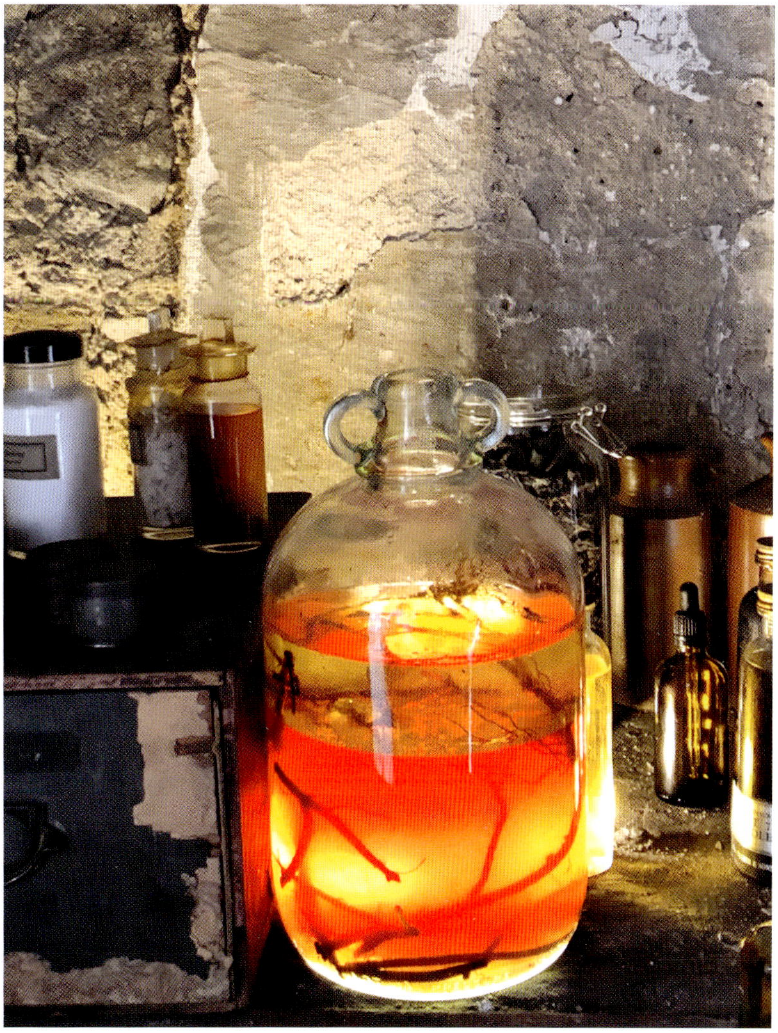

Madder and its multiple outputs

The madder plants informed multiple creative outputs. After our early experimental printing and dyeing workshops, it also appeared as a motif: the prickly plant tops used for contact prints with a printing press (converted from a locally made 1920s Ewbank mangle). Digital images of madder plants and maps from archives were projected onto the wall of Gatty's small laboratory as part of *Mr Gatty's Experiment Shed*, an installation that reimagined the building as a workshop 150 years since it was last in use. These images flickered over large specimen jars filled with vegetable oil bought at a supermarket across the road built on the site of the former dyeworks

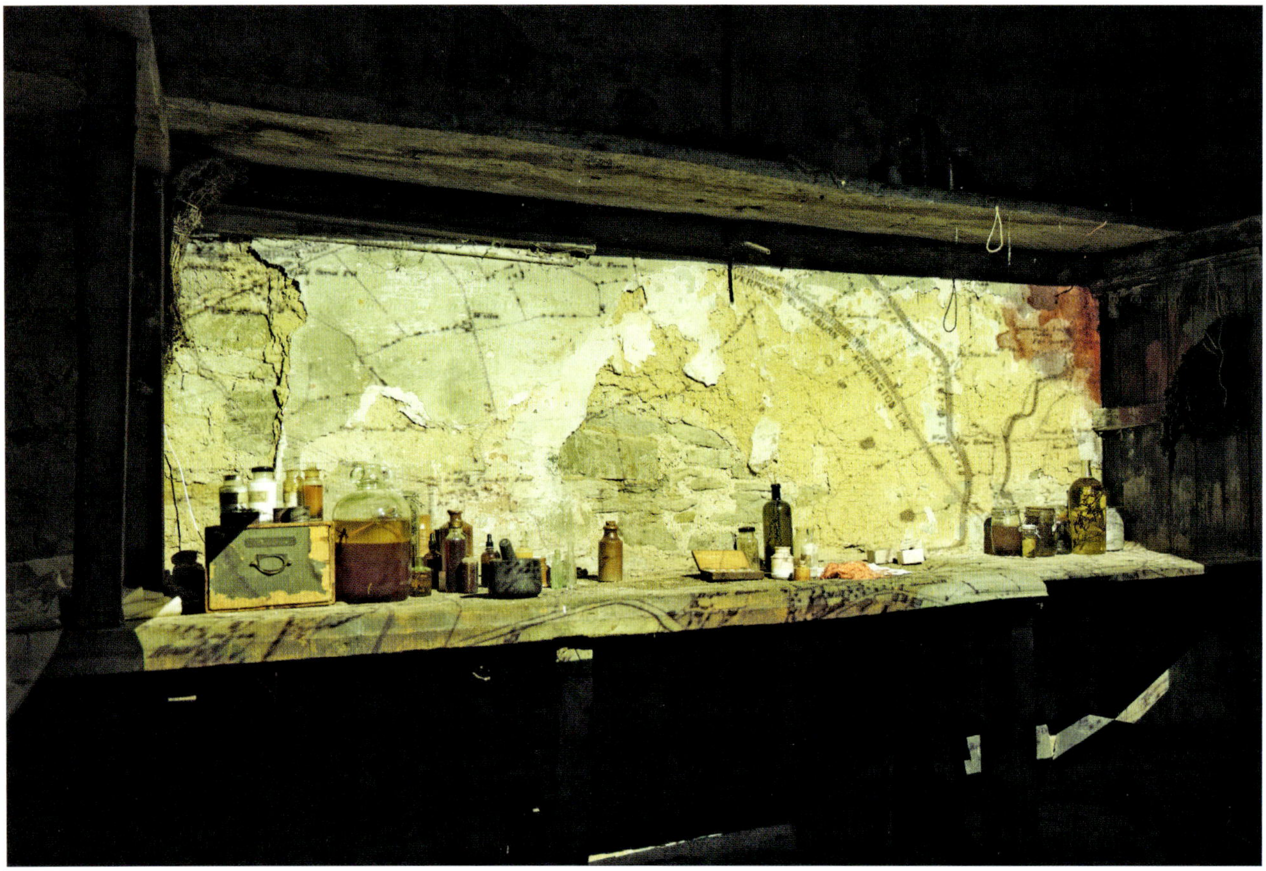

reservoir. Madder root dug from the garden was suspended in the liquid and lit from below. The outcomes were both fast and slow; they referenced the heritage of the place using what was available in the present, informed by the conversations in the project sessions and around the dye beds as we worked.

In conversations during walks and at the weekly meetings, participants, some of whom had worked in the local textile industry decades earlier, said that 'just walking slowly through these areas where there were factories, you're looking for leftover signs that you can relate to how it was a hundred years ago.' They went on to describe new skills learned during sessions and how they connected them to the differences they found living in a post-industrial town today.

The multiple material outcomes described above came from co-produced work with participants and are evidence of the slow time that informed the project, durational work emerging from the conversations while making we had during our weekly sessions. As artist-researcher I looked for ways to navigate collections of community stories and reminiscences about

ABOVE
Mr Gatty's Experiment Shed (2019), installation view of projected 1848 map on the wall of Gatty's laboratory.
OPPOSITE
Mr Gatty's Experiment Shed (2019), Madder root reproduced as a laser cut on MDF for printing.

working life. I mapped the local landscape, the industrial from memory, and the post-industrial today. I sought to sift, collate and offer spaces for the actions that involved the madder plant.

In my field notes two years into the residency I found the following, 'Gardens as gifts: what do we give? Social space, materials source, skill exchange, learning opportunity. Creating a space where any conversation can take place'. Through making practices that developed around the madder bed and the conversations alongside, the plants became a material motif, that in turn offered ways in – to more thinking, making and research and new trajectories for the project.

One plant and the transformations it offered brought local geographies to life. As the madder plants grew and took up space in a community setting, they offered multiple ways of reconnecting stories from the local industrial heritage with the very different work of a community setting in the twenty-first century, and the loss experienced in the period of deindustrialisation.

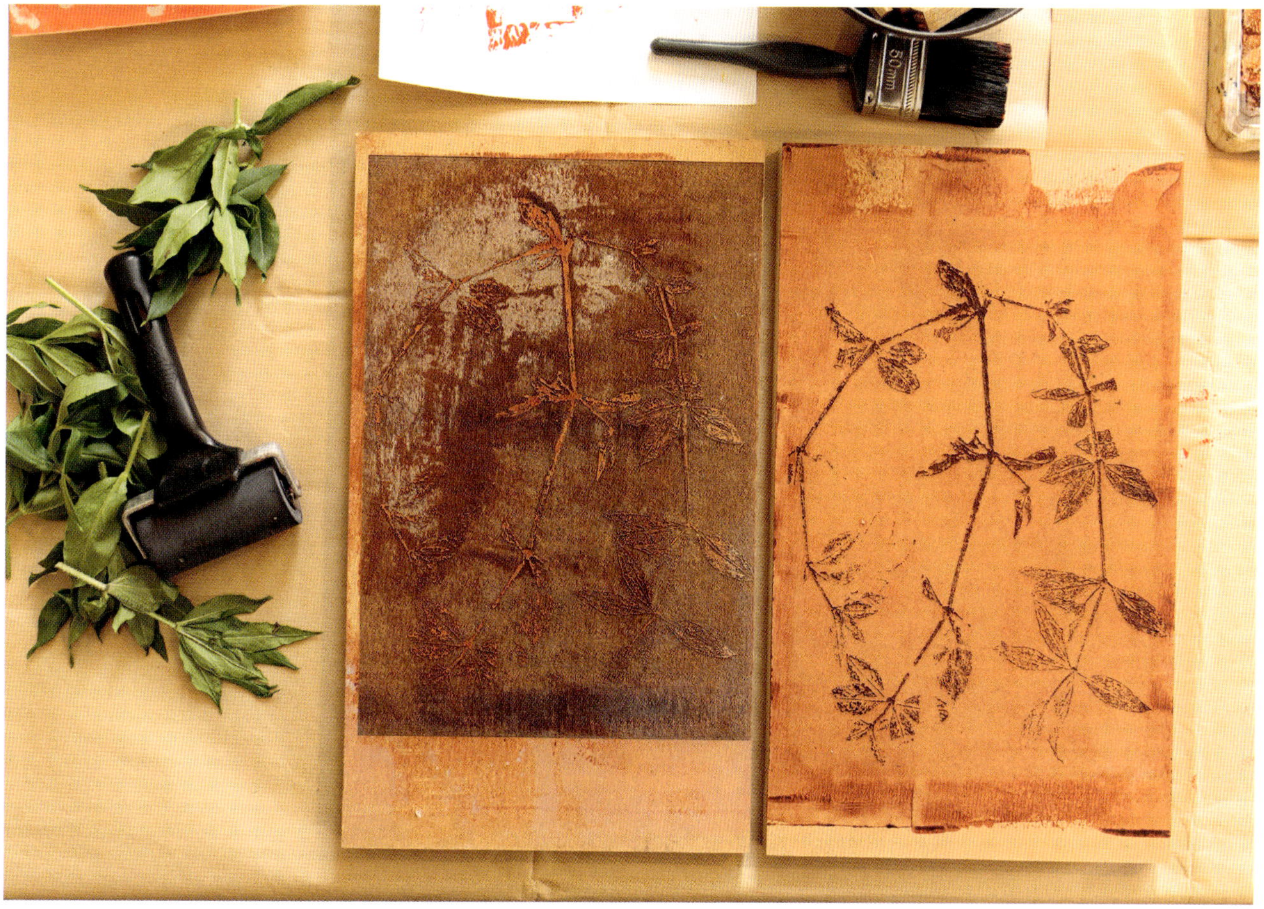

Make your own colour story

The 'Local Colour' residency spent time investigating the heritage of colour production in east Lancashire. Through a red dye, links and connections were made in multiple ways. This activity offers a way into colour through a simple observation and recording exercise. Observations such as this can lead you to focus on one colour and develop work around it.

For this activity you will need a box of coloured pastels and a small notebook.

1. **Pick a location** – Choose somewhere to observe from: a garden or allotment, the view from a window, a local park or other green space.

2. **Look for colour** – Spend a few minutes observing the colours you see. Think about colour in the built environment, street signage, passing cars, the clothing of passers-by as well as from the natural environment.

3. **Collect the colour** – Record the colours you see through making a mark with the corresponding-coloured pastel.

4. **Reflect** – After doing this exercise, reflect on the colours you collected. Is there a story that emerges through them? Did you find a colour you wanted to learn more about? How might you achieve this?

To extend this idea you could use coloured thread and fabric, taking stitched lines for a walk corresponding to the colours you see.

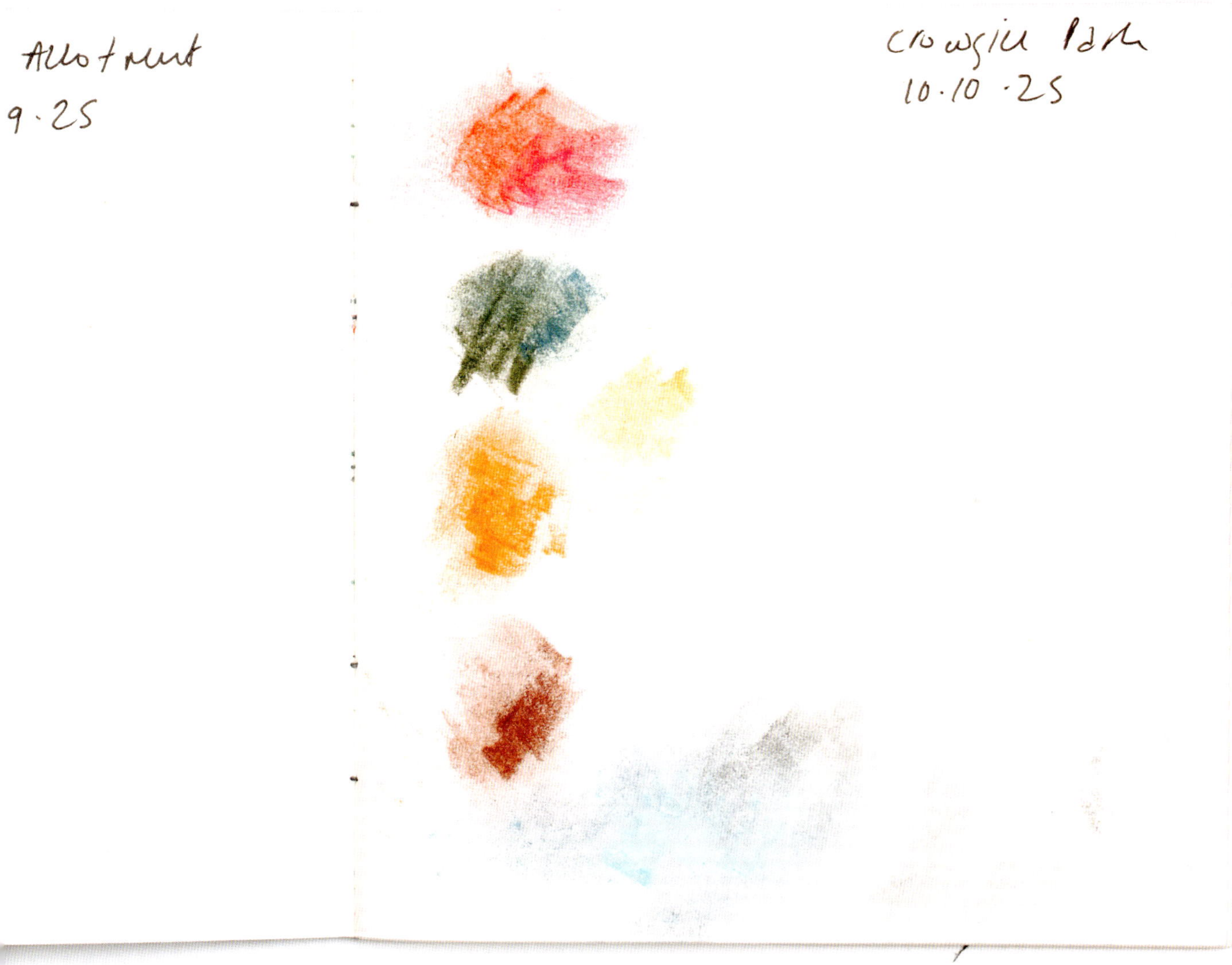

ABOVE
Capturing colour with chalk pastels at Red Beck allotments and Crowgill Park, Shipley (2025).

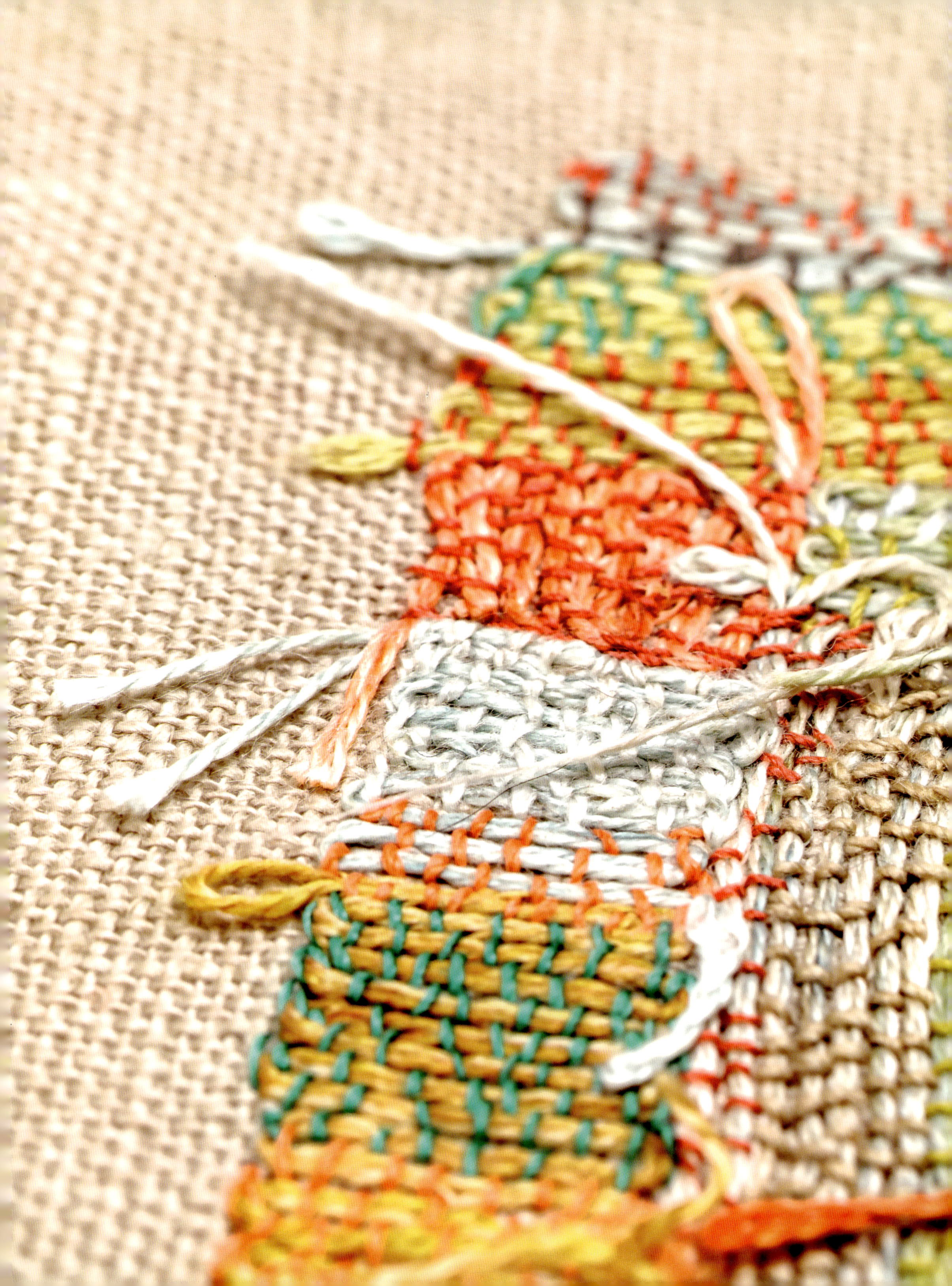

Reflection

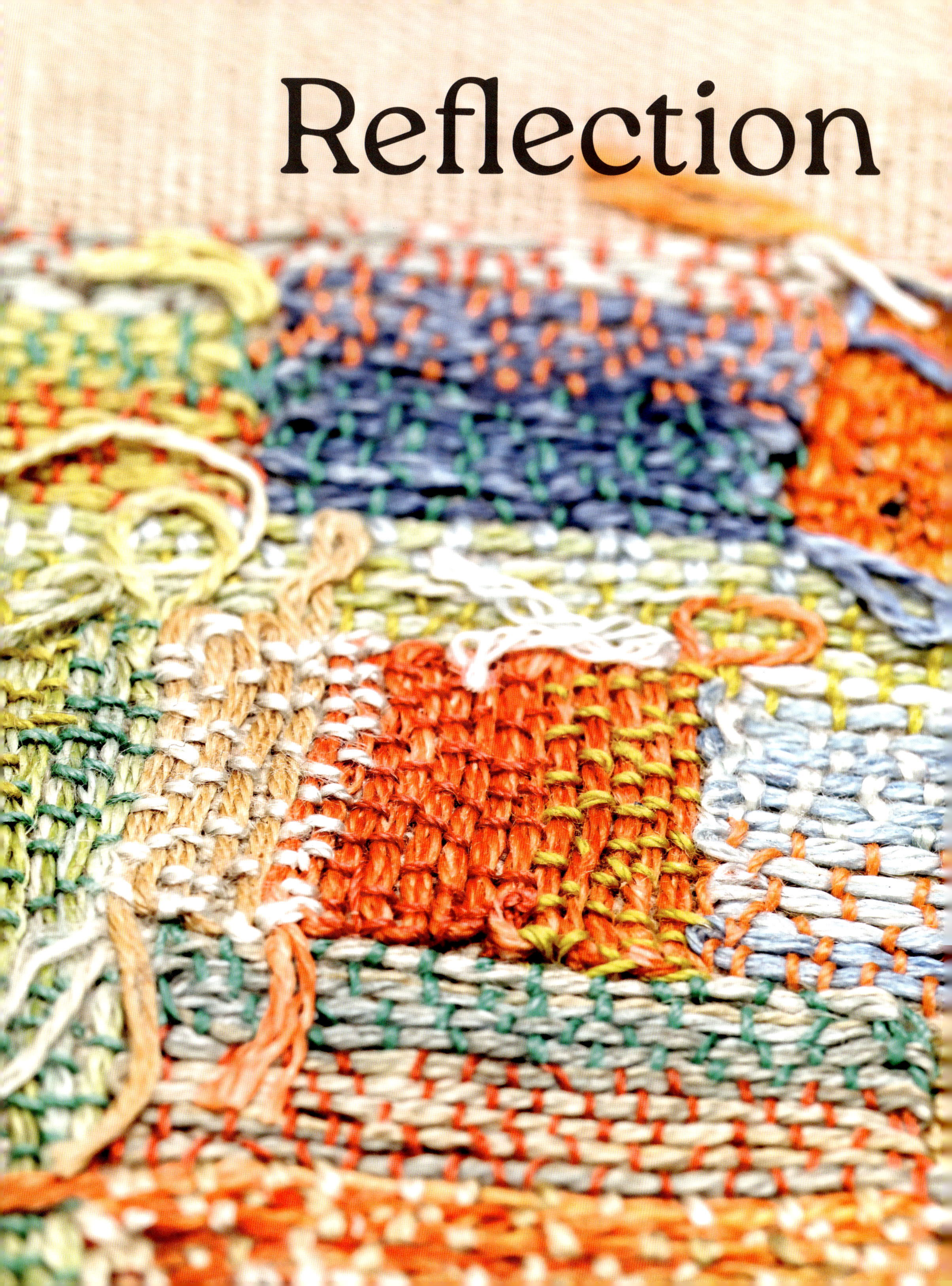

Reflecting on time and place offers spaces for individuals and groups to think about their lived experience; use of textile as a medium is a deeply expressive way of communicating personal stories. Stitches made to mark time can be reflective of joyful or difficult periods of our lives.

In both my work with communities and in my personal practice, reflections on embodied experience have been a significant part of projects, particularly for those living with change or displacement, with illness, and the experiences of care that accompany these challenges. In *Stitching the Self: Identity and the Needle Arts,* Amos and Binkley describe textiles 'that clothe the body and the home, and which, like the body, are ephemeral, wearing and fading out of existence ... have strong associations with individual and collective identity.'

Handkerchief

Handkerchief is a piece that began out of a necessity to make something, back in 2010, while sitting watching my youngest child poorly in hospital. The large white handkerchief I had in my bag, some red thread and a needle in a pocket sewing kit and hexagons cut from flyers found in the foyer kept my hands busy while I waited. The piece contains areas constructed through stitching fabric hexagons together, but also some hexagons made using stitch in negative space.

After ten days we came home, thankfully recovered, and I continued the work. I included other scraps of white fabric but continued using red thread in the construction. Reflecting on that time, one where stress featured heavily in my life, on a piece of textile that appears calm and ordered, offers me a way to understand lived experience as a series of layers. These are overlaid but, at first glance, disconnected. At once still and calm, and alive with the stresses and activity of daily existence – but always, in truth, connected by place and time.

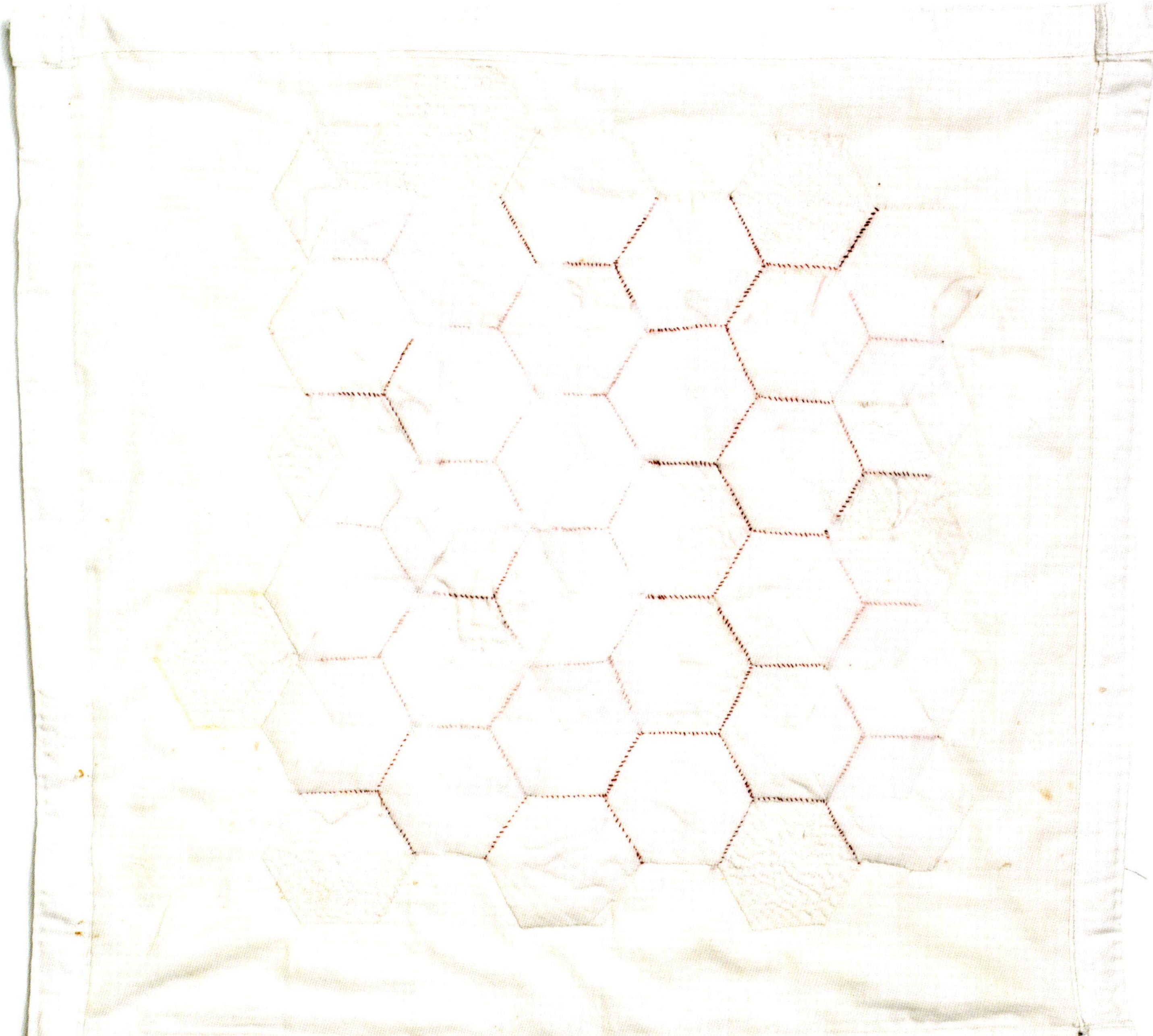

ABOVE
Handkerchief (2010), cotton handkerchief, cotton lawn, cotton organdie, red thread 40×40cm (15.7×15.7 in).

Rasi/Twine Together

Making string, twisting and twining, has played a big part in community work for me over the last few years. Stories come together in the recycled fabric strips used – the tensioning of the twine is an accessible way to share the physical work.

This twining together offered a project in Bradford, 'Rasi/Twine Together', ways of exploring, sharing skills and hearing stories of making over generations. Rasi translates in Urdu as 'to twine'; the women in the group are mainly from the South Asian diaspora. My twining method (shared in *Resilient Stitch*, 2021) involves twisting away from oneself with tension offered by another person, a door handle or chair. This proved to be one of many methods shown to me by women in the group. Far quicker versions of the technique emerged – all involved working alongside a partner, sometimes with long lengths of recycled rags extending across the room. The connections made between physical action, communication and connection were shared alongside a passage from *Braiding Sweetgrass* by Robin Wall Kimmerer: 'Will you hold the end of the bundle while I braid? Hands joined by grass, can we bend our heads together and make a braid to honour the earth? And then I'll hold it for you, while you braid, too.'

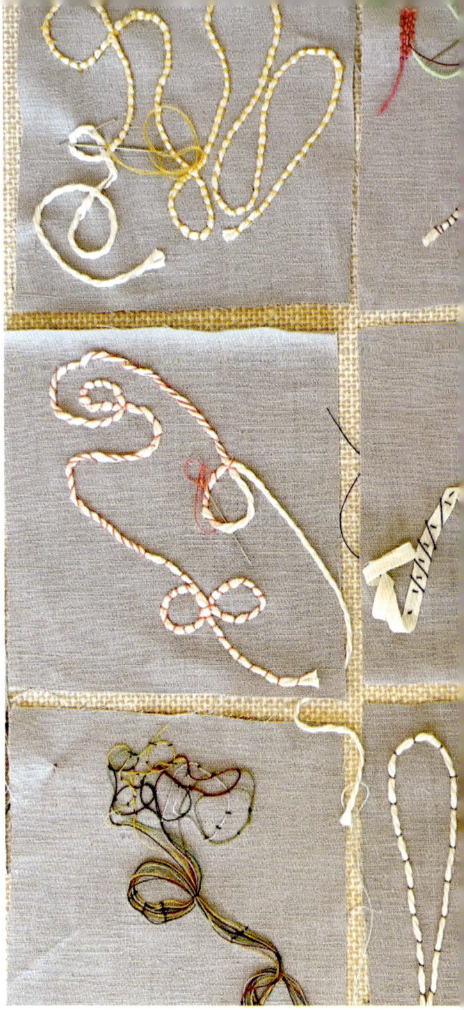

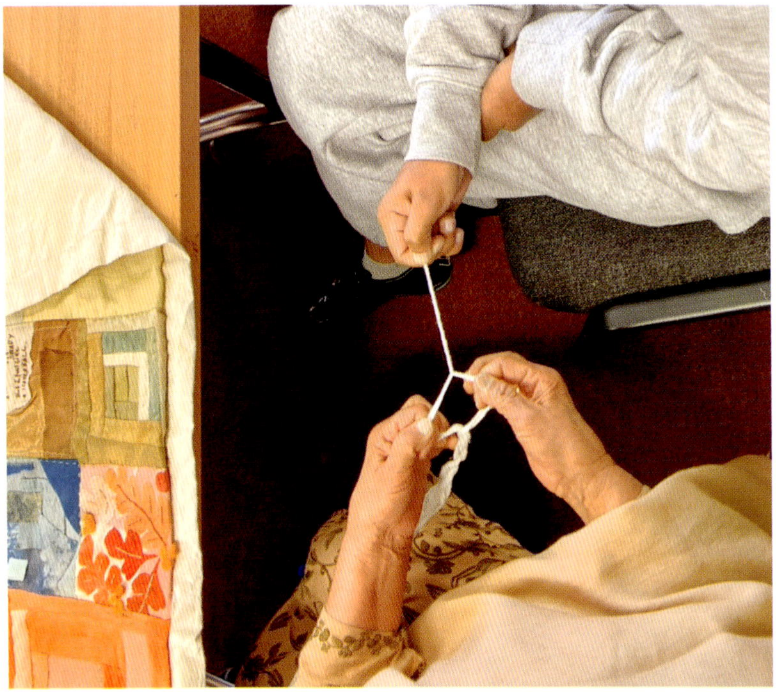

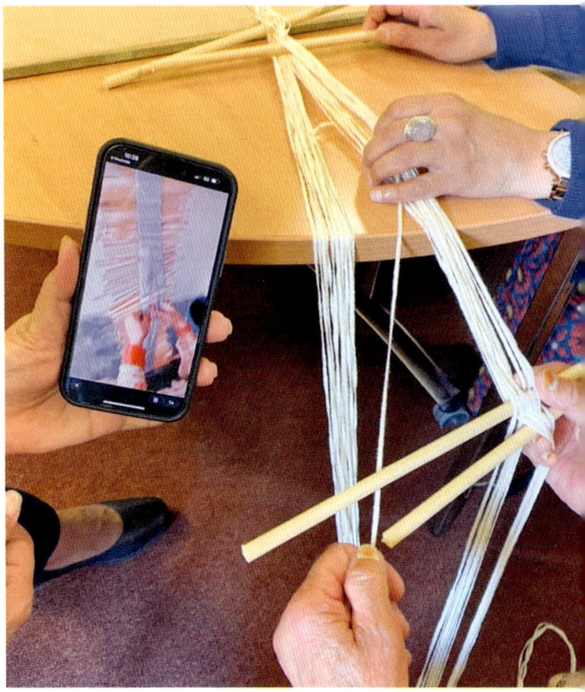

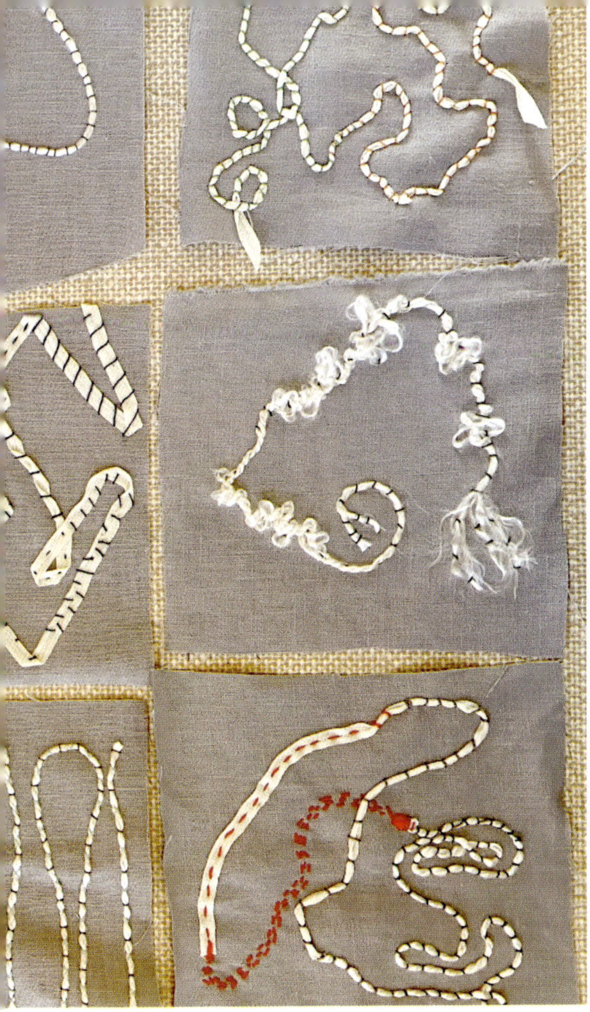

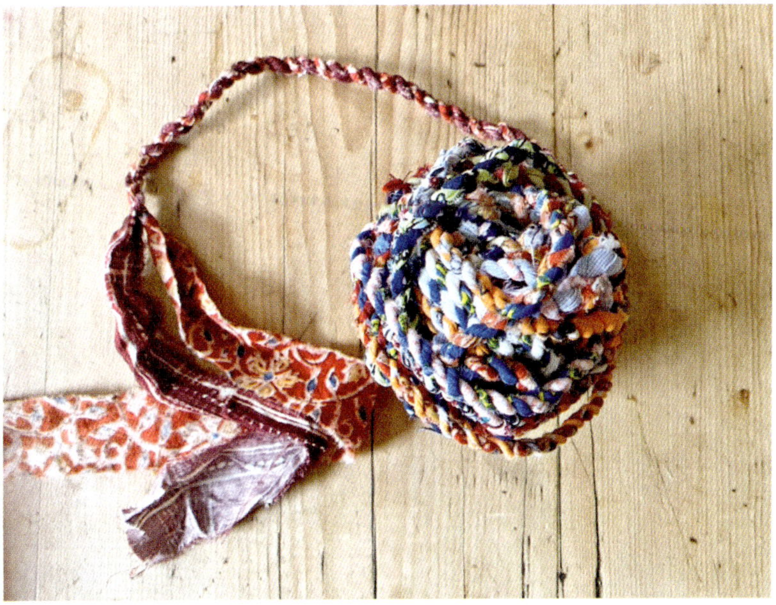

In our twining experiments we began with colourful scrap materials, moving on to white cotton lawn and silk to make finer strings, later dyed with plants from a small community garden we planted. The creation of new threads and strings led to Salma, one of our group, describing the *nara* drawstring ties for shalwar kameez that she learned to make as a child alongside her mother in Pakistan in the 1950s.

We used cotton tape for an experimental prototype, working to-and-fro in a corner of the community centre. Our references included reminiscences from other group members of making them or watching family members doing so. TikTok offered videos of the process, traditional technique and new technology working together perfectly. In the improvisatory way of many community projects, when we ran out of dowel rods to separate the warp threads we used a box of ballpoint pens. The simple process of creating string gave us new ways of connecting and tying our ideas together. In later sessions, couching stitch was used to make small, stitched assemblages or samplers with the twine we had created.

OPPOSITE
'Rasi/Twine Together'. Twining and weaving with help from TikTok videos. South Square Centre, Bradford, 2025.

ABOVE LEFT
Couching samples using handmade white silk twine.

ABOVE RIGHT
Twine made from recycled fabric scraps.

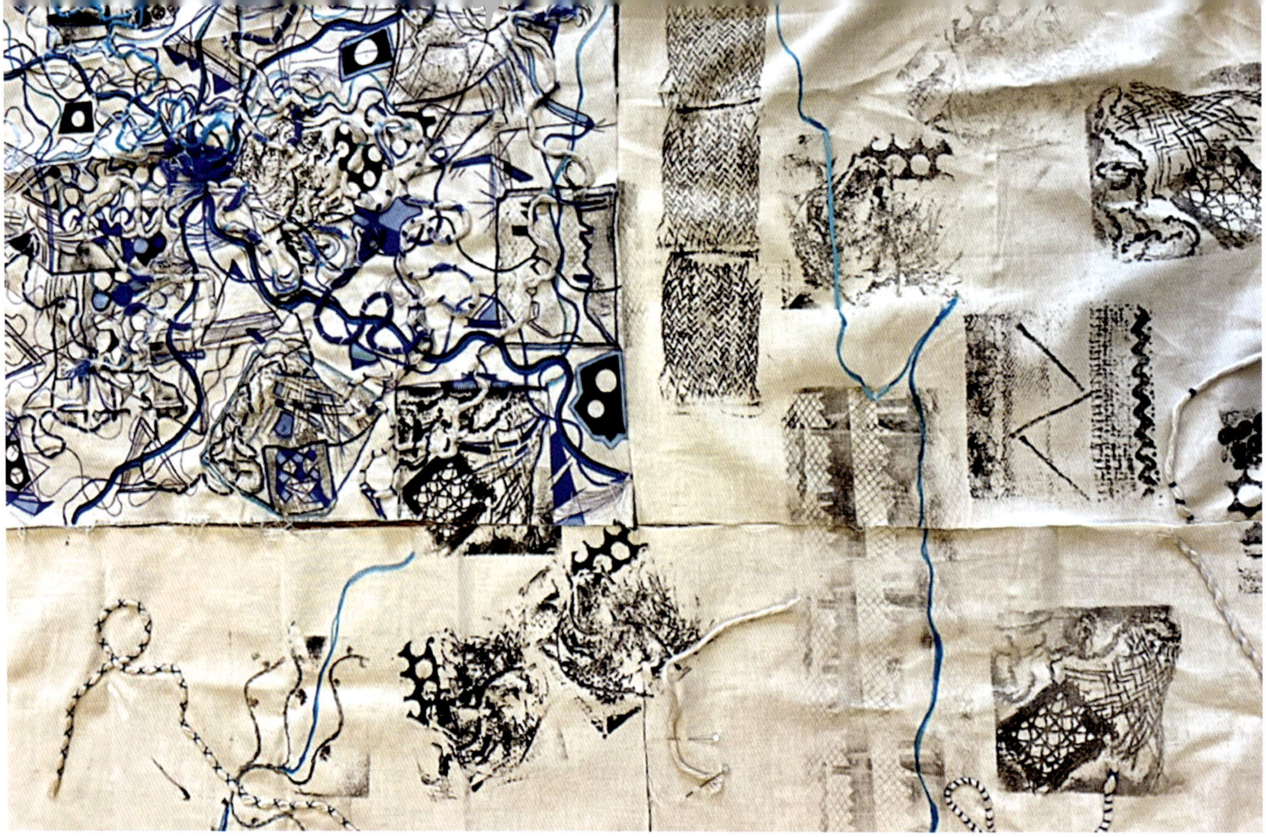

Couching

Mary Thomas describes couching in her 1934 book, *Embroidery Stitches*, as 'working a bold, unbroken line'. Couching stitch involves laying a surface thread on your chosen cloth, over a drawn line if you wish and stitching over it to secure it. It works particularly well as a filling stitch, in blocks or other shapes. Thomas' materials-based description of the process also offers me a directness – the idea of a stitch process actively moving forwards. During workshop sessions a couched line can be 'taken for a walk' and used in conversations about mapping place. This could be related to a physical journey or a personal one.

In community textile work, I like to use the most available materials – the things you might find in a kitchen drawer. In a creative health project for Bradford 2025 City of Culture, *Pathways to Wellbeing*, the medium we used was ordinary household string. Not only can string be used as a couched line, but it offers other possibilities. One participant chose to stitch the string down, then colour it in using fabric pens and permanent markers. In this way the string became something new and organically worked with the background fabrics and other colours of the piece.

ABOVE
Pathways to Wellbeing, HALE/Bradford 2025, City of Culture (2025), collaborative participant work mapping a local park through collagraph printing and stitching.

Couching tutorial

Couching is a versatile stitch that can be used as a continuous line or in bold blocks of texture and colour. Since the thread is laid on the surface of the cloth it offers many options for the stitcher in terms of thread composition. Thicker or boucle yarns, or metallic threads that might normally be difficult to pull through the surface of the cloth can be used to great effect.

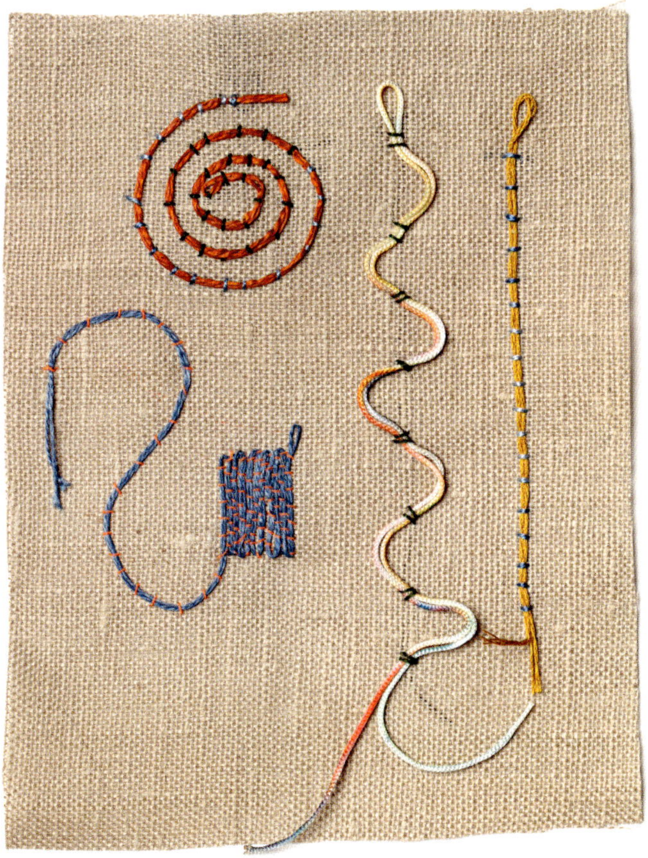

MATERIALS

- Linen or cotton base fabric
- A pencil or erasable embroidery pen
- A selection of threads, cords or string for the laid line
- Pins
- Finer threads for the stitching thread
- Beeswax
- Embroidery hoop (if using)

METHOD

1. To get an even finish use an embroidery hoop to keep your base fabric taut.

2. Mark your fabric with a line or shape as you wish, using a pencil or erasable embroidery pen.

3. Lay the thread for couching over the marked line, pinning it down at intervals so that it maintains its shape.

4. Working from the back with a finer thread, add small catching stitches to hold the laid thread down. The choice of thread colour here, or changing the colour as you go, can give additional interest to the surface.

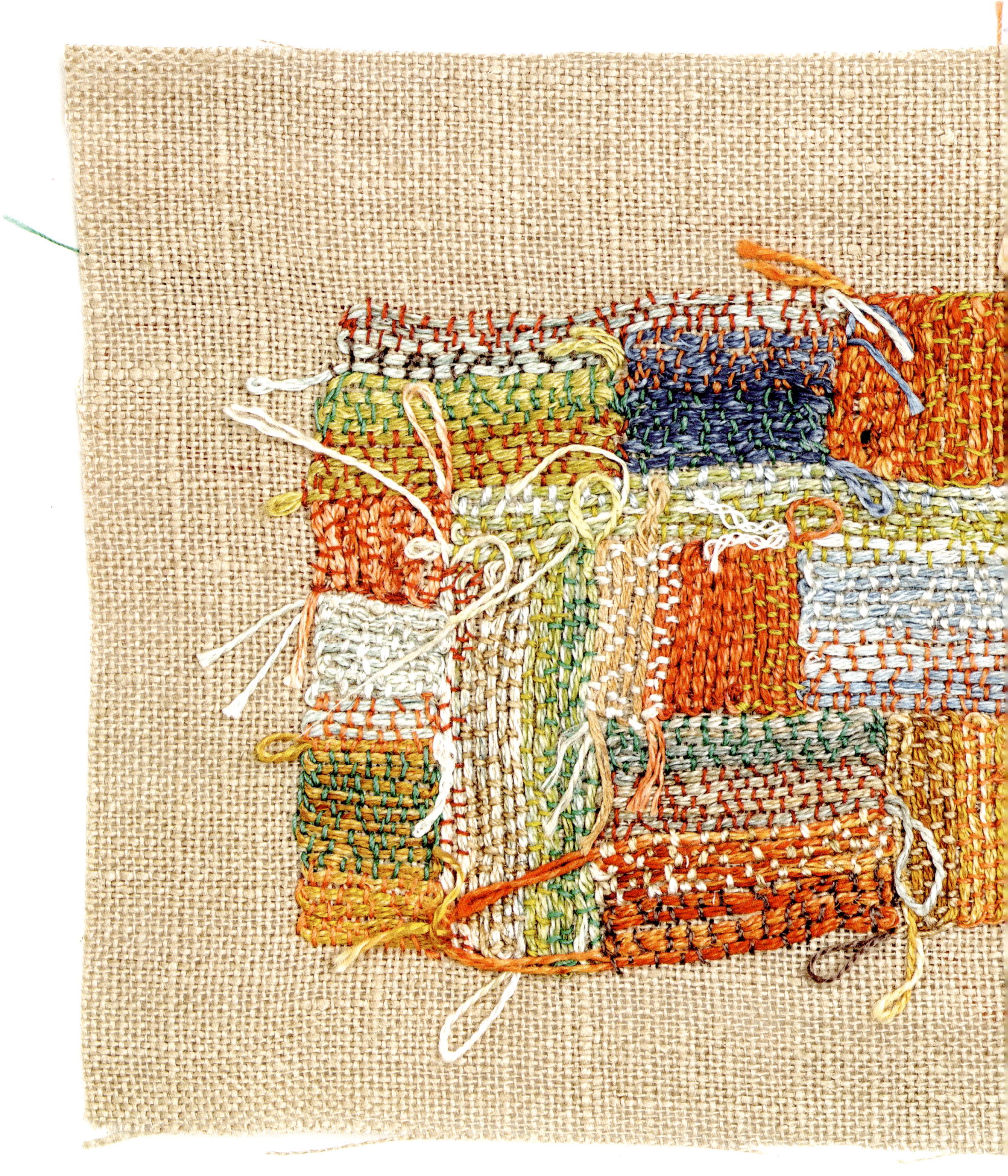

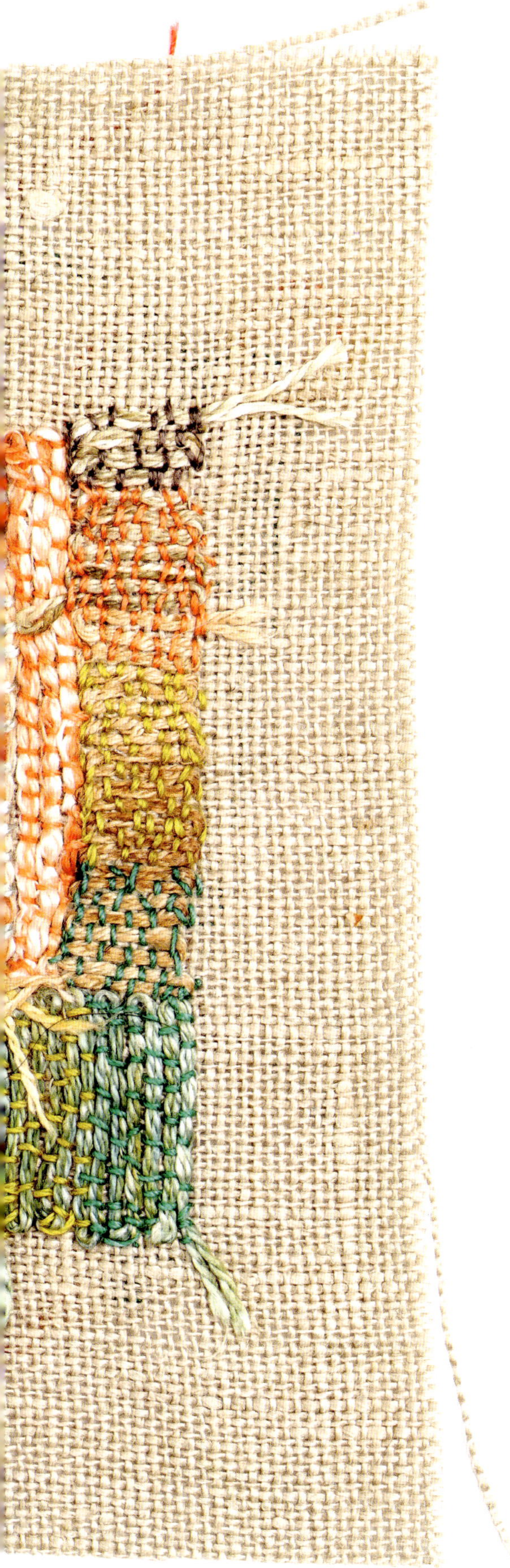

Redbeck sampler

This sample is made using couching to cover a surface. The threads reflect a growing season at my allotment and are dyed using colour found on-site. Joining blocks of couching creates a new patchwork-like surface and could be used as a decorative mending technique on clothing.

LEFT
Redbeck Sampler (2024), plant-dyed silk threads and beeswax on recycled linen 15×20cm (5.9×7.8 in).

Circling

These pieces use couched thread conditioned with beeswax, a method that has been used with couching for centuries. Running the thread over the wax coats and conditions it and helps it adhere to the next line of thread when couching. You can also wax the thread, then, between two pieces of greaseproof paper, iron it so that the wax penetrates the thread evenly. The fabric base for this stitching is black linen recycled from a shirt; the seams remain in some places.

The circles are started in the centre and worked outwards, raising the surface of the work. Doubling the thread before waxing gives a neat loop with which to start couching from the centre. Circular stitching without an embroidery hoop means that the fabric undulates between the stitched areas. A circle created from the outside-in would create the opposite effect – that of a depression in the cloth. The undulations remind me of map topographies, showing the features of the land. The textile surface created is given added interest and tactility.

Circles as a motif appear frequently in my work. The process of creating them offers me focus but also a sense of completion, as the curved stitching meets to form a circle.

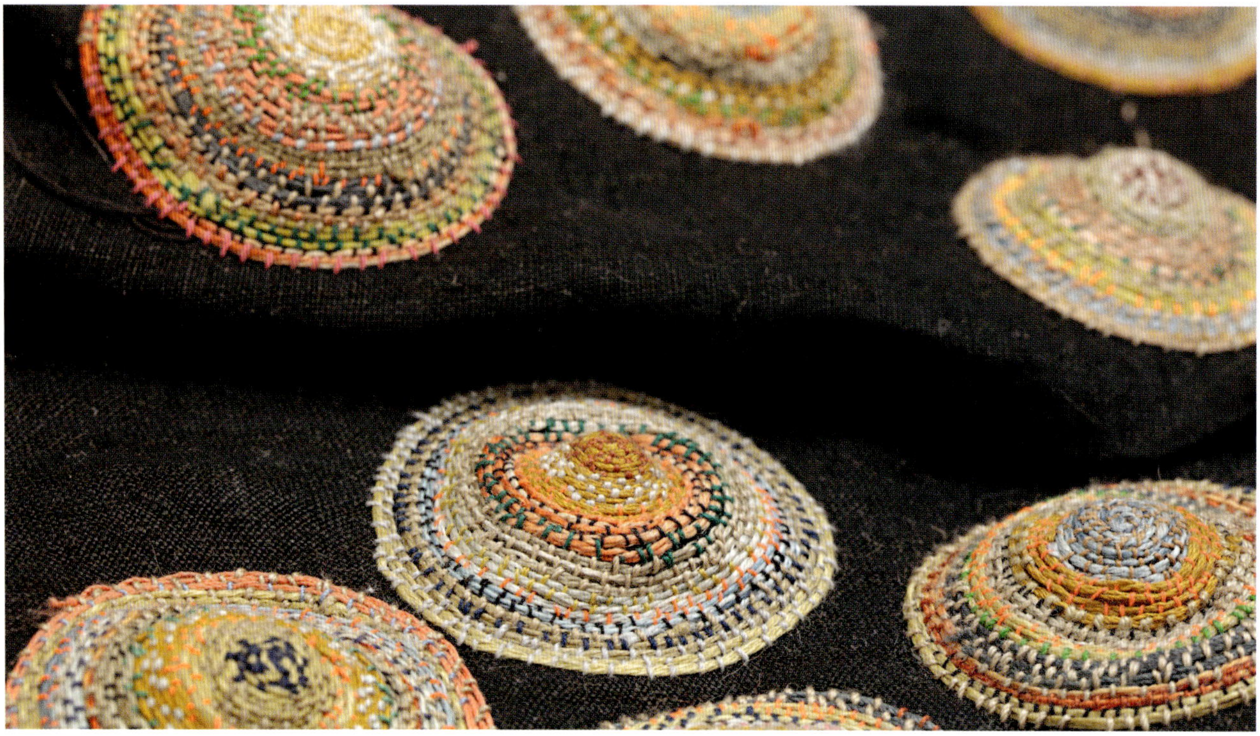

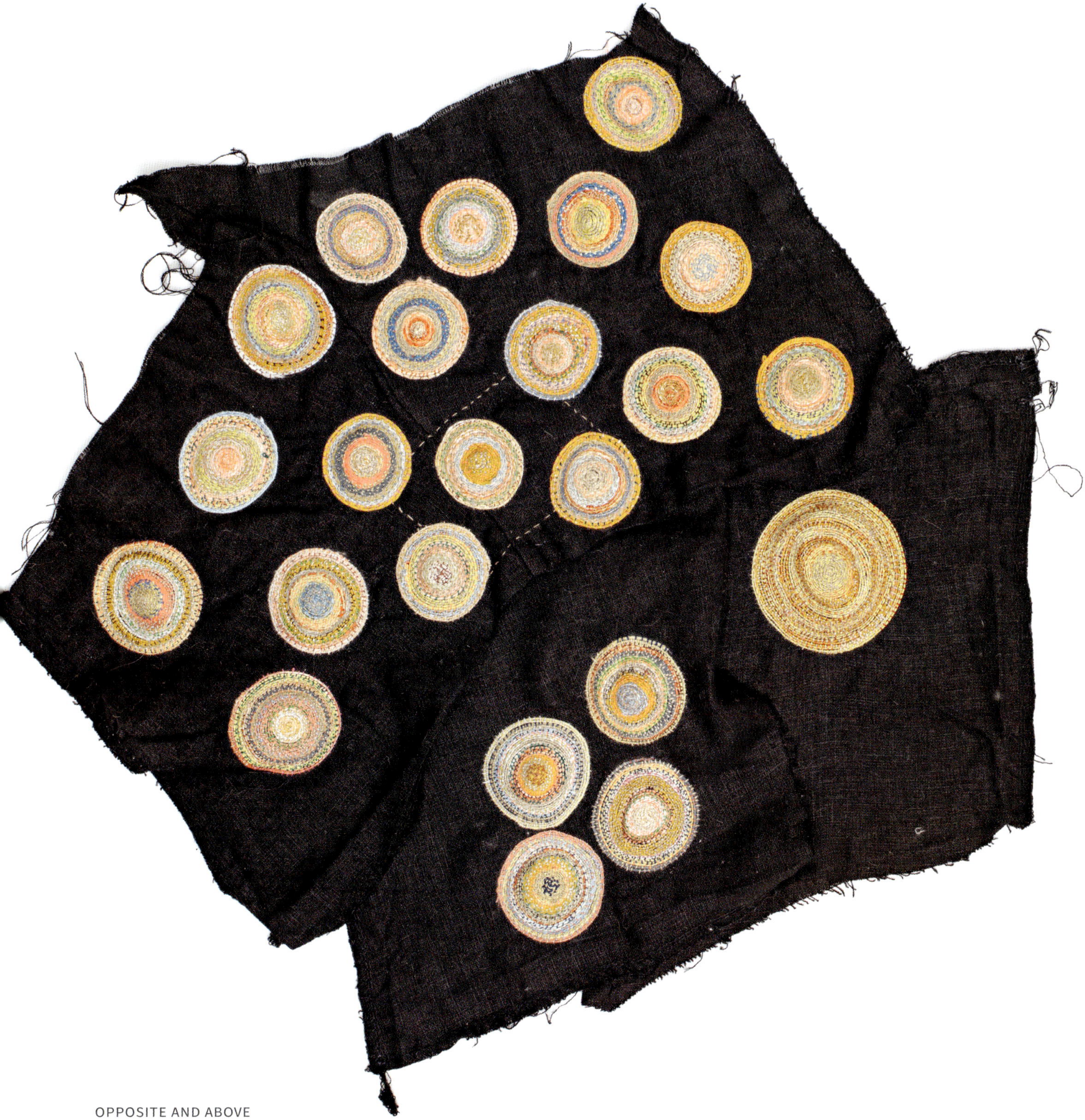

OPPOSITE AND ABOVE
Circling (2024-2025), plant dyed silk threads and beeswax on recycled linen 30×50 cm (11.8×19.6in) at widest point.

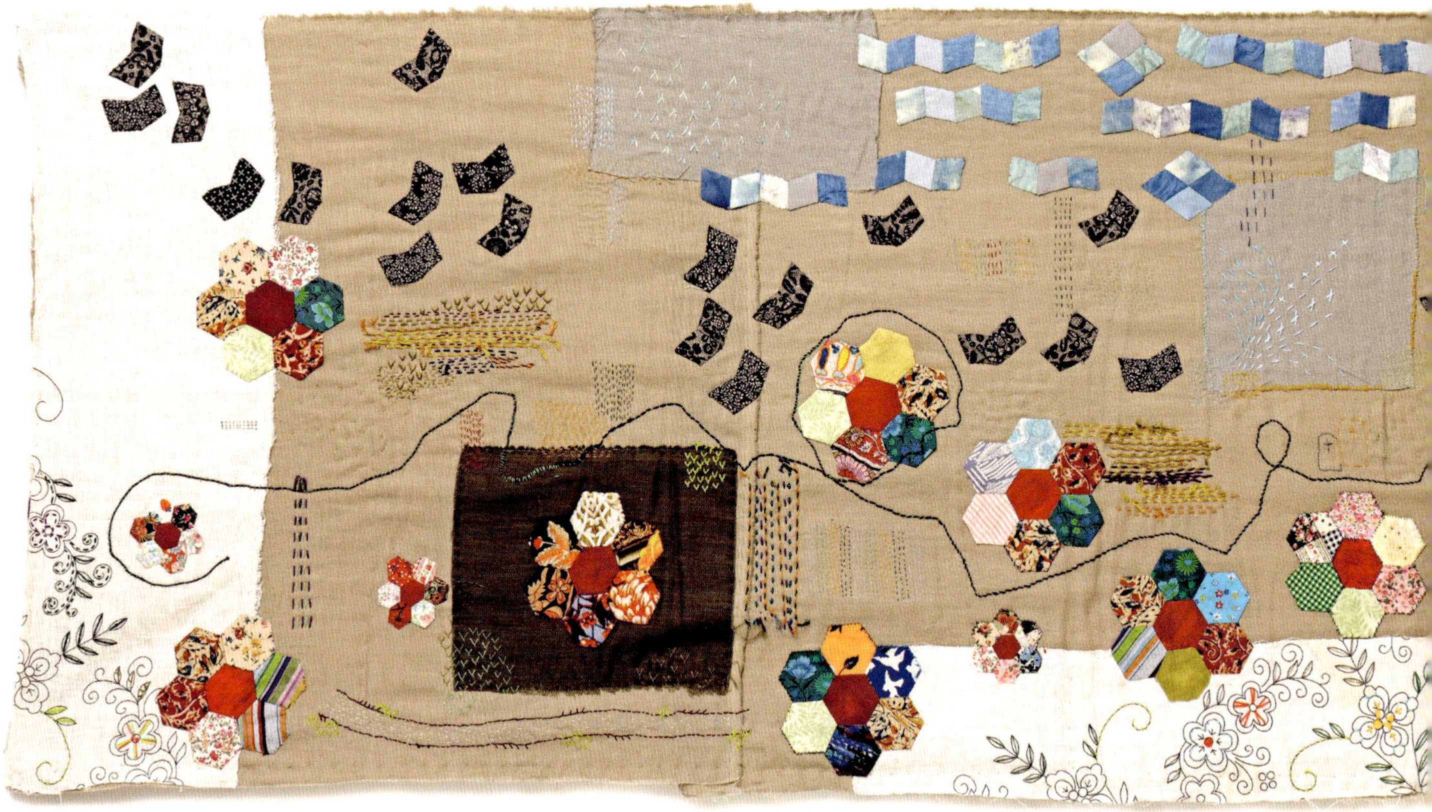

Threaded Journeys

Over an 18-month period I worked with the Brontë Parsonage Museum in Haworth, the former family home of the nineteenth-century novelists Charlotte, Emily and Anne. A group of women who lived in different parts of Bradford district came together on a project called *Threaded Journeys*. We spent time thinking about journeys and connections: how we came together as a group, the landscape that informs us, and the criss-crossing of paths in our everyday experiences.

For this group, these journeys involved urban to rural and back again, partly inspired by a line from a short poem by Emily Brontë, 'Twas one of those dark, cloudy days', particularly the line 'And deeper green is on the hill'. This speaks to the landscape around the city which is surrounded by moorland.

The sessions included opportunities for textile storytelling shared over stitching and working with naturally dyed fabrics created during summer workshops. The group took 'lines for a walk' with wandering stitches and couched laid work, crows in

ABOVE AND OVERLEAF
Threaded Journeys (2025)
Claire Wellesley-Smith, Brontë Stitching Group, Keighley Association for Women and Children.
Linen, hand stitch, recycled fabric. 150×350cm (59×137.7 in).

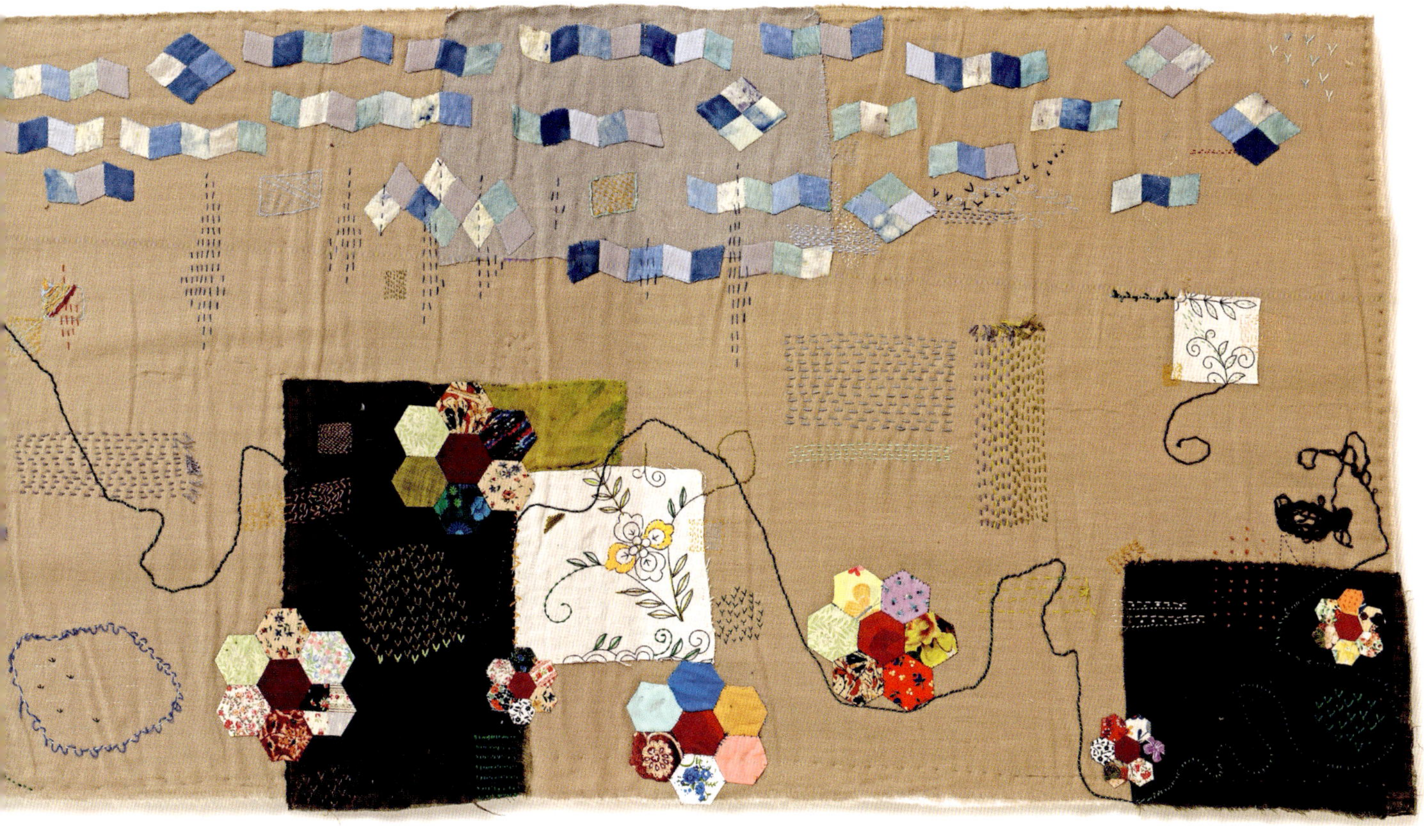

the church graveyard appeared as patchwork diamonds, the canal and the changing colours found in the Parsonage garden all found their way into the piece. The project was also inspired by an unfinished quilt in the museum collection, made by the Brontë sisters and their Aunt Branwell. Too fragile for display, it is a combination of pieced and appliquéd contemporary dress fabrics.

The group paid close attention to the changing seasons and shared their own journeys that led them to this community project. In some instances, these involved living in multiple countries and on different continents. The group also contributed fragments of cloth that we incorporated as we hand stitched the panel on a collaborative stitch table, reminiscing and sharing everyday stories. Lines were made by walking/stitching in a meander along the cloth. Geographer Doreen Massey talks of 'seek[ing] to understand the use of particular materials at a series of key moments and locations'. *Threaded Journeys* is an amalgamation of material memories, shared moments and movement through a diverse and changing landscape.

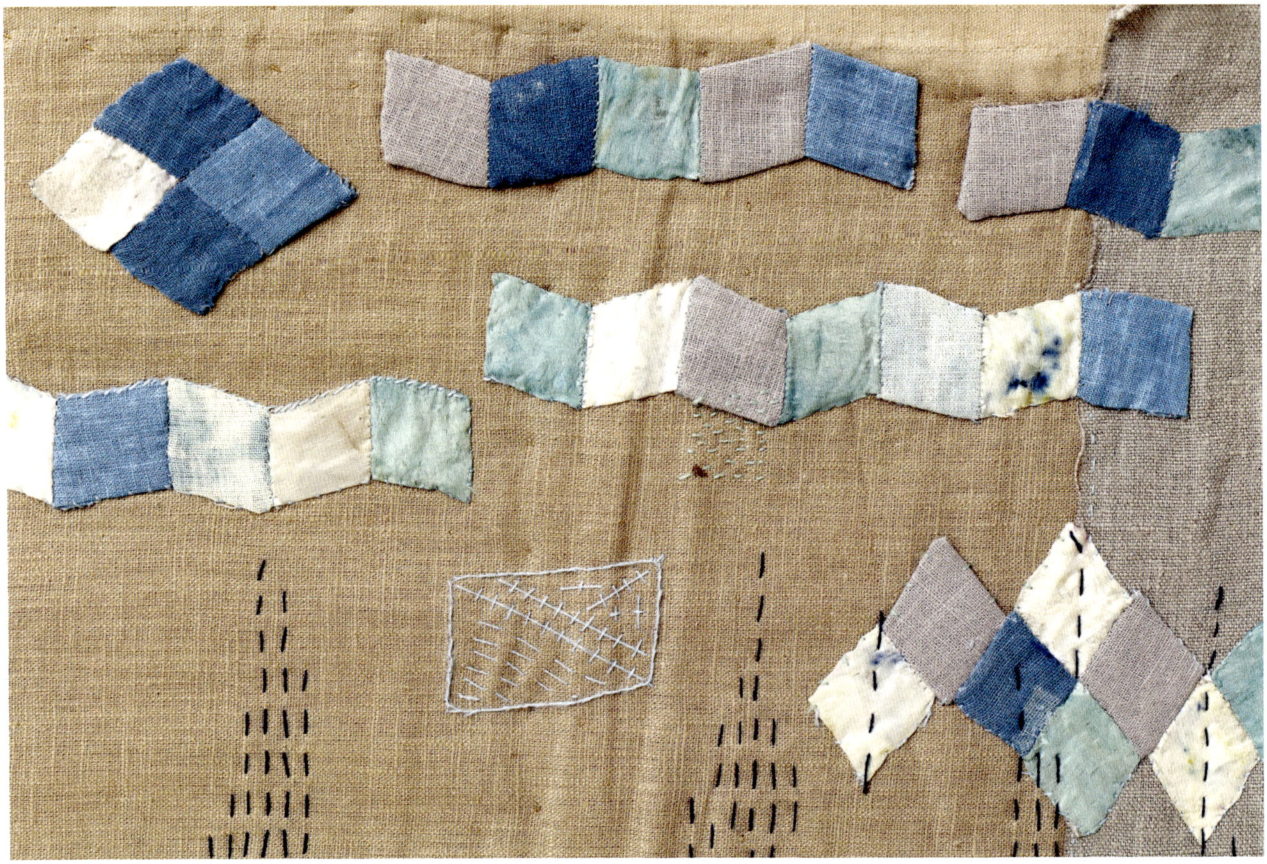

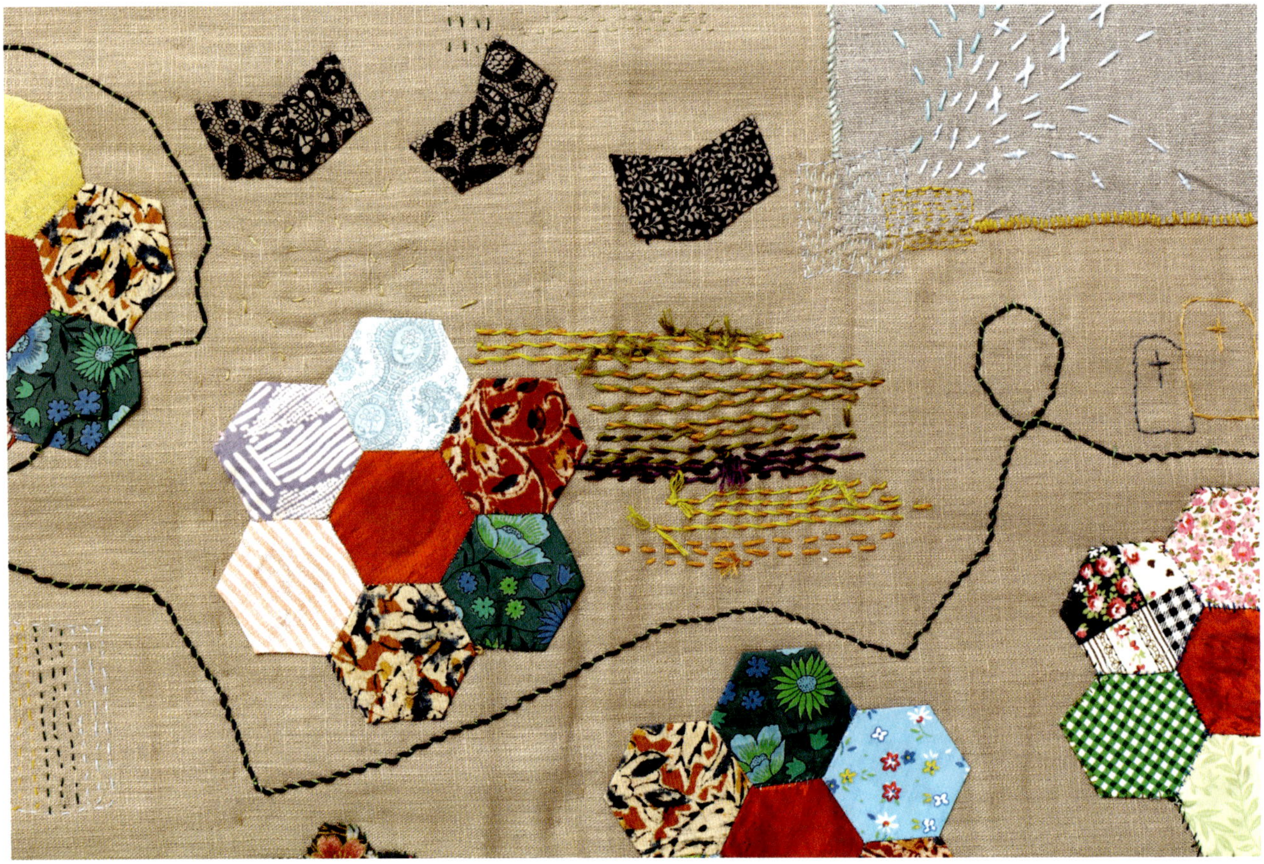

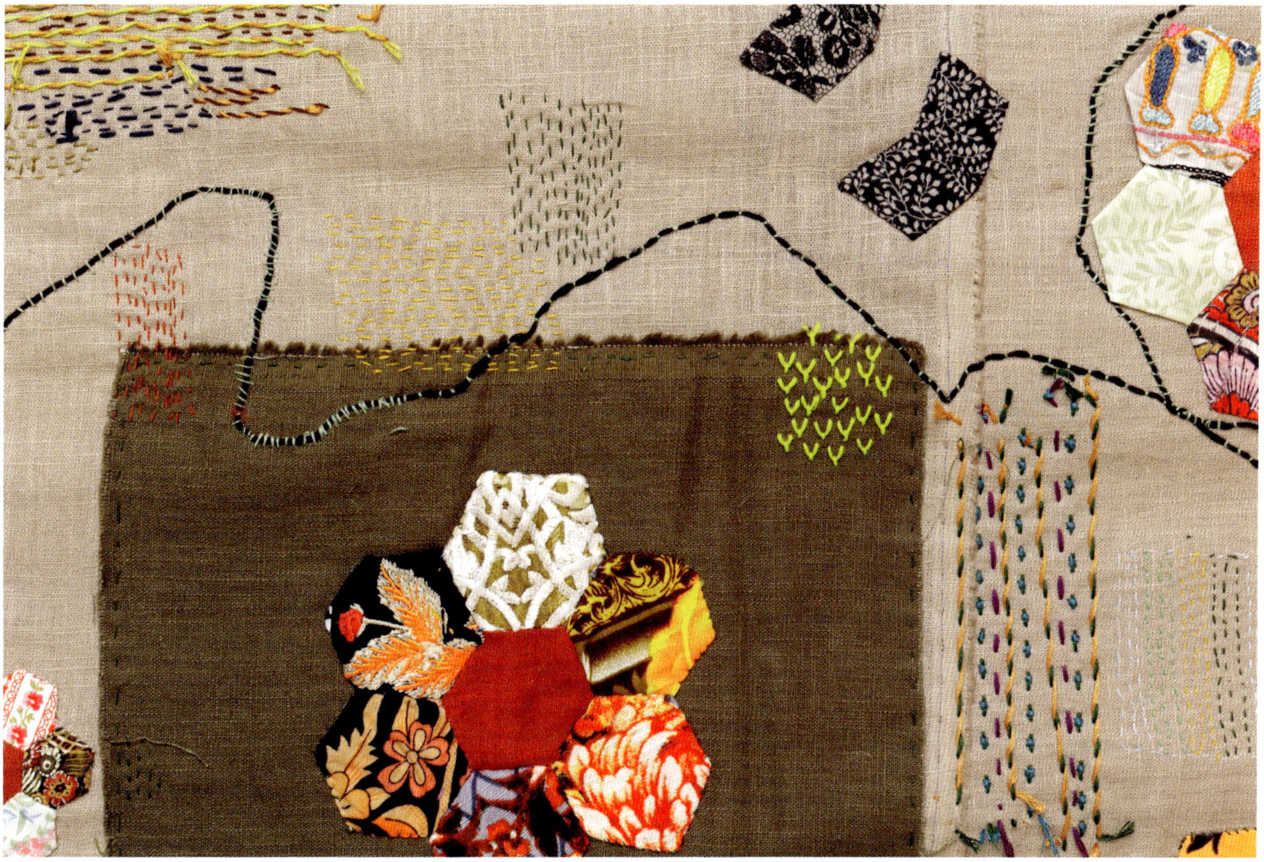

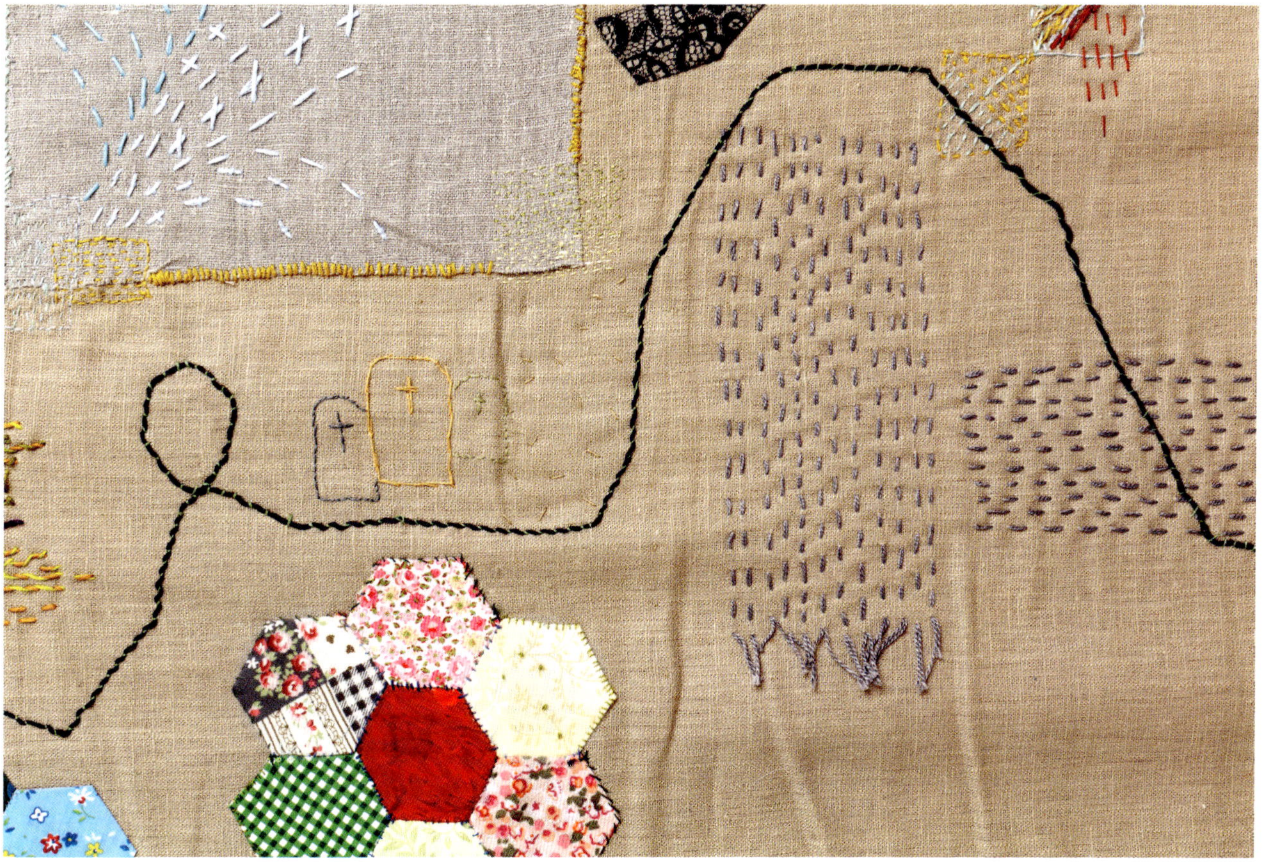

Rachelle Francis

Rachelle is a socially engaged textile artist. Originally from a couture embroidery design background, the death of her mother, Diana, in 2019 and the uncovering of more than 1,000 titled, signed and dated artworks sparked a shift in her practice away from fashion and into art. Bittersweetly with the clarity of grief came the artistic collaboration Rachelle had always wished for.

Diana (b.1951) experienced trauma, mental illness, suicide attempts, anxiety, depression and a subsequent fatal alcohol addiction. Compulsive pattern doodling – private calming acts of self-expression – provided both sanctuary and escape. Hidden in the wardrobe but quietly shared with her children, these intricate felt-tipped artworks deeply influenced Rachelle's career in textile design.

After her mother's death, Rachelle turned to Diana's artworks with questions, stitching patterns and words for catharsis and connection. Engaging with Diana's archive was a transformative process: the sculpting of an afterlife through the creation of new works from old; impossible conversations between mother and daughter now realised. From this new dialogue and artistic enquiry emerged the 'With & Without Diana' project. Funded by Arts Council England, this project promotes creativity for wellbeing, delivering creative health workshops to charities and universities. The book *Mind to Pen*, a posthumous collaboration between Diana and Rachelle, was acquired by the Wellcome Collection in 2024.

My Hands are Dancing

'Why throw away those small pieces? See how they have a life'

(Diana Francis, 2006, from a handwritten note found amongst her artworks)

'It's as if this quote of Mum's was a prophecy for the creation of this artwork. *My Hands are Dancing* is a home for the 'small pieces' of embellishments created during chapters on the cusp of significant life events: motherhood, a house move, a career shift, a mother's death and a posthumous exhibition. The first of these "small pieces" – handmade fabric-covered buttons and sequins –

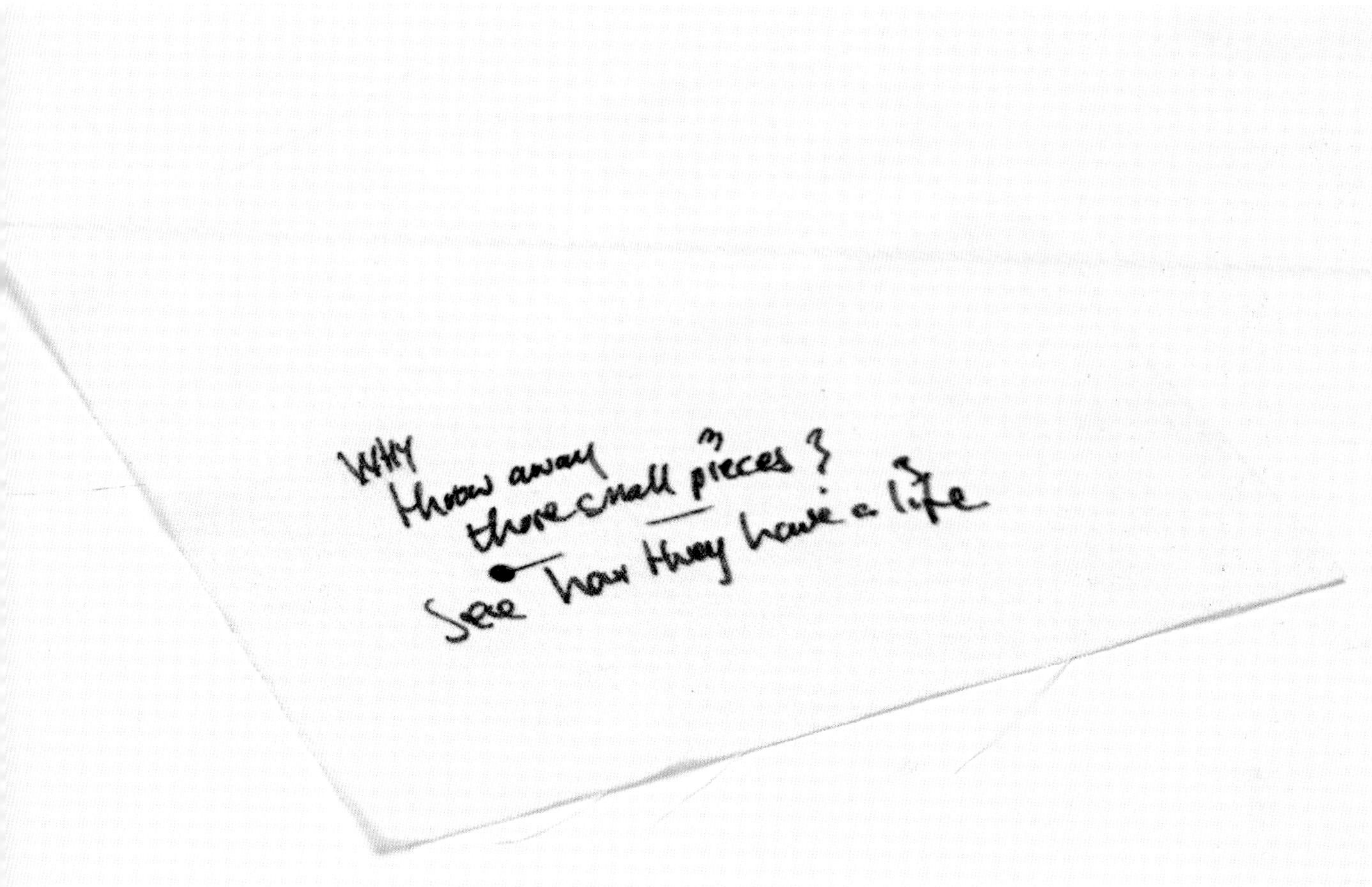

was born in 2013 while pregnant and surviving an absent mother held captive by an alcohol addiction. Small pieces paradoxically representing both comfort and fear, the repetitive nature of their construction (skills honed as a couture designer) provided safety and a controlled yet creative meditation for a scared daughter about to become a mother herself.

'Five years on, with two young children and the primal urge to connect with my now terminally ill mother, I unearthed a folder of her drawings, photographing my small pieces of embellishments placed on top of her patterns. Rediscovering both together felt necessary and right. Despite the silence in our relationship, our creative voices had been in constant dialogue – artworks handcrafted decades and miles apart but speaking the same language in colour, shape and line. They belonged together.

'I made more small pieces. Mum died. The small pieces were boxed away, again.

'Three years later, preparing our first posthumously collaborative exhibition, I reopened the box with a certainty about its contents' destination. Closely guided by the mother

ABOVE
'Why throw away those small pieces? See how they have a life.'
Sublimation print by Rachelle Francis (UK) (2025) from a note on paper by Diana Francis (2006).

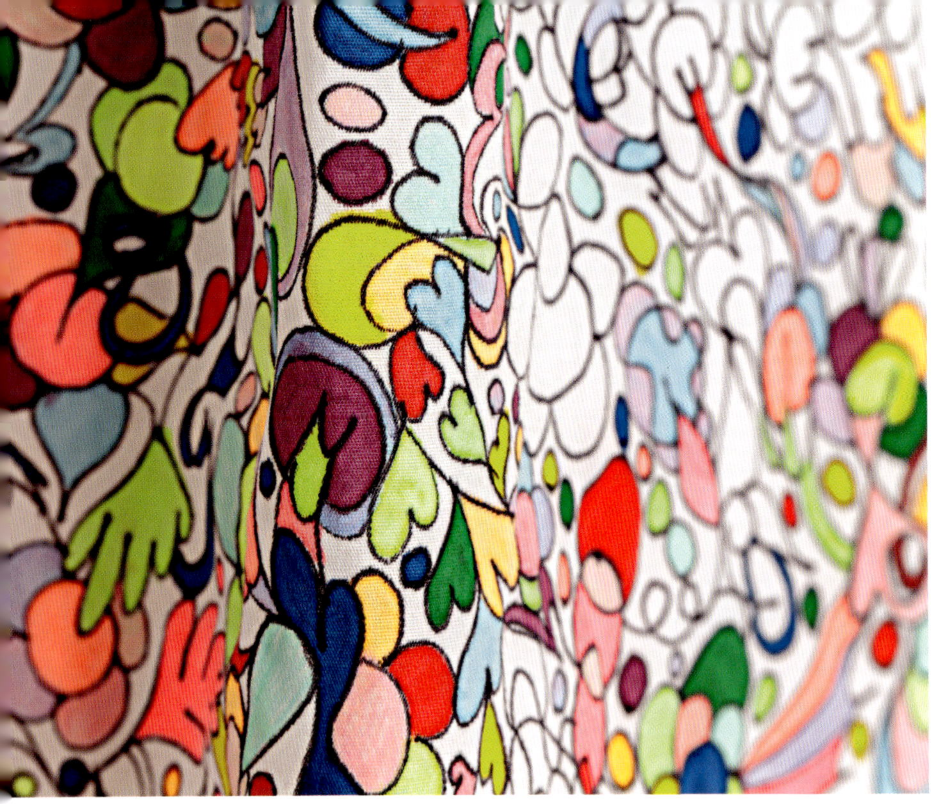

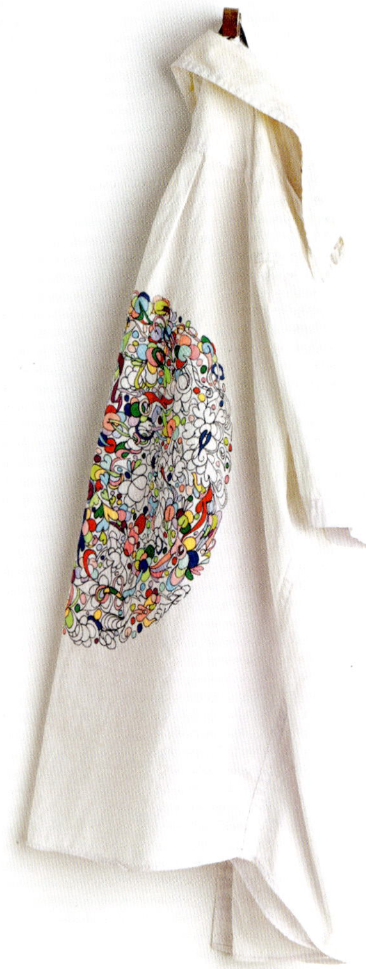

who had once scared me, with a patterned shirt of hers as inspiration, I now felt free to stitch the salvaged small pieces into new terrain. I embraced Mum's spontaneity, suddenly no longer confined by the familiar repeat-pattern methods of my design work. The small pieces became my pen – fluid, intuitive and alive. My first pattern doodled with stitch, the composition and process an echo but not a copy of Mum's felt-tipped drawings – quilled hearts and vertical tears, seeking connection while conscious of the need for separation.

'This reparative piece tenderly binds multiple materials squirreled away from life's sharpest chapters: a frame of transparent mesh made but abandoned in Mum's final isolated months and leftover handmade silk ribbons created in the weeks following her death. Their black fluidity mirroring Mum's felt-tipped ink, these remaining ribbons now had a purpose, surrounding and connecting the lost souls of my small pieces on canvas. Precious but homeless humble jewels cathartically created years ago alongside life's unstable events were now safely secured within the rhythm of a pattern inspired by Mum, but made by me.

'Though anchored, there is still movement within this stitched community – the small pieces floating onto and trailing beyond the canvas edge. A cloud formation: light, suspended and free. Airy and dynamic, opposed to the static weight of the past. Addiction's heavy cloak of silence had suffocated the last decade of my relationship with Mum. In her final years, oxygen and words

ABOVE
Diana Francis (1951-2019) (UK) *Untitled* (2006), fabric pen on second hand shirt.

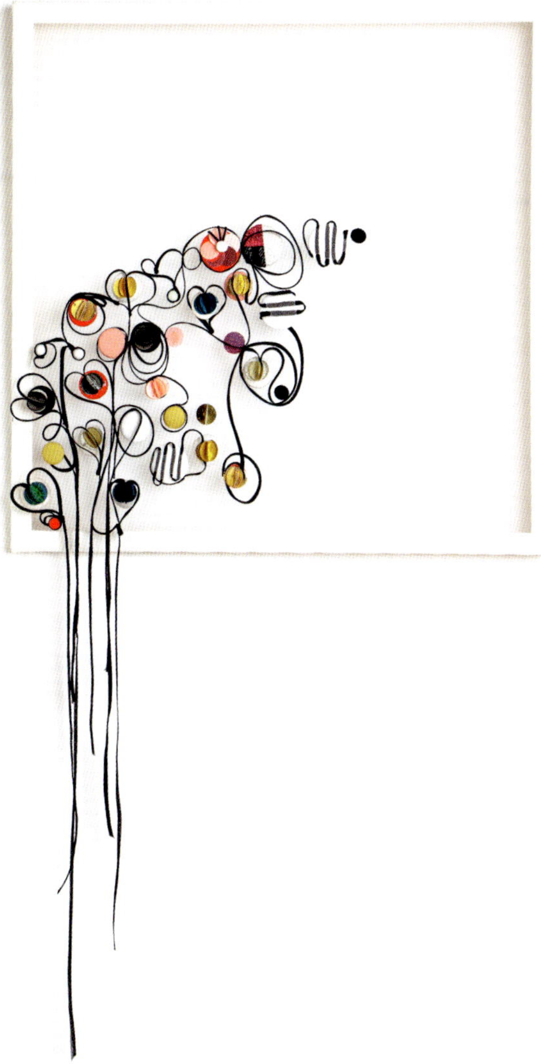

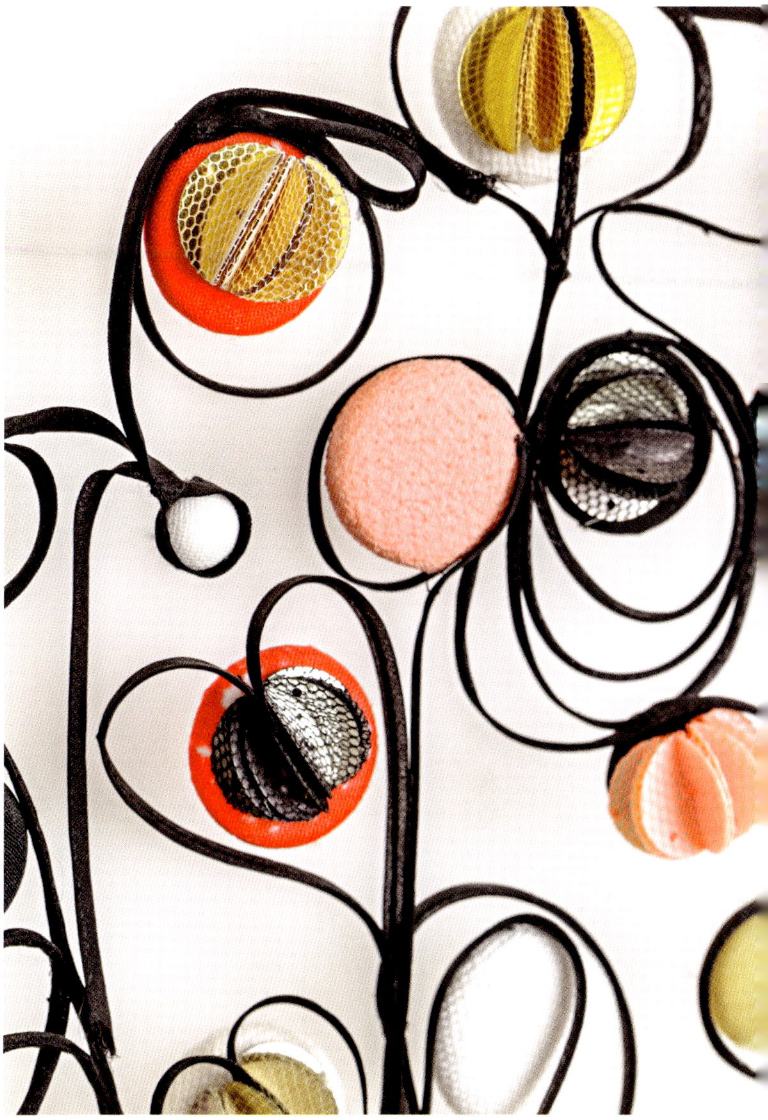

ABOVE
My Hands Are Dancing (2018-2023) Rachelle Francis (UK), mesh embellished with handmade silk rouleaux; sequins wrapped in tulle; handmade buttons wrapped in silks, tulle and aida [Individual embellishments created during a period of hopelessness and disconnect during Diana's final year (2018-19) cathartically stitched into place in 2023. The final composition was inspired by a 2005 doodle of Diana's. Title derived from: '*My hands are dancing, ideas are there, natural, uninterrupted.*' Diana Francis 2006. 52×52cm (20.4×20.4 in).

faded entirely, a terminal lung disease (caused by liver cirrhosis) literally taking her breath, whilst chronic anxiety and depression locked her inside. A meeting point for our re-connected souls, my reflective and reparative stitches bridge the space between silence and dialogue, life and death, Mum and me.

'*My Hands Are Dancing* is an open portal between us. Its title – taken from Mum's handwritten note discovered amongst her artworks, 'My hands are dancing, ideas are there natural, uninterrupted' – a quiet collaborative smile from our eyes. Through my needle I have been able to listen, hands exhaling to create this new dance of small pieces reassembled. A softly sculptured offspring from the mother of Diana's doodles, its stitches thread together chapters in our shared history: cared for and complete – but still breathing.'

Robin Bray-Hurren

Robin Bray-Hurren is an artist working primarily with textiles, using traditional embroidery techniques, cyanotype printing, patchwork and appliqué to explore ideas around queer and non-normative bodies, identities and histories. He is interested in the ways that socially constructed categories overlap and interact with the less rigidly defined boundaries of the biological world and sees visual art as one way we can try to bridge empathetic gaps. His work draws from his experiences as a queer trans man, and as a disabled person. By making work that is quiet and intimate he wants to invite people to get up close and consider the object in detail. By dedicating time and care to a piece of work he hopes to signify the ideas within the piece are worth that time and care. Art can create a space where different ideas and experiences are explored, and Robin wants his work to open up space to people who have historically been marginalised. Hand work is central to Robin's practice. The repetitive nature of hand sewing, lettering or cutting a lino block is something he finds satisfying and meaningful. Keeping the maker's hand present in the work is a reminder of the human experiences he explores.

Busy Hands Quiet Mind (Meralgia Paresthetica)

'This piece started as a series of improvised patches made during Artquest's "30 Works 30 Days" project. Each patch was made with no set goal, but once I had a small pile of them, they needed to become a quilt. I experience chronic pain and find that hand sewing calms and focuses my mind, allowing me to sit with my body more easily. The fluorescent pink ripstop path loosely references one of the sensory nerves of the leg. Several of the other patches include cyanotype printing, evoking elements from my own medical imaging along with other biological diagrams.'

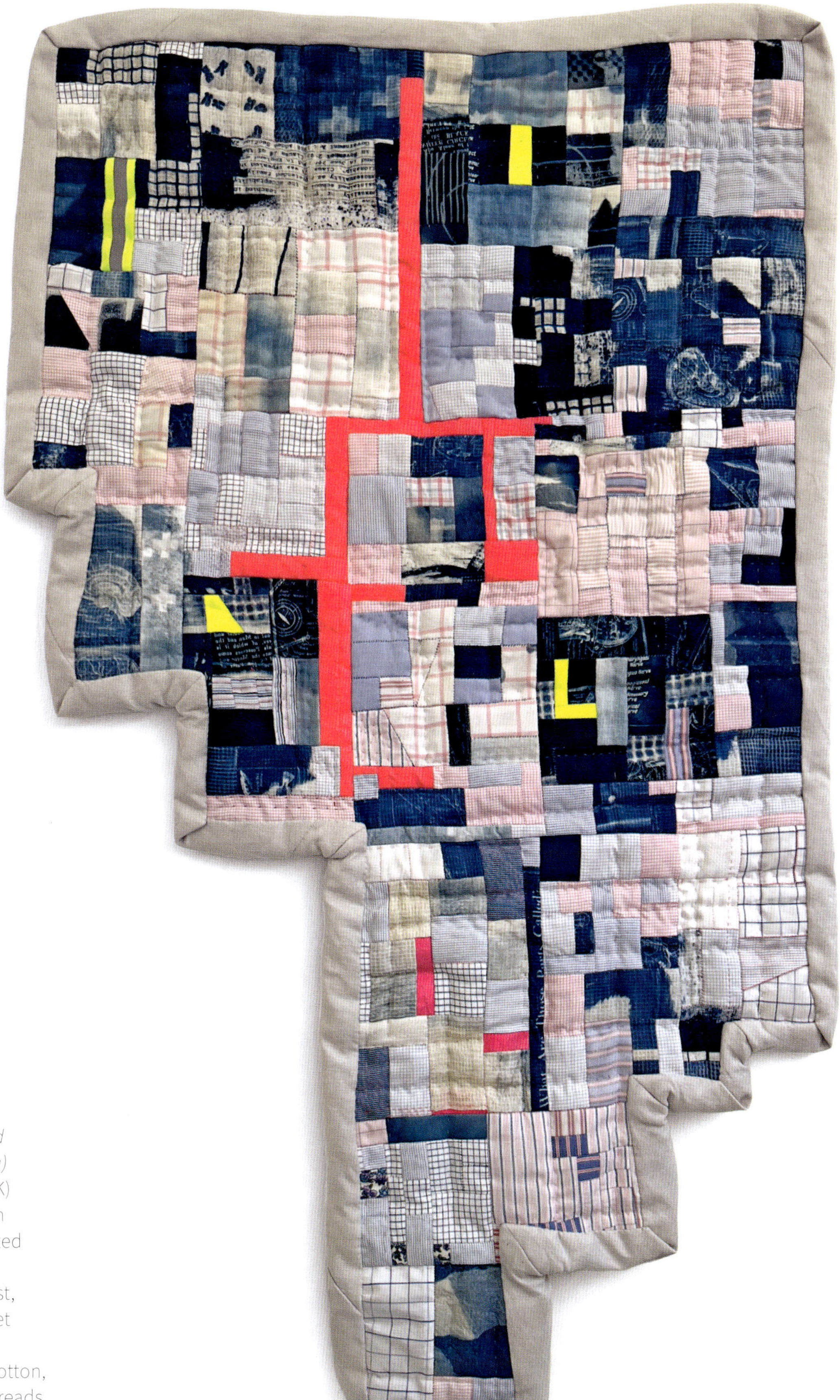

RIGHT

Busy Hands Quiet Mind (Meralgia Parasthetica)
Robin Bray-Hurran (UK) (2025), recycled cotton shirts, cyanotype printed cotton / linen, ripstop nylon, Tyvek, hi-vis vest, repurposed linen duvet cover, recycled wool insulation wadding. Cotton, polyester and linen threads. 100×62cm (39×24.5 in).

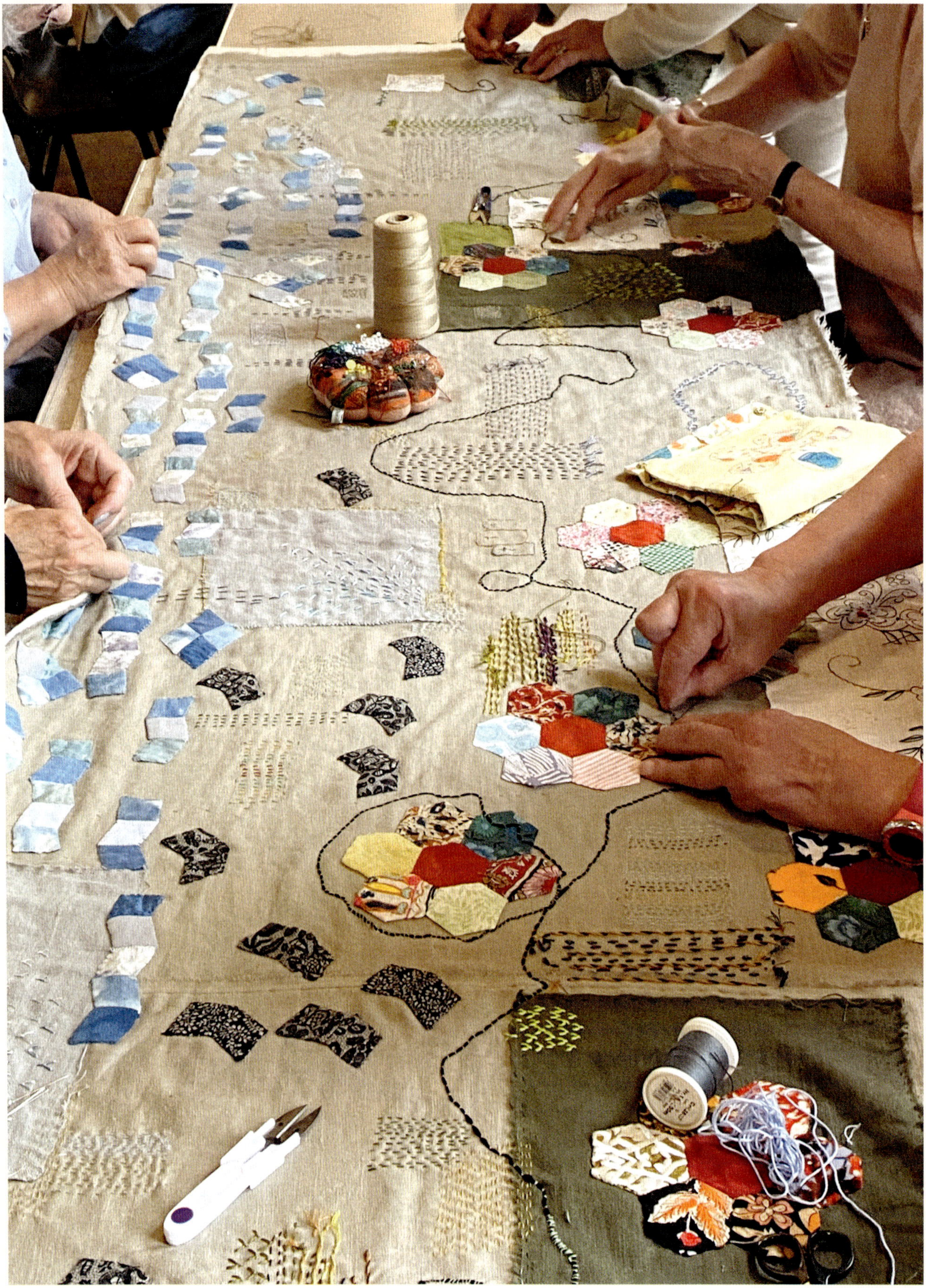

OPPOSITE
Threaded Journeys (2025), collaborative stitching workshop, Brontë Parsonage Museum.
BELOW
Crafting Resilience (2025) details.

Conclusion

From a patch of green space in an urban environment to the difficult spaces of hospital waiting rooms, inspiration for textiles with connection to time and place are everywhere. Starting where you are and using what you have can give your textile work immense richness and help you to tell those important smaller stories.

Textile work can allow us to see and feel these connections and to express them in a multitude of ways. We can share them and explore them, whether doing so alone or collectively, through conversation and quiet, collaborative work. Place and time are connected and ever changing.

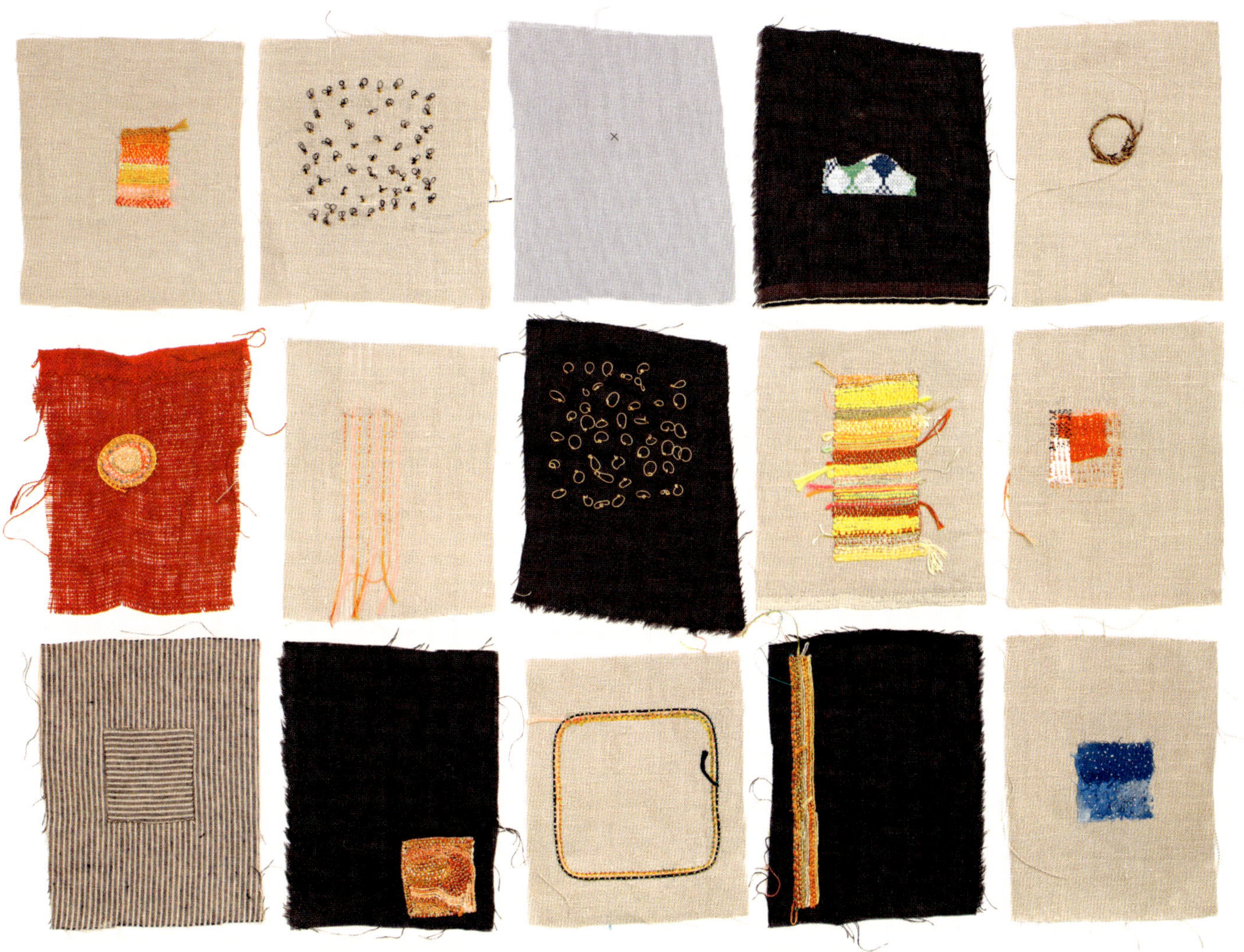

Acknowledgements

Many thanks to the organisations, participants, funders and commissioners of my work.

Bradford Arts Centre
Brontë Parsonage Museum, Haworth
Community Solutions North West, Accrington
Health Action Local Engagement (HALE), Shipley
HIVE, Bradford
Keighley Association for Women and Children
South Square Centre, Thornton

Arts Council England
Arts and Humanities Research Council
Bradford 2025 City of Culture
British Textile Biennial
Economic and Social Research Council
National Lottery Heritage Fund
The Open University
The Super Slow Way

Contributing Artists

Robin Bray-Hurren – www.rjbray.art / @inkysloth
Ruth Broadway – www.ruthbroadway.com / @ruth.broadway
Jordan Cunliffe – www.jordancunliffe.co.uk / @artisan_embroidery
Rachelle Francis – www.rachellefrancis.com / @with_and_without_diana
Sue Green – @sue_green_art
Carol Tulloch – www. caroltulloch.co.uk/ @this_is_not_all_that_i_am

Resources

Whaleys Bradford Ltd – Undyed and prepared-for-dye/print fabrics
Uppingham Yarns – Undyed threads and yarns
John James – Needles

Bibliography

Amos, Joanna and Binkley, Lisa (eds.), *Stitching the Self: Identity and the Needle Arts* (Bloomsbury Visual Arts, 2021)

Chenciner, Robert, *Madder Red: A History of Luxury and Trade* (Routledge, 2000)

DeSilvey, Caitlin, *Curated Decay: Heritage beyond Saving* (University of Minnesota Press, 2017)

Hackney, F, Maughan, H, & Desmarais, S (2016), The Power of Quiet: Re-making Affective Amateur and Professional Textiles Agencies. *Journal of Textile Design Research and Practice* 4(1)

Ingold, Tim, *Lines: A Brief History* (Routledge, 2016)

Ingold, Tim, The Textility of Making, *Cambridge Journal of Economics*, Vol. 34, Issue 1 (2010)

John, Edith, *Needleweaving*, (B T Batsford, 1970)

Lacey, Suzanne, *Mapping the Terrain: New Genre Public Art* (Bay Press, 1995)

Lawrence, Anna M (2022), Listening to plants: Conversations between critical plant studies and vegetal geography. *Progress in Human Geography*, *46*(2)

Lynch, Kevin, *The Image of the City* (Harvard – MIT Center for Urban Studies, 1960)

Kettle, Alice (2019), Textile and Place. *Textile*, 17(4). pp. 332–339

Massey, Doreen, *For Space* (Sage, 2005)

Nenadic, Stana and Tuckett, Sally, *Colouring the Nation: The Turkey Red Printed Cotton Industry in Scotland C.1840–1940* (National Museum of Scotland, 2013)

Tharp, Twyla, *The Creative Habit: Learn It and Use It for Life* (Simon & Schuster, 2003)

Thomas, Mary, *Mary Thomas's Embroidery Book* (Hodder & Stoughton, 1936)

Wall Kimmerer, Robin, *Braiding Sweetgrass* (Penguin, 2013)

Index

Picture credits

All pictures by Michael Wicks except for the following: Claire Wellesley-Smith: p.12, 14, 68, 81, 86, 88, 89, 104, 105, 106; Claire Wellesley-Smith/Brontë Parsonage Museum p.8, 122; Carolyn Mendelsohn, p.6; South Square Centre, p.13; Carol Tulloch p.40; Jo Hounsome, p.48, 50, 51; Jordan Cunliffe, p.52, 53; Phillip Jackson, p.69; Nadine Lamb, p.75; Sue Green, p.76; Richard Tymon/British Textile Biennial, p. 95, 96, 97; Robin Bray-Hurran, p.120.

First published in the United Kingdom
in 2026 by
Batsford
43 Great Ormond Street
London
WC1N 3HZ

An imprint of B. T. Batsford Holdings Limited

ISBN 9781849947541

A CIP catalogue record for this book is available from the British Library.

10 9 8 7 6 5 4 3 2 1

Reproduction by Rival Colour Ltd, UK
Printed and bound by Toppan Leefung Printing International Ltd, China

This book can be ordered direct from the publisher at www.batsfordbooks.com, or try your local bookshop.

Distributed throughout the UK and Europe by
Abrams & Chronicle Books, 1st Floor, 22–24 Ely Place, London EC1N 6TE and
57 rue Gaston Tessier, 75166 Paris, France

www.abramsandchronicle.co.uk
info@abramsandchronicle.co.uk

FSC www.fsc.org MIX Paper | Supporting responsible forestry FSC® C104723